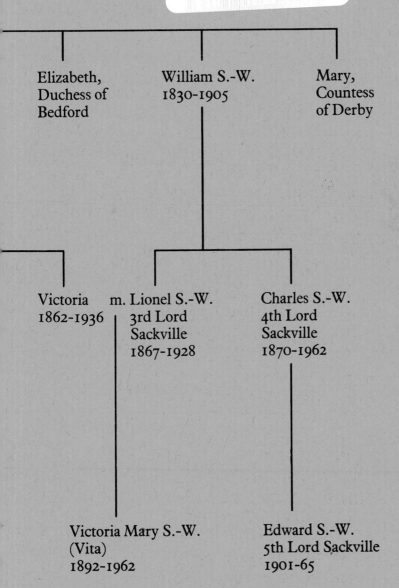

Elizabeth,
Duchess of
Bedford

William S.-W.
1830-1905

Mary,
Countess
of Derby

Victoria
1862-1936

m. Lionel S.-W.
3rd Lord
Sackville
1867-1928

Charles S.-W.
4th Lord
Sackville
1870-1962

Victoria Mary S.-W.
(Vita)
1892-1962

Edward S.-W.
5th Lord Sackville
1901-65

LADY SACKVILLE

LADY SACKVILLE

A Biography

Susan Mary Alsop

Weidenfeld and Nicolson
London

For

Katherine Winton Evans

and for my son and daughter

William S. Patten and Anne Emily Crile

First published in Great Britain by
George Weidenfeld and Nicolson Ltd
11 St John's Hill, London SW11
1978

ISBN 0 297 77477 8

Printed and bound in Great Britain by
Morrison and Gibb Ltd
London and Edinburgh

Contents

Illustrations

Acknowledgements

It was my English publisher, Lord Weidenfeld, who inspired this book. Doubleday in New York and Weidenfeld and Nicolson in London wanted me to follow a book of my own letters with a biography; highly flattered, I looked about for a subject but couldn't find one. George Weidenfeld thought of Lady Sackville, and all his authors know how he communicates faith and optimism. Rereading that marvellous book, *Portrait of a Marriage* by Nigel Nicolson, I saw what an opportunity I had, but how to persuade Mr Nigel Nicolson to allow a perfect stranger to write the story of his grandmother's extraordinary life? I owe the selling job to George and to my dear friend, Nigel's cousin Lady Katherine Giles, to whom Nigel is devoted, and after a weekend at Sissinghurst Kitty Giles and I packed four huge suitcases with the original documents from which the book is mainly derived, and she drove me to London Airport, after stopping at Knole, where her cousin Lord Sackville handed me a green satchel full of papers which he hadn't even had time to inventory. I was desperately worried about the responsibility, but, typically generous, Nigel said that if the plane went down it went down, and that it would be too expensive for me to stay in London having the papers copied.

It will be three years later when the book comes out, during which time I have worn down Lady Sackville's descendants with further trips to England, endless letters and requests for further help; and my reception has been kind beyond description. Nigel has borne the brunt, but I particularly want to thank Mr Benedict Nicolson, Lord Sackville and his brother and sister-in-law Mr and Mrs Hugh Sackville-West for their help. Bridget Sackville-West all but tore down Knole finding the unique copy of *My Mission to the United States* and collecting photographs, and she and

Lionel Sackville opened Knole for me so that I could see it as my heroine knew it.

I have been very lucky. That great Doubleday editor, Mr Ken McCormick, took me through my first book, with Miss Carolyn Blakemore as co-editor; he will never leave me but he preferred to have Carolyn edit this alone and it is due to her unwearying commitment that I have been able to finish it. Beyond her professional skill, I am indebted to her for a personal dedication to *Lady Sackville* that cannot be measured and for her rare sense of style.

The book is dedicated to my research assistant, Katherine Winton Evans and to my two children. Kay Evans is a brilliant and intuitive researcher, but her job was a hard one, especially the American years, for there we had no diary to go on, few letters, only that remarkable fragment, the *Book of Reminiscences* (see Appendix) which I implore you to read, and the girlish scrapbook. Kay hit Victoria Sackville's trail like a tireless truffle hound, and the results of her chase are rich indeed. Several times I have used her notes *verbatim*. I thank her particularly for the cheerfulness with which she accomplished the parts that were real drudgery; it is no fun to read seven years of newspapers on the 1880s in microfilm.

My children and their spouses have been loyally supportive of my effort and I am deeply grateful to them. And I owe so much to Miss Debbie Wichter, who typed and retyped draft after draft of the manuscript with infinite care and skill. I wish that the list of the other people who have helped me could be more detailed than space allows. In France my friend the Comtesse de Rougemont spent hours working in the Musée Rodin doing careful research, and Madame Pol Roger's monograph on the town of Arcachon written for me was an immense help before I visited the place myself. In London Mrs J. G. Links not only gave me her time and her sensitive insight to help me with the last chapter of the book, but wrote me immensely helpful letters to Washington following our interviews, and Mr Robert A. Cecil has been a wonderfully generous friend, not only in his official capacity as Assistant Keeper of the Wallace Collection but as the great-grandson of Lady Derby, who played such an important role in Victoria Sackville's life. In Washington the Swedish Ambassador, Count Wachtmeister and Mr and Mrs Edward Glover of the British Embassy came to my rescue again and again with information that only they would have taken the trouble to discover for me, and a very special source was Mr Perry Wheeler, who shared his great horticultural knowledge with me. In New York, Miss Alice Butler gave her time and her skill with words to conjure up the picture that I use to illustrate life in a great English country house as seen by a servant. To these friends, and the others whose names follow I can only acknowledge my debt and offer my deepest thanks.

In the United States:
The Hon. William S. Moorhead; The Hon. L. Richardson Preyer; The Hon. James W. Symington; The Hon. Clement E. Conger and the Curatorial staff of the White House; Mr Irving Williams, Chief Gardener, The White House; the staff of the Library of Congress; the staff of the District of Columbia Public Libraries; the staff of the New York Society Library; the staff of the Boston Atheneum; H.E. The Ambassador of Sweden, Count Wacht-meister; Mr and Mrs Edward Glover, British Embassy, Washington; Miss Janet A. Kaye; Mr Leo Lerman; Mr Arthur Schlesinger, Jr; Mr Henry Villard; Mrs June Bacon-Bercey; Mr Donald Smith, Chief Gardener, Dumbarton Oaks; Mr Alberto Raurell; Mr Jesse Stiller; Mrs Luis Bolin; Dr Joanne Trautmann; Monsieur Germain Seligmann; Mr Philip Carroll; Mr John B. Trevor, Jr; Mr Michael Mangan; Mrs Peter A. Jay.

In the United Kingdom:
Miss Belinda Giles; Miss Pamela (Honey) Harris; Lady Diana Cooper; Lady Jones; Sir Claus Moser; Sir Robin Mackworth-Young; Miss Barbara Tate; Mr and Mrs Mazur; Mr and Mrs Strang-Steel; The Countess of Perth; The Viscount Hood; Mrs Georgina Battiscombe; Sir Sacheverell Sitwell; The Countess of Birkenhead; Lady Arthur; Mr Justice Edward Clarke; Sir Derek Walker-Smith; Mr H. Montgomery-Hyde; Mr Christopher Hibbert; the staff of the London Library; the staff of the British Museum Reading Room.

In France:
Madame Monique Laurent, Directrice, Musée Rodin, Paris; Monsieur Emmanuel de Margerie; Prince Jean de Faucigny-Lucinge; Comtesse Jean-Louis de Rougemont; Monsieur Jean-

1
Lionel and Pepita

The weather in Paris was hot that September, monotonously and unusually so. The Imperial Court, as was its habit, remained throughout the month at Biarritz, prolonging its stay until 8 October because of the merciless heat in the capital. Biarritz was a summer resort on the south-west coast of France made fashionable by Empress Eugénie; in September the winds blew briskly and the ladies would have fastened their tweed golf capes at the throat, murmuring to each other how fresh and invigorating was the breeze off the Bay of Biscay and how fortunate they were not to be in sultry Paris.

There were, however, several million people who had to be in sultry Paris in September of that year, 1862. At No. 4, Avenue de l'Impératrice an odd little party awaited the birth of a baby born on 23 September, Victoria Sackville-West. She was baptized a Roman Catholic in the parish of St Honoré d'Eylau under the name of Victoria Josefa Dolores Catalina, daughter of Josefa Duran and an unknown father. The legal phrase is an icy one: '*Fille de père inconnu*'.

The *père inconnu* was in fact very much on the scene; his name was Lionel Sackville-West, and he had taken leave from his diplomatic post at a small Italian principality in order to join his mistress Pepita in Paris for the birth of their second child. And he had arranged things very luxuriously for her, taking a furnished flat on the sunny side of the splendid Avenue de l'Impératrice; newly built by the exuberant city planner Baron Haussmann, who had flung out its elegant length from the Arc de Triomphe to the Bois de Boulogne. It was the loveliest of the twelve avenues radiating from the circle called the Étoile, in the middle of which stood and stands, high over Paris, the arch commissioned by Napoleon the First to symbolize the grandeur of Empire. Around the circle were built a series of similar houses of a dignified if somewhat mechanical classicism; No. 4 was divided into apartments. It was the heyday of the Second Empire, and the opulence of the times was perfectly expressed by the shiny brilliance of the new quarter.

But in spite of the comfort, regardless of the pleasure with which Sackville-West and Pepita must have looked forward to the new baby, for they both loved children, it is hard to imagine a more disparate group than the one gathered in the rented apartment. Besides the two lovers and their little boy Max, aged four, there were Pepita's mother Catalina Ortega and her sleazy companion Manuel Lopez. Catalina, the daughter of a poor sandal-maker of gypsy blood from the back streets of Malaga enjoyed stormy rows, the stormier the better, castigating Manuel at the top of her strong lungs, hands on hips. Then would come dramatic, noisy reconciliations. Everyone who knew Catalina associated her with noise.

Sackville-West, a reserved young British aristocrat, hated rows and noise all his life. At Buckhurst, his home just across the Channel, the partridge-shooting season had opened and the cool beeches in the park would have been hinting autumn, while his people spoke in quiet voices of pleasant things. What in the world was this handsome and independent young man of thirty-five doing shut up in a stuffy Paris apartment with a band of Spanish adventurers? The story could have come straight out of an Offenbach operetta of the period.

Ten years before, in 1852, the Hon. Lionel Sackville-West, fifth son of the fifth Earl De La Warr, had come to Paris for a week's leave from his post at Stuttgart, capital of the Kingdom of Württemberg, where he was serving Her Majesty's government as attaché at the British Legation. Of medium height, with blond hair and the deeply hooded blue eyes that were characteristic of his family, he could be very charming, but he was also singularly reticent, cautious and outwardly conventional.

He would have fitted Balzac's conception of the British aristocrat perfectly, the haughty young 'milord'. In more recent times he would instantly have been placed as a member of British Intelligence, that mysterious body, easily identifiable to every Paris taxi driver, because of his reserve and lack of small talk.

Trained as assistant précis writer to the Foreign Secretary,

Lord Aberdeen, he was everything that his relations could have hoped of the younger son of a great house as he started to climb the ladder of Victorian diplomacy. 'Sound' was the adjective, 'brilliant' perhaps too much for which to hope. A safe marriage to an appropriate well-born girl with a nice fortune could later be managed by one of his sisters, who as Marchioness of Salisbury (later Countess of Derby), and the Duchess of Bedford were powerful ladies indeed. They must have pleasantly anticipated the comfortable career which could lead eventually to one of the great embassies: Paris, Vienna, St Petersburg or Rome. Then, provided his uncle Mortimer should die without an heir, Knole, one of the largest and most historic of English country houses, would fall to him, bringing with it the title of Baron Sackville. Could any life seem more predictable?

Instead, chance took Lionel to the theatre one evening in Paris. Seeing the beautiful dancer, Pepita, he arranged to be introduced and fell instantly and deeply in love. They spent every night of that intoxicating week together; he was twenty-five, she twenty-two, and the liaison that began so passionately lasted, with intervals of separation, for nineteen years. There is no record of what Lionel's grand relations said; but it can be imagined.

Pepita. How to capture her radiance? She was born in Malaga in 1830, the child of an obscure barber, Pedro Duran. Dying young, he left his widow Catalina to bring up their daughter as best she could and Catalina's strength and courage must be admired. An ambitious mother, she determined that Pepita should become a dancer and to this end Catalina worked as a washerwoman, and later peddled clothes from door to door. Pepita danced first at the theatre in Malaga, 'like a bird in the air', said an admiring witness. But Malaga was a provincial town and Catalina wanted a national stage for her beautiful daughter. When Pepita was nineteen, they moved to Madrid, accompanied by Catalina's lover, Manuel Lopez. God knows what sacrifices this supreme effort must have entailed on Catalina's part, but the formidable stage-mother immediately addressed herself without introduction to Don Antonio Ruiz, director of the ballet of the foremost theatre in Spain, the Teatro de Principe. This was as if the Director of the Royal Ballet at Covent Garden had been asked to add a poorly trained dancer from the provinces to his company, but the startled Don Antonio agreed to dancing lessons, and the ill-assorted trio of Andalusians returned in triumph to their basement lodgings. If Don Antonio had remained unmoved by Pepita's grace and charm he would have been unique among men.

Technically, the dancing lessons were not a success and she never attained the perfection of style demanded by the Teatro de Principe, but her likeable dancing teacher, Juan Antonio de Oliva, fell in love with her and they were married in Madrid in 1851. The marriage lasted only a few months; why it broke up can only be conjecture, but Oliva's sister blamed Catalina.

Pepita then left Spain, and, dancing abroad as 'The Star of Andalusia' became an international figure within a year; news of her engagements in all the capitals of Europe beyond the Pyrenees reached Madrid and it was known that she had been able to install Catalina and Manuel in luxurious circumstances in the southern town of Albolote. Catalina made the most of her new grandeur, and boasted to her awestruck neighbours of Pepita's triumphs abroad; as the dancer who had been turned down by the Teatro de Principe was now acclaimed at Her Majesty's Theatre in London, was packing houses throughout Germany from Frankfurt-am-Main to Berlin, where the German audiences had screamed for her to let down her wonderful chestnut hair on stage to prove that it was not a wig. Vienna – Copenhagen – there was no end to the path of Pepita's glory, and the best of it was that it was all true, an extraordinary success story.

How did the great star and the young British diplomat manage their private life together? At first they were as extravagant as they were reckless. When Lionel moved from post to post he took a villa for Pepita nearby the capital in which he was serving; and they met whenever they could between her professional engagements. He took houses at Heidelberg, Hackenfeldt, Como, Genoa, Arona on Lake Maggiore; even the names of these places ring romantically to the ear. Passionate, sensual and headstrong, the private Lionel was the very opposite of the correct and detached man the world knew. Had there been any way of disposing of Juan Antonio de Oliva, the inconveniently legal husband in Spain, Sackville-West would certainly have married Pepita.

There was a remarkable episode in Malaga in 1855 during which the British Consul was obliged to lock Lionel into his hotel room in order to prevent him from undertaking some sort of marriage with his mistress. The Consul succeeded in sending him away on a boat before this impossible ceremony could take place, but the fact that Lionel Sackville-West could even have contemplated an adventure that would have broken the law of the country and the rules of his own code illustrated the depth of his feeling. During the years of their long liaison, seven children were born to Lionel and Pepita: Max in 1858, Victoria in 1862, the short-lived baby Eliza Catherine, born in Bordeaux in 1865. The next year Sackville-West bought a large villa at Arcachon, not far from Bordeaux and there in 1866 Maria Flor, known as Flora, was born, to be followed in 1868 by Amélie Albertine, called Amalia by her family, and in 1869 Ernest Henri Jean Baptiste, Henry. The last child, Frederic, was born in 1871. By 1866 Lionel was serving as first secretary at the British Legation, Madrid, and it was impossible to think of installing Pepita and the children in the city in which her legal husband still lived. The Foreign Office remained blind to Lionel's double life due to the skill with which he led it and at the same time accomplished his official duties conscientiously, but this was a risk he could not take. What better solution than the little seaside town of Arcachon, south of Bordeaux, so unfashionable, so discreet, so healthy for the children? Sackville-West could and did cross the Spanish frontier and join his family four or five times a year, for visits sometimes lasting several weeks. It would only have been an overnight trip. Pepita at thirty-five had given up her professional career and wanted the contentment of having her children around her and Lionel's visits to look forward to as often as his duties permitted. But the Arcachon years were bitterly lonely ones for her, and Victoria became her chief consolation.

In the 1860s the town, population 800, was a charming place, provincial in tone. The fishing port gave and gives onto the protected Bassin d'Arcachon, but in winter the Atlantic winds blew hard and the fishermen in their picturesque red trousers drew up their boats waiting for better weather. Inland from the small port was the so-called Ville d'Hiver (Winter Town) filled with villas then inhabited by Bordeaux merchants on holiday, or visitors from colder temperatures who sought the healthy climate; it was especially recommended for lung patients. It was impossible to imagine a more delicious climate, for the smell of sea and pine was everywhere, and the villas had large gardens in which the grass remained green all winter long and January brought camelias and

5

mimosa. Later came the waxy magnolia blossoms and the flaming judas trees, against a background of deep green ilex. Palms flourished, and the town was and is proud of its specialty, the umbrella shaped tamarisks planted in neat rows on the broad walk by the seaside. The villas were marvels of Victorian fantasy, details from Tudor cottages were happily married to bits of the *châteaux* of the Loire, reckless of proportion, merry in use of colour and material. Each bend in the little piney road brought the visitor a new delight, and one sensed the owners' pride in his carefully tended beds of salvia and begonia.

The architectural triumph of the Arcachon that Victoria knew was the casino, always described by the residents as the Moorish casino. Its minarets and domes carried the brightest of banners, and the architect had added a grand stairway worthy of Persepolis which led to a graceful balcony of generous proportions inspired by pictures of the Alhambra. The colours were gold, vermilion, yellow and purple.

Arcachon was a cheerful place and Sackville-West had done his best for his family. The Villa Pepa, as Pepita had named their home, was among the finest of the houses. It had high iron gates bearing a coronet and a monogram, and the builder, Monsieur Desombres, made a fortune out of the alterations and additions in which Pepita delighted. Eager for respectability, anxious to establish herself in a new, fulfilling life, Pepita told everyone that her husband was called Comte West, that she therefore was Comtesse West, and she had engraved visiting cards carrying this fictitious title and a crown. The local people on the whole believed her and thought no more about it. She was a generous client and beloved in the town for her charities. Madame Dubern, the butcher's wife, would tell her who needed what and it would be given to them at the Villa Pepa. One neighbour said of her, years later, 'She was better known to the poor than to the rich.'

Pepita and the children were ostracized by the sixteen English families who lived in Arcachon. Next door lived the Harry Johnstons, well-established wine merchants from Bordeaux. The two gardens were divided by the lowest of walls and the Johnstons had little girls of Victoria's age, but she was not allowed to play with them. Mr Johnston recalled that Pepita, having been a dancer, could not be received by Arcachon society, adding that he took good care that his children should not associate with the West children. Oh, those pathetic visiting cards, yellowing between their fine layers of tissue paper; there was no one on whom it was possible to call. The English chaplain Mr Radcliffe sounds especially sanctimonious, although he was reported to have been a 'popular figure in the best society'. When he came to the coroneted gates of the Villa Pepa, he passed by on the other side.

This must have been mysterious to a little girl, and Victoria never forgot a terrible night at a children's ball at the Casino when nobody danced with her or her sisters, she came home and cried and Pepita never let them go to another ball, although they were frequently held and were the great events of the year for the neighbourhood children.

But Victoria did not remember the Arcachon years as unhappy; on the contrary, she looked back on them as the wonderful time when she was the chief companion of her radiant 'Mama'. Pepita was a devoted mother, although her temperament caused her affection to be spasmodic. A small misdemeanour could bring on a tantrum, followed swiftly by demonstrative forgiveness. Seizing one of the babies to her breast in an actress's gesture, she would cry, 'Oh, my poor darlings', and burst into the great Spanish dance, El Olé, skirts flying and castanets clicking. The children particularly loved the castanets, and Victoria never forgot one special dress that Pepita put on when she danced to them, it was long and lacy and ruffled. She had the small feet of the Andalusians and her black satin pumps would kick back the flying ruffles in the imperious gesture which climaxes and characterizes El Olé. Pepita grew a little stouter as she neared forty, but was still very lovely. She was tall, with almond-shaped black eyes, and her chestnut hair which dropped to her knees was described again and again by witnesses.

Victoria received no formal education whatever. Although there was a governess in the house, she appears not to have learned to read or write. Instead, she slept in her mother's bed and spent the days with her while the little children were in the nursery and Max, the eldest, was busy with his studies. There were long lazy afternoons in the garden under the magnolia trees, watching her mother embroider and listening to her stories. They were marvellous stories. There had been the first night in Vienna, when Pepita drove back to her hotel in a carriage filled with bouquets and with the ovations of the crowd ringing in her ears, to find the hotel sitting room full of more flowers for 'The Star of Andalusia'. The cards that accompanied the bouquets often bore very real crowns above the titles. There had been, among many other admirers, Prince Youssoupoff, the richest man in Russia. He owned, it was said, a hundred thousand serfs and ten times as many acres. There had been the night in Copenhagen when the students went mad and, taking the horses out of their traces pulled the dancer's carriage to the Hotel d'Angleterre, shouting, 'Pepita, Pepita'. Later, on that same Copenhagen tour there was the evening when she looked down in surprise from her window to see that a crowd had gathered and was standing in motionless admiration. She had been brushing the famous hair, and it was a moonlight night. London, Paris, Rome, Munich, Berlin – how much more fun than any geography lessons the stories of the triumphs were; how dashing the admirers; how delicious the details of the presents of jewels. As Victoria wrote in the *Book of Reminiscences** of those sunlit days, 'I was always with her; she was so beautiful and I loved looking at her. She had a very happy disposition and was always so cheerful.'

Perhaps these wonderful stories made up to Pepita and her little girl for the snubs of Arcachon society. What could the opinion of the Harry Johnstons have mattered to a beautiful woman, who had had Prince Youssoupoff at her feet? Of course, it did matter, and it hurt. But far graver than social ostracism was religious ostracism, and it was the hardest trial of Pepita's life that as a woman living in adultery she could not receive absolution nor take communion. However, unlike the English chaplain, the social lion of Arcachon, the Catholic priest of Notre Dame d'Arcachon was a kind and compassionate adviser. He told Pepita about a little unconsecrated chapel in the woods at nearby Le Mouleau, and there she and Victoria would repair to pray undisturbed. It is comforting to go to Le Mouleau today, for it is exactly as one would wish it to be. Still unvisited, the small sanctuary is a holy place; even its name is consoling: La Chapelle de Notre Dame des Passes. It was built for the fishermen, who as they left harbour and pointed to the open sea would turn at the *passes*, or passage, and their last sight of land before facing the Atlantic would be the Chapel of Our Lady, high above them. It makes one think of Cape Sounion, where the ancient Greeks built a noble temple towards which their sailors could turn

* See Appendix, p. 237.

to invoke protection from their god, Poseidon, as they saw the last of the mainland sink below the horizon. Pepita found solace during her tranquil hours in this cool and shadowy place, the little girl quietly beside her. They would emerge into a sunny garden full of the sound of birds. Arcachon is everywhere a birdy place, but Our Lady of the Passage is especially sweetened by the song of the thrushes in the woods that enfold its rounded choir.

Later, Pepita had a private chapel built in the garden of the Villa Pepa, and to her great joy, the kindly priest from Notre Dame d'Arcachon consented to say Mass there for her and the children. Still she could not receive the two supreme consolations of her church, but she had only to cross her garden to pray at any time.

What did Sackville-West hear of the family problems when he came on visits? Very little indeed, probably, for no woman ever kept a lover for nineteen years by meeting him at the train with a long face. His arrivals were great occasions. Pepita and the children would go to the station, dressed up and excited, hoping that he would notice the garden of the villa in which they had festooned the dark branches of the trees with red cherries. The local shop-keepers remembered the domestic felicity of these visits, and were appreciative of how the accounts of the Villa Pepa increased when Lionel was in Arcachon.

They also noticed Pepita's ravishing dresses and beautiful jewellery. No, it is highly unlikely that she would have spoiled Lionel's visits with self-pitying complaints. Her nature was naturally optimistic and cheerful and she could not risk boring her lover. From his point of view, the society of Arcachon was of no interest whatever, as he remarked later he could not have met anyone there with whom he would have cared to associate. Lionel simply could not imagine the misery of social insecurity. He could have very well seen himself, in the unlikely event that he would have been reflective enough to think about it, becoming a bore or a drunk or a cheat at cards, such things could occur to a gentleman. But it was perfectly unimaginable that he would enter a drawing room at the Tuileries Palace or a peasant's hut without the unconscious certainty that he would be accepted for what he was. He was not vain, but the modern term 'identity crisis' would have been un-intelligible to him. To this simple and natural man, Pepita's whims were tiresome, but unimportant. The ridiculous title, Comtesse West, the visiting cards, and the fact that without consulting him she chose royal personnages as godparents for their children, who were always represented by proxies at the christenings, were small concessions which he accepted, shrugging his shoulders. 'What did it matter?' he said later, wearily.

In the nineteenth century, a man could lead his private life as he wished, *provided that there was no confusion*. Lionel's English family, his career, his colleagues and friends were in one compartment, his mistress and illegitimate children in another. If a mistress stayed within the bounds of her compartment, she would receive affection and generous material comforts: it seemed fair to Lionel, and while it is impossible today to conceive of a young secretary of embassy keeping his mistress in a luxurious villa conveniently contiguous to his post, it is a sad fact of diplomatic history that this is no longer financially possible. It was immensely romantic, immensely good fun, and did not interfere with Sackville-West's work. He rose steadily in the career which he had chosen, and we can feel sure that if his *'chefesse'* (an old-fashioned word for the wife of the chief of mission) required his services at a reception or dinner, Sackville-West would have been there, handsome and charming, apparently engrossed in the conversation of the *principessa* or *Gräfin* who might be his dinner partner. Otherwise, as a colleague of the 1850s described, after leaving the chancery at the end of the day, Sackville-West and he would go their separate ways. He said that everyone knew about Pepita, but it never occurred to him that he would meet her or that her lover would speak of her; and he never did.

The Villa Pepa was a happy house despite the real pain of religious and social ostracism. Victoria remembered her mother singing as she went about it; and there was a charming slapdash quality to daily life. Instead of learning to read and write and do arithmetic as other little girls did she would drive out with her mother and the smaller children to the wide white beach; it amused Pepita to watch them fill their drawers with sand and let it trickle out at the ankles, shouting with laughter. Their costumes were short little skirts or smocks with the frilly pantalette drawers of the time reaching far below the skirts, and everyone wore sailor hats with wide navy blue ribbons.

But even the most amused and loving mother must have longed for the society of a grown-up during the long intervals between Lionel's visits. The builder Desombres was a pleasant man, who often stayed for meals when his work was over, but about three years after Pepita had settled in Arcachon a more important companion entered her story. This was the Vicomte de Béon, the son of a small landowner in the Bordelais region. He was employed as assistant stationmaster at the Gare du Midi in Bordeaux, and on one occasion did Sackville-West a favour by stopping a train for him. In return he was invited to the Villa Pepa with his mother who, Victoria said, was the one and only lady who ever came to call on Pepita. Henri de Béon and Pepita became such friends that he gave up his job at the railway station and became her secretary and superintendent, eventually moving in permanently to the villa. At this distance, it is impossible to judge Béon: we have no record of his appearance or personality as a young man. Naturally, there were some unpleasant rumours in the town about his relationship with Pepita, but there is no evidence whatever that the friendship was more than it appeared on the surface.

In 1868 Lionel Sackville-West was appointed to H.M.'s Embassy at Paris as Secretary of Embassy and Minister Plenipotentiary. This was a very different position from that of attaché at Stuttgart, secretary at Turin, or even first secretary at Madrid. It followed a brief appointment to Berlin where he must have done well, for it was a highly sought honour to serve as a senior official in Paris, the most important British Embassy in the world, directly under the Ambassador, Lord Lyons. His family in England must have been proud of him, but they would have worried about what he would do with Pepita and the embarrassing brood of five young illegitimate children. What he did was what he had always done, showing, as usual, generosity and skill in playing his dual role. He bought a house for the family at 200 Avenue d'Eylau, now called the Avenue Victor Hugo; a pleasant and fashionable part of Paris not far from where Victoria had been born. They were to spend the winters there, the summers at Arcachon. Again, Pepita entertained no one; and we have the first and only time recorded in which she kicked against the pricks of her position as a kept woman. She longed to have Lionel take her to a *fête* at the Tuileries; it would have been such fun to be presented to the beautiful Empress Eugénie whose pictures were in every illustrated paper. She cried and stormed, but Sackville-West was implacable and she had to watch him drive off alone in his handsome diplomatic uniform.

It was a lovely walk from the Avenue d'Eylau to the British

Embassy and Victoria was allowed to accompany her father in the mornings to within ten minutes of his office in that great eighteenth-century house. Regularly, at a certain place on the Champs-Elysées, she and her governess were sent back. This was bewildering, and even more disappointing was not being allowed to play in the gardens of the Avenue Gabriel, the hoop-rolling rendezvous of upper-class children. Her Majesty's Minister Plenipotentiary was taking no chances.

In the winter of 1870, the Franco-Prussian war brought German occupation, the fall of the Second Empire and a new French government provisionally installed in Bordeaux. The British Embassy staff moved with it, and the winter of 1870-1 must have been a happy time for Pepita. She was expecting another baby in the early spring and awaited it with the rest of the children in Arcachon, so conveniently close to Bordeaux and Lionel. It must have been a blow when Lord Lyons ordered Sackville-West to return to Paris to take charge of the deserted Embassy and the worst of luck that he should have been the officer chosen, but it was thought that he would not be gone long and when he left on 16 February 1871, Pepita's natural optimism reasserted itself and she settled down cheerfully enough to wait for the arrival of her seventh child.

He had hardly been gone three weeks, when the frightening telegrams began coming to Paris, signed by Béon. The baby, Frederic, had been born on 6 March, to live only briefly, and Pepita's condition was alarming. The frantic Sackville-West obtained permission from Lord Lyons to rush to Arcachon, but arrived too late, Pepita had followed her baby two days later and it was little comfort to hear that she had died with his name, 'Lionel', upon her lips.

Poor Sackville-West was confronted with Victoria, a desperate little girl of eight and a half, and his four other children. Max was by now twelve, Flora five, Amalia three and Henry a baby of two. The practical Desombres and Béon were there to take charge of the funeral arrangements. All the tradespeople and all the poor in the little town came to the service; for, as has been said, she was more beloved by the poor than by the rich in Arcachon. She had requested burial in her own garden under the little chapel, but even this last favour was denied her by the authorities and she lies in the bleak grey general cemetery, where today it is impossible to identify the grave.

Lionel's position was appalling. To whom could he entrust the care of the children? Their grandmother Catalina was still alive in Spain, but despite Pepita's generosity she and Manuel Lopez had sunk back into the obscure life from which they originally came; their money spent, they were said to be living in decayed and straightened circumstances in the poorest quarter of Malaga. The English family? Kind friends? There seem to have been no offers of help from England or if there were they were not recorded. And there were no friends, except for the Béons, mother and son. So Béon was chosen as guardian, and Sackville-West left the children with him and his mother at the Villa Pepa for the next two years. Then Madame de Béon and her son moved to Paris, established themselves in an apartment paid for by Sackville-West and left only Max, the eldest boy, at his school in Bordeaux. The little children lived with the Béons, the eldest girl, Victoria, was put in the Convent of St Joseph, on the rue Monceau, where she remained for seven cruel years. The nuns were not unkind but it cannot have been easy for them to assimilate this unusual child. Illiterate, emotional, accustomed to the enchantingly happy-go-lucky ways of life in the Villa Pepa, possessed already of the charm and beauty of her dancer mother, spoiled, as the nuns would have seen it, and full of the arrogance that little girls exhibit when they are desperately unhappy. It would have been hard even today for one of the sisters at St Joseph, now so well and wisely trained in child psychology, to handle Victoria. In 1873 it was impossible. '*Oui, ma Mère. Oui, ma Soeur. Merci, ma Mère.*' That was the vocabulary. She must have been dying inside, longing to make it seem that praying to Our Lady for warm feet in bed was not a sin. It was hard to explain that she had always slept in her mother's warm bed, that she had been accustomed to Spanish elasticity of hours, to loving maids who had understood that she could spoil her frilled pantalettes rolling on the lawn and getting grass stains on them, and that her indulgent mother would laugh over the catastrophe and say that there were always new pantalettes to buy, and that rolling down a sloping lawn was a natural thing to do.

What did she in fact learn at the convent? Above all, 'morale', the tenets of her Church, as applied in that day. She learned how to sew expertly and she knew by heart the names of the rivers of France and their tributaries, the names of the departments of France and their capitals. Of French history she learned a great deal, and could recite the names of the kings of France backwards. Of other histories she learned nothing, and of modern literature nothing. The great nineteenth-century novelists were closed books, as were the scientific and philosophical writings of the day. Holidays were either spent with the nuns at the singularly gloomy resort at Berck-sur-Mer, where the winds from the English Channel were supposed to restore health to the tubercular patients who filled the pensions and sanatoriums of the town; or with the Béons. The Béon holidays were spent getting out of the way when visitors came for, sleek and prosperous with Sackville-West money, the Béons were now entertaining their friends and one must assume that they were extremely sensitive to the embarrassment of explaining the *raison d'être* for their new-found prosperity. Victoria must not have understood, but noted later that whenever Madame de Béon received, it was made most clear that she should remove herself to her bedroom for the afternoon or evening. One can imagine the Comtesse de Béon offering those rich *pâtisseries* from the most fashionable pastry shop in Paris (the strawberry tarts, always encrusted in their crisp paper cases, so that no one would mistake their origin), and saying, 'Do have another cup of tea . . .'

Sackville-West had gone to the Argentine in 1872. It must have been a relief to him for several reasons. It was his first post as head of a mission, and not an unimportant one, for commercial interests made Buenos Aires a capital of considerable interest to the United Kingdom. Above all, it was far away. Before leaving he made the best arrangements he could. Max was to attend Stony-hurst, a famous Roman Catholic boarding school in England, to be followed by little Henry when he was old enough. First, Henry was to stay with the Béons, then to proceed to a *lycée* in Vannes, Brittany, preparing for Stonyhurst, then later on both brothers were to be sent out to South Africa to farm. By the time Henry arrived, Max would presumably have established himself and could help him. Remittance men, but what were Sackville-West's alternatives? The girls we have seen disposed of with the Béons, Flora and Amalia to follow Victoria into the convent.

It was the best Sackville-West could do. Victoria, embattled, wretched, was fighting for what would now be called her identity in the convent. She, who was known as 'Mademoiselle 42' summoned courage and strength to help her little brother, Henry, the saddest of all. A very early letter from him to her, written in French, undated, but in such a childish hand that it must have been written in pre-*lycée* days, and still while he was living with the Béons:

> My dear sister,
> I remember that when you left for boarding school I cried, I don't know why. Write me a letter a little longer than your last one. Pepita, send me a stamp and I will write to you. Send me some pictures to look at. I send you all my love. Goodbye. Write as soon as possible.

Henry always called Victoria Pepita as a child, as did the other children.

There were later affectionate letters, always begging Victoria to write again soon, thanking her for the news she sent him of the other children, sending her little pictures to be given to Flora and Amalia at their first communions, and so on. By the time Henry was ten, his writing was good and his feelings well-expressed.

Far-off Papa wrote charming letters to Victoria from Buenos Aires. In 1873, when Victoria was eleven, he said how glad he was that she was doing well in her studies; he described the Argentine flowers and birds, which were unlike any in Europe, and he told of his expeditions into the interior where he had seen lions and tigers. He promised to teach her to ride when he returned. Above all he implored her to look after little Flora when she came to the convent, because she was so tiny and less strong than the others. 'You are a big girl now, and I greatly count upon you, my dear daughter, to take care of the family.'

Later he decribed the official business which delayed his coming to Paris and went on to promise her that he would not leave her at the convent much longer. (But he did leave her there for another six years.) He urged her to do whatever Madame de Béon said and to try and please her.

During his infrequent visits to Europe – there were two or possibly three – Sackville-West, a kind and conscientious father and an experienced man of the world, must have observed that his oldest daughter was growing up without friends in a cold and hostile environment from which she begged to be removed. However, his choices were limited. That he worried about the children was evidenced by the fact that he consulted Mrs Mulhall, who with her husband were among his English friends in Buenos Aires. Something had to be done about Victoria, who was due to leave the convent in 1880 with nothing but a certificate enabling her to seek employment as a governess and a blind faith in her remote father. Mrs Mulhall came to Paris, scooped up Victoria and on the Channel crossing to England told her that she was illegitimate. At first Victoria did not understand what this meant; and the first record we have of her mentioning it to anyone came a year later, in 1881, when she felt that she must inform Henry before he entered his English boarding school, Stonyhurst, in order to protect him from the shock of learning it from anyone else. Meanwhile, she had been placed in a convent in Highgate for what amounted to a crash course in English, and on the death of Madame de Béon, Mrs Mulhall offered to take the children in and carried them off to her own house, Grasslands, at Balcombe in Sussex.

But the children couldn't be left with the Mulhalls forever. Something had to be done, and at last Victoria's English relations entered the story. Her two aunts, the Duchess of Bedford and the Countess of Derby, both invited the girls to their houses. They were received alone, and it was understood that if other visitors arrived, the embarrassing nieces were to be dismissed. Lady Derby was the kinder of the two; she lent them her box at Albert Hall, and went to see them in Highgate, and after the grim, lonely Paris convent Victoria was very grateful to Aunt Mary Derby. It had been nearly ten years since Pepita died, and she had known no affection since except from her unreachably far-off father. Accustomed to her humble and ambiguous position in life, she probably did not guess as she climbed the stairs of Derby House that the great lady was observing her with a keen and experienced eye, weighing an important decision.

Lady Derby had first been married to James, second Marquess of Salisbury. As a widow she married the fifteenth Earl of Derby, Foreign Secretary under Disraeli from 1874 to 1878 in which year he resigned the Conservative whip. He became a Liberal under Gladstone and joined the Liberal Government as Colonial Secretary in 1882. Thus, in the year 1881 Lady Derby was in an unassailable position to use influence in order to obtain a favour from the Liberals, who were courting her husband, or, indeed, if she needed Conservative help she would not have hesitated to canvass the other side of the family; the third Marquess of Salisbury had succeeded Lord Derby as Foreign Secretary in 1878.

She was a formidable figure, and very fond of her brother Lionel, who had returned from Argentina and was looking for a job. The Washington Legation was open, and Sackville-West was appointed; the exchanges between the two governments on his appointment were of a routine nature. The Foreign Office proposed the name of Lionel Sackville-West and James G. Blaine, Secretary of State under President Garfield gave the *agrément*. There is only one unusual note in the correspondence. James Russell Lowell, United States Minister in London informed his chief in Washington that he had known Sackville-West well in Madrid, where they had served at the same time, and that he could assure the Secretary that in his view Sackville-West would be socially acceptable. An odd phrase in view of the appointee's historic name, but Lowell must have known about Pepita and was assuring the Department of State that Sackville-West could be trusted in every sense of the word. For Lady Derby this hurdle was nothing compared to the problem of Lionel's hostess, and hostess he had to have.

The British Legation in Washington only became an embassy in 1893 and would not have compared in importance to one of the big European embassies in 1881. Still, it was all the same important, and Her Majesty's Government expected the British Minister to entertain often and well; yet Washington custom was that ladies could attend no entertainments given by gentlemen who had no hostess to preside for them. What to do?

Lady Derby took a gamble. Having observed her eighteen-year-old niece with the shrewd eye of a woman of the world, she decided that this ill-educated, insecure, illegitimate girl had the potential that was required; and she threw all her power and influence into persuading Lord Granville and Queen Victoria that Victoria should accompany her father to Washington as his hostess. The Queen agreed, contingent on the approval of Washington society. A committee was composed of the wife of the President, Mrs Garfield, the wives of the Secretary of State and the Under-Secretary of State, and the wife of a leading Republican senator, Don Cameron of Pennsylvania. The question put to these ladies was whether society could accept as the hostess of the most important diplo-

2
Political Washington

The new British Minister arrived on 5 November 1881, and moved into his Legation, which had been built eight years before on the corner of Connecticut Avenue and N Street. It had been bold on the part of Sir Edward Thornton, Sackville-West's predecessor, to insist on this then-remote site; a good fifteen minutes on foot from the White House on Lafayette Square. He had foreseen that the Washington of the early seventies would expand and that the dusty wilderness north-west of the White House would be developed, reflecting the vertiginous development of the United States. London thought that he had delusions of grandeur, and Sir Edward's pleas for a very large house were treated by the Office of Works as the ravings of a lunatic, the thinly veiled implication being that, lost in his dim outpost, he had begun to imagine himself Ambassador to Vienna or even Paris. Sir Edward fought back gamely; there was a note of pathos in the correspondence as he pled for a smoking room on the grounds that a good cigar could open the heart of the Secretary of State. A tenacious man, he won the argument and the house was large, built of the dull dark-red brick so admired in Victorian times. The style was bastard Louis XIII, the fine plain lines of the French seventeenth century were broken by many a whimsical touch in what was later called 'Newport Renaissance' style, and a golden minaret sprang unexpectedly from the central tower above the mansard roof. There was a heavy *porte-cochère* carrying the arms of Great Britain; twelve stone steps led up to the front door. In cheerful photographs Sackville-West is sitting on these steps on a sunny day surrounded by his small staff; there is a family feeling about the scene, and there was in those days a sort of countrified charm about the quarter in which the Legation stood. The only noise to disturb the peace of N Street was the cry of vendors selling watermelons, red ripe, at five cents apiece, the musical sound coming through the wide windows on warm evenings.

Sackville-West had sent over an advance guard of a dozen French and English servants with his plate and personal possessions, and his steward had bought many of Sir Edward's furnishings at a legation sale held before his departure. The government supplied more, but as a younger son Sackville-West did not have many things of his own and Mrs James G. Blaine, the wife of the Secretary of State who dined at the Legation just before the arrival of Victoria remarked on the forlorn bareness of the house.

But the new Minister had more immediate things on his mind than housekeeping, and would have cared little had he known that his private life was already the subject of speculation. President Garfield had been shot by a disappointed office-seeker in July, and lingered on until September, when he was succeeded by the Vice-President Chester A. Arthur. Arthur was a widower, and Mrs Henry Adams, the keenest observer of her day, noted that the arrival of the bachelor British Minister and the new President promoted the eagerest interest among the widows of Washington. The President was, of course, the first prize in the race, but the British Minister not a bad second. Sackville-West was to prove a disappointment to the dashing widows; for a spring had broken within him that terrible day in Arcachon 1871, and this handsome man of fifty-four was not looking for a wife. His mind was on his job, and success depended on the man who was the dominant figure in American politics of the day, James G. Blaine, then Secretary of State.

Blaine was important to Victoria's story as he was to her father's. He was a big man, brilliantly intelligent, a compelling orator, possessed of flair and charm, and the first national figure since the Civil War to be deeply interested in foreign affairs. He should have been just the man to harness the energies of the 1880s in America, the virility, youth and raw power that so typify that decade. But he was a flawed hero. The source of his wealth was mysterious; while Speaker of the House he refused to expose his holdings or to make public the crucial evidence, the 'Mulligan papers' which contained the information on a supposed deal between Blaine and the Little Rock and Ft Smith Railroad. Although never proved, it was widely assumed that in return for a favour he gave the railroad he was given the opportunity of selling their bonds at a secret and lucrative commission. By a superb speech to the House he saved himself with the loyal Republicans, but the suspicion of corruption could never be erased and although he was a perennial candidate he never achieved the presidency. But he was a remarkable man, and even Mrs Henry Adams who 'cut' him socially recognized the waste of talent. 'What a pity', she wrote to her father in Boston, 'that so much ability should be unsupported by enough moral sense to make him an honest public servant.' Blaine's wife, born Harriet Stanwood of Augusta, Maine, was as perceptive and shrewd as Mrs Adams; her letters are with Mrs Adams's the most literate and interesting records we have of Washington. The two women were made for each other and should have been close friends had they not been hopelessly divided by politics.

Blaine as Secretary of State was publicly a violent anglophobe. He had described his policy to Sir Edward Thornton in simpler words than he generally used: 'England as against the United States,' he said, 'was always wrong.'

When Sackville-West arrived the four central questions preoccupying the Secretary of State concerned British–American relations; on all four the two countries were adversaries. What was the new British Minister to do? He knew exactly what he was going to do; he was going to make friends with Blaine and he went about it immediately.

The Adamses watched with interest. It was a lovely autumn, and the Indian summer weather continued for much of November and December, the Virginia hills were ablaze with red, purple and yellow. On 4 December Mrs Adams was able to pick a gay bunch of chrysanthemums in the garden on H Street, and there had been a day in November on which she preferred the shady side of the street on Pennsylvania Avenue as the temperature rose over seventy degrees. It was a delight to ride out through sleepy Georgetown to the Virginia shore of the Potomac, as the Adamses did every afternoon, letting their horses go over the slopes leading to wooded Arlington. They came home to dine (possibly taking the Long Bridge to vary the excursion), and after dinner, which was at seven, came the evening call at about nine or ten. Gentlemen wore evening dress with white waistcoats; the ladies awaited them in long sleeved evening dresses, their tight bodices whaleboned, and tea was served as gossip was exchanged. Henry Adams, professor, historian, son of the house of Adams in Boston, which had already given the country two presidents and a line of distinguished diplomats, had moved to Washington with his brilliant wife in order to watch how the wheels of power moved. Nothing could interest him more than to observe those turning in the house around the corner on 15th Street in which lived the Secretary of State and Mrs Blaine. In his brilliant, recently published comedy of manners, the novel *Democracy*, Adams had given the name Senator Silas P. Ratcliffe to Blaine, of whom he was thinking when he wrote these lines:

A certain secret jealousy of the British Minister is always lurking in the breast of every American Senator, if he is truly democratic; for democracy, rightly understood, is the government of the people, by the people, for the benefit of senators, and there is always a danger that the British Minister may not understand this political principle as he should.

If the new British Minister was nervous as he entered the drawing room of the Secretary of State on the evening of 16 November, ten days after his arrival, he showed no sign of it. Mrs Blaine, wife of the Secretary, had been very anxious about her dinner. The house was large and comfortable; Mrs Blaine, an experienced hostess, was a wise and witty woman; but had it been a good idea to invite both the new President and the British Minister, the two newest lions in town to the same party? And by the worst of luck, the usually well-ordered household was in disarray; she had only a substitute cook, one man and her maid. Dinner was at seven, and although we do not have the menu for that night, it would have been considered vulgar to serve more than ten courses. One of Mrs Blaine's luncheon menus gives some idea of the generous table she set. 'Oysters on shell, mock turtle soup, broiled chicken and fried potatoes, sweetbreads and peas, asparagus, Roman punch, partridge and salad, ices, charlottes, jellies, sweetmeats, fruits, coffee and tea.' For the President and the British Minister, she would have outdone herself, and it appeared that not a moment dragged, although the party did not break up until nearly midnight. Sackville-West was thought to be the most agreeable and cordial of men, very ready to be entertained; the President was always a delightful conversationalist and Blaine was one of the most brilliant talkers in the country. The food was as great a success as the dinner was gay, and the undercurrents were undiscernible. The Blaines, of course, were tensely aware that the President was going to replace his Secretary of State, and it was about this time that lovely young Mrs Don Cameron encountering her dear friend Mrs Blaine remarked to her in a moment of malice, 'What are your plans, Mrs Blaine? Shall you pass the winter in Augusta?'

Sackville-West, a professional diplomat, had no illusions about his charming host, and a few weeks later was writing privately to the Foreign Secretary, Lord Granville:

> Every man in office in this country consults solely his political future, and if a secretary of state sees his way to advancing his own interests in this respect by appealing to national prejudice he will do so regardless of the consequences. Such have been Mr Blaine's motives in the present case.

The present case to which the Minister referred was the problem of the proposed canal to link the Atlantic with the Pacific Ocean, a weary business which was ultimately decided twenty years later by Theodore Roosevelt when he modified the Clayton–Bulwer treaty of 1850 by which the United States and Great Britain had agreed that the Isthmian canal, as it was then called, would be placed under joint guarantee. Blaine insisted that the canal must be built under the unilateral auspices of the United States and that it should have no other protector. Pages flowed across the Atlantic on the subject, as they did on the issue known as 'America for the Americans'. Blaine found the Monroe Doctrine too negative and wanted the United States to assume the role of 'elder sister' to the Latin-American nations. Latin America was very important to England commercially, and no one knew it better than Sackville-West, former British Minister to the Argentine. The Hawaiian Islands were another sore spot, the State Department considered them to be part of the American hemisphere, but feared that the British planned to take them over. These matters were, however, pinpricks compared to the running sore of the Irish question, the bitterness of which was to poison Anglo-American relations throughout Sackville-West's tenure of office. His private letters to his chief were interesting. Outwardly, the agreeable new British Minister was busy getting to know his staff, relaxing on the gravel tennis court at the Legation in that lovely Indian summer autumn, dining out night after night as the dashing widows had hoped he would. His private correspondence with Lord Granville showed another Sackville-West, firing off competent and well-drafted reports to London succinctly outlining the problems before him, above all Blaine's public support of the Irish extremists. The Irish-American vote was crucial to any American politician, and the Secretary of State was already looking to the presidential elections of 1884.

It was a delicate and difficult mission for a British Minister. The arrival of Victoria on 22 December 1881 must have distracted his mind. She landed in New York accompanied by Mademoiselle Louet, a French lady-companion of infinite respectability, chosen by Lady Derby. On shipboard she had been in the charge of the estimable Boston merchant Mr John Sturgis, who wrote to thank Lady Derby for having put Victoria under his care and for giving his daughters 'so sweet a sister'. He said,

> I quite envy her father the possession of a child at once so docile and of so good a temperament. You must not consider my expression extravagant, but must remember that 12 days' intimate association on board ship is equal to an equal number of years acquaintance on land.

This charming letter must have been warmly received at Derby House, St James's Square. In Washington, Victoria had reason to be docile that winter night she arrived. The large number of servants, for instance, all awaiting her orders as their mistress; grand French and English servants who would have been observing her keenly. There was the big, bare official residence, which Papa expected her to administer, and Papa himself with his carefully planned schedule. It would have been an intimidating prospect for an experienced woman; to Victoria it must have been terrifying.

The day after her arrival, her father took her to call on Mrs Blaine, who found her extremely pleasing and pretty. It is significant that Sackville-West wished her to make her first call at this house. Blaine had been replaced by Frederick T. Frelinghuysen as Secretary of State four days before, so there was no official necessity for the call. Possibly, Sackville-West was indirectly paying a debt, for it must be remembered that Mrs Blaine had been one of the four members of the crucial 'Ladies' Committee' that had voted to accept Victoria in Washington. Also, Mrs Blaine was a warm and intelligent woman; Sackville-West liked her as he did her husband. He wrote to Lord Granville that he considered Blaine as a personal friend, who in private was the first to deplore the Fenians, the Irish-American Society whose terroristic acts he applauded in public speeches for their twisting of the British lion's tail. Sackville-West saw much of Blaine when the Secretary of State was out of office, partly because he was likely to become the next President, perhaps because he was grateful to the Blaines for their support of Victoria.

The next crucial call was on Mrs Adams, a few days later. It would not have done to go immediately from the Blaines to Mrs Adams, who cut Mrs Blaine as the wife of a tainted politician, but this was the most interesting house in Washington. It has been said that Henry Adams had come to Washington to study the machinery of power; this is an incomplete picture of a serious man who was worried, for the country's early moralism and Civil War idealism had been replaced in the seventies by a national binge of greed and corruption. He came to Washington to help.

By then, in the early 1880s, there existed a small band of reformers who demanded something better; there was a new smell in the air. They wanted civil-service reform which would exchange the spoils system for a merit system; and they wanted honest public servants. There were the influential journalists, who did much to alert Americans to the need for change; Carl Schurz, George Curtis, Edwin Godkin. They were joined by Henry Adams and his friends Theodore Roosevelt and Henry Cabot Lodge, sons of some of the most respected families in the country. Well-educated, high-minded, the 'machine-smashers' as they were called, were a force to reckon with and while Sackville-West would not have thought of trying to explain the political importance of the house at 1607 H Street, he could easily have told Victoria that she would meet the most interesting people in Washington there, and that it was fun, for despite Mrs Adams' highmindedness there was a cheerful informality about the little dinners of six or eight carefully chosen spirits, and one likes the descriptions of pretty young women like Mrs Cameron and her friend Miss Emily Beale tapping on the windows of Adams's study with their umbrellas, explaining that it was so much better than ringing, as he couldn't say that he was out, and they were dying for a good cup of tea. It is possible to caricature the fastidious Adamses, and their friend Henry James did so when he described in his story, *Pandora*, a Washington gentleman, Mr Bonnycastle, suggesting to his wife that for once they ignore the social niceties in preparing a guest list. 'Hang it . . . let us have some fun – let us invite the President.'

Mrs Adams herself was a brilliant caricaturist and her letters were sometimes cruel in their observations of the new hostesses such as Mrs Levi P. Morton of New York with her English butler and footmen, but she went to Mrs Morton's; she even went to the White House, returning to report every terrible detail to her father in Boston. It was important for Victoria to make a good impression on the Adamses and Lady Derby would have been delighted could she have seen what Mrs Adams wrote:

> West, the new Minister, and his daughter, who has just come over, came in . . . and I thought her charming; she is the daughter of a Spanish ballet dancer, now dead, has been educated at a convent in France, is quite pretty, rather elegant, and speaks with a most charming foreign accent. It's a curious position for a girl of eighteen to be put at the head of a big establishment like the British Legation. She is delighted with her first week here. As I can't endure English misses, it's a great relief to have this pretty girl after Lady Thornton with her neuralgia and sharp tongue. Tomorrow, we are to dine with them at the Bancroft Davises' . . .

In all the letters of the first weeks in Washington, there is a note of surprise that the little daughter of the Spanish dancer should be so pretty and so elegant; her charming foreign accent amused people. She was always described as a shy *ingénue*, sitting quietly over her embroidery, or once, being persuaded to play the piano, while others waltzed. The newspapers were kind although Mrs Adams wrote:

> The Sunday papers opened fire at first but were instantly throttled – probably by Blaine as he holds them all even today, and Mrs Blaine, so one of her intimate friends told me, was consulted by West so she has to stand by him. Luckily for him the girl is sweet and refined in manner and attracts everyone; she will help him rather than hinder him – still, it's a horrid position; there are *three* other children in England. You had better not show this . . . gossip travels fast enough.

On the whole probably most of Washington society felt as did a woman who said that what was good enough for Queen Victoria was good enough for her. Docile, refined, shy were the adjectives most frequently applied to Victoria in the first weeks. Mrs Adams, after several meetings, wrote 'She is a funny little church mouse in contrast with the sharp-clawed grimalkin who preceded her.'

On New Year's Day 1882, ten days after her arrival, Victoria accompanied her father and his staff to the President's New Year Reception. This was always an important occasion, but this year it was a fascinating one for devotees of Washington's favourite indoor game, *White House watching*. In any president's first term the social atmosphere is charged, for the curtain has gone up and every move of the players seems important, from the colours chosen for the presidential bedroom to the photographs in that room, from the name of the Secretary of State, to the name of the family dog. Not a detail of the President's choice in china, his reading habits, his breakfast menu, the hour at which he rises, and the hour that he goes to bed escapes the public scrutiny. So it has been since the earliest days of the republic, and so it will always be, but it was in some ways a crueller game then than it is today. Since Andrew Jackson's tenure of office, it had been the accepted rule that presidents must live as economically, as meanly as possible, in order to have the world perceive how truly republican were their principles. Any ugly tendency towards monarchical grandeur, such as requesting funds from Congress to maintain the White House as a clean and comfortable gentleman's dwelling brought the eagles swooping, screaming from Capitol Hill; and that the President should demand even a small portion of the privacy of an individual citizen would have given the cartoonists of the day a splendid opportunity to race to their history books in order to find an image of Emperor Nero on which to impose the features of the present incumbent. The dignity of the office between the terms of Abraham Lincoln and Chester Arthur was hard for the foreign visitor to perceive; all engravings of the hall of the White House during the seventies showed it jammed with office-seekers slouching about hard by the adjacent spitoon, and even in Cleveland's administration later in the eighties, any citizen could call on the President simply by presenting his card to the guard. Unless the visitor was obviously deranged, he was admitted. The public receptions were indeed public. People of every age, colour and station of life lined up for four blocks from the front door of the White House down Pennsylvania Avenue.

The casual manners of the pre-Arthur period are typified by the description of a dinner for thirty-five people given by President Hayes in 1881, at the end of his term and less than a year before Arthur took office. The German Minister remembered that Senator Schumacher of Ohio said to him that he always thought it best to accept a dinner, and then when the time came you could do what you liked. The wife of Senator Conger of Michigan remarked that neither she nor a Kentucky lady on the Minister's left had answered their dinner invitations to the White House at all, not thinking it a thing to do. Mrs Henry Adams and her husband, who were at this dinner, fell ill the next day and attributed the cause to having drunk 'Potomac water' at the teetotal Hayes White House; Mrs Adams was not however too unwell to resist a description of the china on the table in a letter to her father in Boston:

> The new dinner set, which is said to have cost fifteen thousand dollars, is fearful. To eat one's soup calmly with a coyote spring-ing at you from a pine tree is intimidating, and ice cream plates disguised as Indian snowshoes would be aesthetic, but make one yearn for Mongolian simplicity.

Chester A. Arthur surprised everyone; his critics and his friends. He was a product of the corrupt machine politics of New York. As a former Republican boss himself, he was expected to accept the crippling spoils system which meant a job awarded in return for a vote, extending down to scrubwomen in public office buildings. Yet, once in office, he pressed for and obtained civil-service legislation which required appointments to be made as the result of open, competitive examinations. Personally, he looked as a president should look: six foot one, handsome, urbane, immacu-lately turned out. The White House watchers noted his charm and easy manners, his love of pleasure, and good companionship. Not an outstanding president; all the same, he had dignity and in his administration, style returned to the White House. Not everyone liked it, an annoyed citizen wrote to the *Evening Star* that it was intolerable that a man was expected to get up when the President came in.

However, critics and admirers were alike in their curiosity to see the renovations at the White House that New Year's Day of 1882.

Arthur's first action had been to clear out the roaches and vermin which infested the old house; and to improve the rudimentary sanitary conditions, for escaping gas from the ancient brick sewer was a serious health hazard. The place hadn't been touched for years, and the President chose Tiffany and Co. of New York as decorators. Famous for their cunning use of glass, they suggested to Arthur that they make a large glass screen of many colours to be thrown across the public entrance hall. This, it was hoped, would ensure some degree of privacy from the ubiquitous crowds of office-seekers. Arthur was delighted by the idea of the screen; and it also helped when he established regular visiting hours; an unprecedented move. The East Room, main reception room of the White House, was furnished in what the President considered an unsuitable style of 'steamboat' furniture, which was alive with insects who had found the sunny room a happy home for years. President Arthur must have really hated this verminous furniture; he is said to have left his office to assist the movers himself, and stood in the middle of the East Room brushing the insects off his frock coat with a French handkerchief of lawn as he lent a hand. Next to the East Room was the Green Room. The improvements here made the White House watchers goggle as they strained over the accounts in their newspapers.

In each corner of the ceiling, a decorative plaster bird had been installed; with the foot of a stork, a pink body and one wing, a tall red comb, a long, red bill and a fish's tail. What would Andrew Jackson have said of such luxury? But the papers particularly revelled in the President's sleeping chamber, as his bedroom was called; it had a ceiling of intense sky blue, the walls papered in silver, delicately flowered in gold.

The President laid in a cellar of fine French wines, engaged an excellent cook, and prepared for his first season of entertaining.

The public, on the whole, loved it. As has been suggested earlier, there was a new breeze stirring in the country; it was a time of transition and Americans were sick of dishonest politicians, of the spoils system, of shoddiness in the White House. They wanted the President's house to reflect a new dignity that the dreary Reconstruction period following the Civil War had lacked; and if the dignity of the new President was combined with a certain lushness in his residence, so much the better; America was bursting with vibrant vitality and exuberance.

President Arthur's first New Year's Day reception began promptly at 11 a.m., on a chilly morning in the year 1882. The Diplomatic Corps were received first, convening in the newly redecorated Red Room with its ruby red velvet and lace curtains, its richly upholstered red plush furniture, buttoned and anti-macassered, its ruby and red Persian carpets. Potted palms were placed in happy conjunction with other plants so beloved by the Victorians, some on pedestals, some in specially designed, round pieces of mahogany furniture. The visitors admired the discretion of the White House gardeners, remarking that nothing was in profusion. This term is, however, relative, for in Victorian times, no drawing room was not crowded. Red flowers were especially popular, the crimson rose, the strident coxcomb, the scarlet salvia, usually in combination with asparagus fern. Against this cheerful background the Diplomatic Corps milled about making conversation as they waited to be summoned into the Blue Room next door, where the President was to receive them in that lovely oval room, the wide windows of which give, as do the windows of all the reception rooms, onto the wide South Lawn with its tall trees. From the Red Room there was an especially fine view of the elm planted by John Quincy Adams, beyond it was the Jefferson Mound, and in the distance rose the slender shaft of the new Washington Monument.

Sackville-West wore the diplomatic uniform of his country, 'levée dress', dark blue cloth tail coat and trousers, gold-lace embroidered collar and cuffs, gold buttons in a line from the high collar to the waist. He wore a sword and carried a cocked hat. This costume struck by its simplicity next to the superb azure-blue satin robe of the Chinese Minister. The French Minister wore the semi-military dark uniform of the time, and carried in his hand a Napoleonic cocked hat reminiscent of Imperial days. His wife, the 'winsome' Madame Outrey, wore a black velvet evening dress with a long train; the popular Turkish Minister, Aristarchi Bey wore the traditional red fez. As the clock struck eleven, the Dean of the Corps, Mr Allan of Hawaii, entered the Blue Room where the President, in morning clothes, stood, flanked by the wives of his Cabinet members. This flashy assembly of diplomats provided the newspaper reporters with rich material for the descriptive journalistic style of the day, and it is quite remarkable that the young daughter of the British Minister should have gotten the attention that she did. Victoria had been received kindly by the press – but now, after only ten days in Washington, she stunned them and the writing became lyrical, to continue so during the seven years she spent in Washington. No other woman in the Diplomatic Corps was to receive such coverage. She kept a scrapbook into which she carefully pasted in references to herself, sometimes writing comments on the margin. But this is as if the great opera singer Melba had tried to keep track of her publicity without the benefit of a clipping service. The scrapbook was an amateur effort compared to what was discovered in the files of the newspapers of the eighties; the tip of the iceberg.

Her great charm was evidently apparent that grey morning of 1 January 1882 at the White House. Yet she was quietly dressed in a heavy, dark green, satin walking dress, with a simple bonnet to match. Never in her life did she wear make up; her skin was always ravishing and unlined. About five foot seven and a half, she had her mother's height and was slim, with a tiny waist. Dark-blue eyes, wonderful eyes according to the reporters, with long dark lashes. Masses of thick black hair (the dancer's inheritance in its abundance, but darker than Pepita's) done up demurely, not in a showy pompadour but looking as if she had done it herself with her long hands; just pulled it up and stuck in a comb or two to keep it in place.

The effect was so unstudied that one gasps looking at the profile photograph (see illustration, section one). The nose was classic, the eyebrows high and arched, the neck Modigliani-long and slender. The French speak of women having 'allure', the English use the word 'alluring'; both are hard to define. Sex appeal certainly – but it was not blatant. The sex appeal was subtle; distinction was the first quality, and in the photograph of the young Victoria, there was gentleness and delicacy, above all freshness. The adjective 'alluring' was applied to her all her life. She could madden people, but ten minutes later she had them laughing, bewitched, fascinated. The charm came across to the reporters immediately, and they rushed for their notebooks to cram them with superlatives.

Did President Arthur notice Victoria? It wasn't an easy day for him; after the departure of the official guests the unofficial ones arrived in such crowds that the police had to be called in. There was always gossip about the charming widower, Arthur, and every year the story of a new romance. Sackville-West had written to Lord Granville that the new Secretary of State, Frederick T. Frelinghuysen, owed his appointment to the attraction of one of his daughters. Victoria wrote in the *Book of Reminiscences*:

> What flattered my vanity as a young girl was the proposal of marriage from President Arthur, after a dinner at the White House; it was the second proposal I had at Washington. I burst out laughing in his face and said: "Mr President, you have a son older than me and you are as old as my father."

There is no reason to disbelieve her, and it is significant that the report was officially disclaimed by the President's brother, under the headline: 'The President NOT to get Married – SPECIAL REPORT TO THE WORLD.'

This flash, datelined Pittsburgh, 23 February 1883, was followed by a brief paragraph denying the rumour. By then, Victoria had been the toast of Washington for over a year and was fighting off suitors. From the way she described the episode after the White House dinner she took it very lightly. Victoria was extremely secretive about her relations with men when they were serious. Reticent, innocent and naive she took refuge in code, in misleading initials scattered about through scrapbook or diary. If the President's proposal had disturbed her or seemed important she would never have written of it so frivolously. It can only be conjecture, but possibly what happened was something like this. Chester Arthur took his seat at the White House table that night between Miss West on his right and the sixteen-stone wife of a leading senator on his left. He was weary, and the responsive young girl with the wide blue eyes seemed to understand everything that he told her. She said little herself, while he might have talked of the wretched day he had had with the uncooperative Congress and complained of his lonely return to the White House to face once again the long table with its boat-shaped centrepiece, a triumph of the White House gardeners that made the room almost sickly with the smell of hundreds of carnations. Victoria could have murmured in her low foreign voice something sympathetic; the bored, middle-aged President had never met anyone like her before and when protocol obliged him to turn the table in order not to offend his other neighbour he would have felt relaxed, appreciated, even young again. Later in the Oval Room the party must have sat about on the cushioned ottomans, the Marine Band, led by John Philip Sousa, probably played a Viennese waltz as the discreet black ushers passed glasses of champagne in the new Tiffany fluted glasses. Flushed with enthusiasm, the President could have suggested to Miss West that she was the only person who understood his problems and his loneliness and then proposed marriage. She would have laughed him off, gently, and he might well have been relieved, for he hardly knew her. Going home in the carriage she would certainly have told her father, who would have been half-asleep and bored. But a proposal from the President, however lightly made and lightly taken, is not a thing that a young girl could forget. At the first opportunity she would have confided the episode in deepest secrecy to her two girl friends Mrs Cameron and Miss Beale. The news would soon have been all over town, for the President had married off Miss Frelinghuysen and there always had to be a new romance. It became necessary for an official denial to be issued.

In any case much had happened to Victoria during her first year in Washington. It is time to ask what was this Washington, and what was her life?

3

Washington Entertains

A few weeks after Victoria's arrival Henry James, who had returned to America after an absence of six years, went to Washington and wrote to a friend in England:

> I should like to put America into a nutshell for you; but like Carlyle's Mirabeau, it has "swallowed all formulas". Things go very fast here, and the change that has taken place in the last ten years is almost incredible. The increase of civilization, of wealth, luxury, knowledge, taste, of all the arts and usages of life, is extremely striking, and all this means the increase of the agreeable ... I believe that Washington is the place in the world where money – or the absence of it, matters least. It is very queer and yet extremely pleasant: informal, familiar, heterogeneous, good-natured, essentially social and conversational, enormously big and yet extremely provincial, indefinably ridiculous and yet eminently agreeable. It is the only place in America where there is no business, where an air of leisure hangs over the enormous streets, where everyone walks slowly and doesn't look keen and preoccupied. The sky is blue, the sun is warm, the women are charming, and at dinners the talk is always general.

This superb description perfectly conveys the flavour of the Washington that Victoria knew. The agreeable quality of the city was largely due to a great administrator, Alexander Shepherd, Governor of the District of Columbia in the 1870s.

Originally, George Washington had first perceived the potential of the site. Enamoured of the river Potomac, with which General Washington was familiar from its source in the Appalachians to Chesapeake Bay, he had a wide vision of a capital strategically secure and at the same time capable of being linked by waterways

34

with the Western frontier. Besides which he and his architect, the young French engineer officer, Pierre L'Enfant, liked the topographical possibilities of the valley before them. The wide Potomac met its eastern branch, the Anacostia River, just south of the Capitol building that they planned; they dreamed of a canal system worthy of Venice to drain the lowland marshes; they asked Thomas Jefferson to lend them his plans of the cities he had visited in Europe, which he laid before them, a bit sceptically. Jefferson was never the enthusiast for the site of the new capital that Washington was.

Washington died before his vision could be carried out; and by 1870, the squalor of the city was such that serious men were talking of moving the capital to St Louis, Missouri. Foreign visitors, American editorial writers and reporters thundered out year after year that the capital was a national disgrace, an ugly and unhealthy overgrown village, and it was officially considered 'a hardship post' by European foreign offices. 'Boss' Shepherd had been preceded by other men, who had hoped to implement the great plan of L'Enfant and Washington, but their efforts were frustrated, and Shepherd happened to suit the time and place. Hundreds of miles of dusty streets were paved with smooth asphalt, a sewer system was built that was to become a model for the nation. A practical man, he was also imaginative. The great avenues were cold and sterile in their treelessness; Shepherd planted thousands of shade trees along them, and L'Enfant's open spaces which had become windy, dusty areas in summer and muddy ones in the winter were transformed into small parks, just as L'Enfant had planned. By 1881 Pennsylvania Avenue was lighted, as Shepherd had directed it would be; and the Army Corps of Engineers were draining the fetid marshes. Between them, Shepherd and the Engineer Corps turned Washington into a delightful town, which was still comfortably small when Victoria arrived. The population was less than 177,000, including Georgetown, the old Virginia port now incorporated into the District. Washington was provincial, cosy, and slow-moving; old inhabitants instantly recognized everyone who kept a carriage, and as Henry James remarked, 'an air of leisure hung over the enormous streets'.

As the far-sighted Sir Edward Thornton had predicted, the town was expanding rapidly to the northwest of the White House, and it was a pleasant walk from Dupont Circle, where the big new houses were going up, down to Lafayette Square; friends stopped to greet each other and to chat under the new sycamores on Connecticut Avenue. It was a great town for chatting. The lonely Congressman, ill-paid at $1,000 a year, could rarely afford to bring his family to Washington for the congressional sessions, which were briefer then than they are now. He lived in a boarding house, spending his evenings relaxing gratefully in the comfortable stuffed chairs at Willard's Hotel or Wormley's, chatting with his colleagues, glasses of whiskey in their hands and the inevitable spitoon beside each chair. Slow as the pace was, there was much to talk about, for power in that epoch lay not with decent Chester Arthur in the White House, but in the Congress.

Senators were another story. In 1882, the year after Victoria arrived, seventeen of them had a combined fortune of $600,000,000, and it was said that it was easier for a camel to go through a needle's eye than for a poor man to enter the United States Senate. These tycoons also enjoyed chatting as they strolled downtown majestically in their well-pressed frock coats, and poorer men bowed to them deferentially as they passed.

For women, there was a special institution for chatting. This was the Center Market on Pennsylvania Avenue, typical of the southern flavour of the town and its lack of hurry. Millionaires' wives and boarding-house keepers alike wandered from stall to stall making their decisions. The boarding-house keepers were the more keen-eyed, as they rapidly calculated how much bad food they dared give their congressional clients and still retain their custom. It was said that many a congressional beard was stained of a morning with the grease of stale eggs fried in oil.

The elegant ladies were followed by black grooms carrying baskets to fill with the delicacies that were so plentiful in those days: terrapin and crab from the Chesapeake, oysters, woodcock, wild duck and wild turkey in season, pheasant and partridge, too. Spring brought the first shad from the river, green asparagus to follow it, and later tiny fresh peas and juicy ripe tomatoes from the Maryland and Virginia countryside. When business was completed with the friendly black and white vendors, there was plenty of time to chat on the sunny sidewalk of the avenue. During the season, which officially opened on New Year's Day and ended with Lent, it was fashionable to be exhausted by the round of dinners, receptions, balls, teas and germans, to say nothing of the calling which occupied much of the ladies' time and followed an etiquette nearly as rigid as that which had ruled at the Court of Byzantium. In fact, the ladies were strong as horses and gradually the season began to extend through Lent. The post-mortems at the Center Market often began with the subject of decoration. Mrs Senator Hearst might congratulate Mrs Senator Stanford on her new candlesticks in the house on K Street – a silver brick had been consumed for the making of each one. Mrs Leland Stanford could gracefully reply that the whole town was talking about Mrs Hearst's reception of last Monday; everyone had been struck by the originality of the decoration in the doorway connecting the parlour with the ballroom. This was an umbrella covered with moss specially brought in from California and sprayed over with carnations. From it fell a pendant fringe of gilded cypress cones, also from the West. The White House was always a subject of conversation. Could one imagine anything finer than the Judiciary Dinner, at which the centrepiece was a scale of justice made of carnations and acacias with a dove bearing an olive leaf poised on top? The entire design was an island surrounded by water in which real goldfish swam. And all was surrounded by pots of stuffed game.

Victoria's first month was a busy one. Mrs Blaine, who had remarked on the bareness of the house before she arrived had also commented on the poor food. Mrs Senator Cameron had stolen the excellent Legation cook before Sackville-West's arrival.

Lovely Lizzie Cameron would probably not have done that to Victoria, who was soon to become her friend; on the other hand, she might have. Food is important in Washington society, and until cooks became practically an extinct species, some of the loveliest ladies in Washington have been known to indulge in the nefarious practice of cook-stealing. Also, Senator Cameron of Pennsylvania was a very rich man; Sackville-West by comparison a poor one, although his salary was generous for the day. He received $30,000 a year; while his opposite number, the U.S. Minister in London, received only $17,500.

Somehow Victoria managed; one never heard of a bad meal at the Legation again, and the house miraculously became charming overnight, according to the same witness. There was a large dinner on 19 January, a dinner and dance on the 26th, and another dinner and dance on 9 February. Henry James, who attended the party on the 26th must have found Victoria enchanting in her pale pink tulle dress, ruffled over satin of the same shade, a pink moire sash around her tiny waist, for a year later he remembered her, writing to Mrs Adams about his memories of Washington. '. . . and Miss West! You see in what a roseate vision Washington appears to me.'

The press raved, and Victoria delightedly pasted in the carefully cut-out clippings. A typical one reads,

> She is not yet nineteen years old and has the sprightliness of a child. Her style of beauty is more Castilian than Anglo-Saxon; [exclamation point in red ink by Victoria] she has expressive blue eyes and white skin, with dark hair; harsh English angles are rounded off by the grace of her Spanish mother . . . [these lines are underlined in red and marked in margin].

The letters must have flown across the Atlantic to Aunt Mary Derby. It would be fun to know what Sackville-West reported to his sister. We have a description of him talking to a visitor in his own ballroom that same season as he stood watching Victoria, amused. He explained that he had been given orders not to receive with her nor to interfere in any way; it was a young people's party and as it was her company, she wished to do the entertaining. He added that this was a surprise to him, for she had been educated in a convent, where dancing and deportment were not taught; yet she seemed to know it all. The two men paused in their conversation to watch Victoria and the visitor noticed how gracefully she danced; but that while doing so, she kept a sharp look-out for new arrivals. At the sight of one, she would break away from her partner, bound to the doorway and cordially greet the new arrivals, introduce partners to girls, and attend to everyone. She led the way from the ballroom to the dining room, saw that everyone was served, and even looked into the dressing room for ladies to see if all was right there.

Any woman reader who has ever been shy will instantly pick up the most important point in this description – Victoria's swift check of the ladies' cloakroom. She was not concerned about clean towels; an efficient maid would have been on duty. She was concerned about the lonely girls, who at all balls seek the ladies' cloakroom as a safe haven, pretending to arrange their hair.

Victoria was kind to the shy in her moment of triumph; unlike the parvenue, who rejects the image of what she herself had been a moment before; the illegitimate girl, who had climbed the stairs of Derby House so humbly a year earlier, must have remembered what it had been like in the lonely convent, the visits to her imposing London relations when she had been dismissed the moment the guests arrived, and the first awkward visits to Washington, where she sat docilely in the drawing rooms, bent silently over her embroidery, or was invited to play the piano so that others could waltz.

There were reasons for the sudden flowering of Victoria. She had never known flattery nor security since her mother's death. Now she knew both and her confidence grew daily, as she developed the potential that Lady Derby had thought was there. A natural executive, she relished the organization of the large household. Also, all through her life, she showed a chameleon-like ability to absorb and adapt to the interests of the man who was central to her life at any given period. During the Washington years this man was her father, and her main aim was to help him. And the political and social climate of the United States during the eighties were particularly congenial to her temperament. She could not have realized the facts: that America was about to pass Great Britain and take over the industrial leadership of the world; and that a decade later, its output would exceed that of England and Germany together; nor that her seven years in Washington were to span the final conquest of America's western frontier. Nor would the question of political corruption versus reform have meant anything to her – Victoria was never interested in political principles or general ideas of any kind; she was interested in individual persons. But such was the air of Washington that the forces affecting American society as a whole were reflected in the society in which she mixed, and these forces, the explosive industrial growth, the materialism, mixed with a gradual return to dignity in political life were all around her, embodied in the men and women she saw every day. She was naturally attracted to rich and powerful men older than she, and Washington was full of them. She must have enjoyed meeting Senator Hearst, who had said that after making all the money he wanted he was going to become a senator, if it took every damned cent he had. His colleague Senator Stanford of California was another big man, so were Blaine and Pendleton and

Cameron and many another whose names were on the Legation list.

And there were private moments in spite of the alarming social calendar; it was a cosy house as British legations and embassies usually are in small capitals. The staff was close to Sackville-West, who considered him a charming chief and were accustomed to his reticent ways. A visiting Canadian journalist gave a pleasant description of the lack of pomp at Connecticut Avenue and N Street. He was impressed by the Legation, which seemed to him like a spacious English manor house. A tall footman wearing a blue livery with scarlet facings answered the door and showed the representative of the *Toronto Mail* into a cheerful reception room full of flowers. The furniture was covered in faded, but freshly laundered pink and lilac linen. A young man in a threadbare jacket introduced himself as Mr Alan Johnstone, Secretary of Legation, and asked if the matter was something he could attend to. The reporter said that he had just dropped by to pay his respects to the Minister, as the representative of the greatest newspaper in the Dominion of Canada. In an instant, Sackville-West himself appeared in the doorway, dressed in an old tweed suit, and made himself perfectly charming to his visitor, praising the delights of the great Dominion, which he and his daughter had recently visited, and promised to render the *Toronto Mail* any service in his power. His warm smile impressed the visitor, and he was particularly appreciative of the cordial way in which the envoy extraordinary insisted on accompanying him to the door, with a careful parting admonition not to fall on the sidewalk. It is not surprising that the *Mail* reported that Mr West was a skilful diplomat well beloved by 'United States lawmakers'. In fact, Sackville-West would have received the Secretary of State or the Chairman of the Foreign Relations Committee exactly as he received the relatively obscure journalist. His manners were of the old shoe kind most likely to appeal to Americans and Canadians, who were in those days alarmed by brilliant, articulate, incisive British diplomats. They could not have known that this casual *grand seigneur*, padding back to his shabby office (the journalist remarked on the bareness of the office, which he glimpsed through the open door) might have been about to tear off a tightly worded telegram to London, which would have made Alan Johnstone whistle as he encoded it, or a long letter to Lord Granville blowing off steam about the machinations of the French Ambassador.

There is always in Washington a certain tension between the French and British embassies, disguised but real.

Old Outrey, who was at the White House with his 'winsome' wife, had been replaced by a cleverer man called Théodore Roustan. Sackville-West, writing to Lord Granville about the Isthmian Canal negotiations, could not resist a condescending line to the effect that Roustan was getting nowhere as he couldn't speak English.

Victoria, meanwhile, was making great friends with the French Minister. Roustan, a bachelor, was immensely flattered when the belle of Washington accepted an invitation for a merry French picnic, at which the small party ate 150 crabs. She was blessed with a good digestion, a consuming desire to help her father, and a sense of fun which is always the essential ingredient in awkward relationships. One can almost hear her saying to Roustan what a relief it was to speak French again; as she downed her thirty-fifth crab, and it would have been true, for although her English became good, both written and spoken, it had not been long since her first language, French, was her only one except for the Spanish of her very early childhood. It would be absurd to suppose that Victoria influenced Monsieur Roustan's views in any way, or that the problem of the future canal came up for a moment at the picnic, but it is always convenient for the French and British representatives in Washington to be on good terms. Sackville-West and innocent, blue-eyed Victoria were a good team.

And there was a family feeling in the British Legation. The Minister was fond of his small staff, they of him; the first tragedy came two months after Victoria's arrival. In spite of Shepherd's improvements to the city public health was still of concern to the residents; President Arthur was claimed to have had trouble forming his Cabinet because his preferred nominees were afraid of Washington's malaria. The defensive D.C. Medical Society reported in November 1881, that the rumoured prevalence of the disease was unfounded, but the papers headlined the malarial cases: 'ex-Senator Conkling of New York has it'; 'the late President Garfield's son has it'.

By the middle of the eighties items such as these disappeared from the press, but there were other illnesses: smallpox, tuberculosis, typhoid and diphtheria, often ill-diagnosed. On 13 March 1882, the *Evening Star* carried the following paragraph:

Lord George Francis Montague, Third Secretary at the British
Legation died yesterday of diphtheria . . . which he contracted
following a severe chill as a result of riding horseback in the rain
from Great Falls a week ago. He was treated by Dr Lincoln and
Surgeon-General Wales. He was 27 years old and had been in
Washington since January 1880.

To readers who have followed the colonial history of the French
and British Empires of the nineteenth century the above will have
a familiar ring. Small, overgrown cemeteries in India and South-
East Asia contain the graves of many gallant young men, who died
of disease in the service of their countries beside the Mekong or
the Ganges. Lord George was in that tradition beside the Potomac
in 1882.

The Sackville-Wests carried on.

Following the dinner and dance at the British Legation on
9 February, there was on 20 February a dancing reception, and on
27 February a dinner for the Chief Justice. In between there were
dinners at the other foreign legations and at the homes of Cabinet
members and senators; there was the President's state dinner in
honour of the Diplomatic Corps. For Victoria there was the oner-
ous duty of calling. Official ladies had special days appointed on
which they received from 3 to 5 p.m. Monday was the day for the
wives of Justices of the Supreme Court and of the General of the
Army and the Admiral of the Navy. On Tuesdays, the 'prominent
families of the West End have receptions'. This meant the
Senators' wives living on Massachusetts Avenue or Dupont or
Scott Circles. Wednesday was reserved for Cabinet wives and the
wife of the Speaker of the House. On Thursday there were diplomatic calls and on Friday and Saturday a mixed bag, sometimes
announced by the newspapers and sometimes by invitation. Even
the strongest ladies in Washington began to wilt under this
exhausting schedule, which entailed three hundred or so calls
during the season (the winter months) and in 1885 there was a sort
of strike and the rigid system was relaxed. Victoria did not have a
regular reception day that first year but if at home, did receive
those who came to call. In the morning during the months of the
season, she did not go to the Center Market herself, but sent the
Legation steward. This mistake born of ignorance was an expensive
one, as the Sackville-Wests later discovered to their chagrin that

the man had been robbing them for years. Victoria never forgot the lesson, and for the rest of her life kept her household accounts with extreme exactitude. She probably spent the morning planning the meals and seeing to the flowers, and writing the notes and letters that were so much a part of the life of the period. Luncheon was at one o'clock, preferably at home with her father and such members of the staff as he chose to invite to join them. Then the carriage drew up under the *porte cochère* and it was time to set out for the calls. Sackville-West paid for his own stables and had three carriages, which had been made in England and were the envy of the other legations. Everyone knew Miss West's turnout, with the English coachman and footman in blue liveries with silver hat bands.

On some other days, there were ladies' luncheons. At Mrs Leland Stanford's, luncheon took two and a half hours to serve and consisted of twelve courses. From Mrs Blaine's luncheon menu given on page 22, we have an idea of the sort of food. Occasionally, the decorations were all of one colour. Miss Bacon, daughter of Representative Bacon (not all congressmen lived in boarding houses) gave a red luncheon at which the shades of the candles and glass globes were red, the bread and baked potatoes were tied up with red ribbon, and a cushion of red tulips formed the centre-piece. The souvenirs were Japanese bonbons with dwarf red roses springing from their tops. Of course, the ice-cream was strawberry. Each hostess achieved her own form of originality – it was thought most amusing a few years later when Mrs Cleveland mingled chewing gum in gaily covered papers with the bonbons on the White House table.

The early ladies' luncheons were useful to Victoria, for they gave her a chance to get to know the women and to choose her friends among them. Her busy official life gave her little time to see women alone and, in any case, she seldom made intimate women friends, preferring throughout her life the company of men. But, women were important in Washington society and probably Mrs Don Cameron had as much influence on her as anyone. She is worth describing.

Mrs Cameron was one of the four members of the Ladies' Committee chosen to decide on whether or not Victoria could be accepted in society. That she was the only woman on that committee besides the wife of the President, the wife of the Secretary of State and the wife of the Under-Secretary of State shows how powerful she was; yet she was only a few years older than Victoria. At twenty-one she had made a dynastic marriage to forty-five-year-old Senator Don Cameron of Pennsylvania, who came from an important Republican family and was one of the most formidable men on Capitol Hill. His bride was Elizabeth Sherman, niece of Senator John Sherman of Ohio and of the great Civil War general, William Tecumseh Sherman. She was ravishingly beautiful, highly intelligent, and with her husband's money and power added to her own connections, she was just the person to lead Victoria through the brambles and thorns of Washington society. Bored to death by her middle-aged husband and his boss fights in Harrisburg, she escaped when she could to the Adamses, where she and Miss Emily Beale rapped on the study window with their umbrellas to gain admittance. She was extremely political and very much of a reformer; Cameron was a 'stalwart' or right-wing member of the party, with no interest in reform and less in the clever people his wife met at the Adamses. Victoria, no intellectual, was not a natural member of the Adams circle, but she went where sparkling Lizzie Cameron and sparkling Emily Beale led. Mrs Cameron must have had great charm; after his wife's death, Henry Adams depended on her and wrote at the end of the eighties that she and Mrs Henry Cabot Lodge were the dispensers of sunshine in Washington.

Sitting beside Lizzie Cameron during one of the two-hour ladies' luncheons must have been an indispensable education to Victoria, and she was a quick study. Who would add to the legation parties and who would not?

Besides the Diplomatic Corps, the Cabinet and the Congress there was a new stratum of Washington society: the winter visitors, well-off families from other parts of America who found the improved capital a pleasant resort, a delightful escape from colder climes. Levi Z. Leiter, the Chicago millionaire, came because his wife wanted a brilliant social triumph in a more cosmopolitan scene than she had known at home. He built a huge house on Dupont Circle and his daughter Mary was to become one of the most admired girls in Washington. As the eighties progressed other families simply rented houses for the winter as now they might take a Florida villa; the John B. Trevors and the James Roosevelts of New York were examples.

Then there were the odd drifting characters who always abound

44

in any capital. Mrs Bloomfield Moore of Philadelphia, for instance, who had given Victoria a pearl necklace worth £5,000 soon after her arrival as a prize for being the most popular girl in Washington. There was no harm in Mrs Moore; one of those rich, well-meaning American widows who like giving presents to young and glamorous persons. She knew everyone everywhere and when King Edward VII said, 'There are three things from which no man can escape; l'amour, la mort, la Moore', there is only one Moore of whom he could have been thinking. She was also a prolific novelist; *On Dangerous Ground; or Agatha's Friendship – a Romance of American Society* is a typical Mrs Moore title.

Oh, to have been a fly on the wall as Mrs Cameron and Miss Emily Beale talked over their new friend Victoria at the end of her first season. They should have been proud of her, for while the British Legation was traditionally the first diplomatic house in Washington, under the Thorntons it had been a bit of a bore in spite of the good food and shining silver. Now it was immense fun to go there and everyone admired Victoria for her early innovation, stopping the silly practice of bunching which had forced impecunious young men to send expensive bouquets of flowers to popular girls every night they went out. She had overcome her difficulty with English and made friends everywhere with her charmingly accented way of speaking; she got on easily with the great and was gentle with the humble and shy; as a hostess she should have been gauche and ignorant; instead, as her father had said, she seemed to know everything instinctively. The shadow of illegitimacy could not be erased, but in less than a year after the anxious meetings of the Ladies' Committee, Washington recognized her quality, for her performance had been remarkable.

4

'Please, Miss West!'

Spring started early south of the Mason–Dixon line. First, the red maple began forming its buds in January or February; they were noted with delight in that year of 1882 by Mrs Henry Adams, just as they had been a hundred years earlier by that other observer of nature, George Washington. Then in Rock Creek Park, even while snow was on the ground, came the first witch hazel, palest yellow, followed by the swamp willow's yellow-green foliage and the delicate wild azaleas, again pale yellow. Early spring in Washington was all pale yellow-green and anticipation, pale blue skies and hope. Mid-April and May were the loveliest and richest times. Behind the mossy banks and fern that bordered Rock Creek were fruit trees: wild cherry, crab apple, pear and flowering plum, followed by the magical flowering dogwood. In the city itself the catalpa trees, so loved by the Victorians for their creamy, tight flowers, the arched elms on New Hampshire Avenue, the giraffe-like, slender gingko from Japan, the luxurious grandiflora magnolias from the South accompanied the brave trees that nobody mentions: the ubiquitous ailanthus forcing its way through the cement, the paulownia, coarse-leaved, vulgar and determined, with its sharp lavender blue flowers.

There were lots of ailanthus and paulownia around the Legation, but Victoria would probably have banished the latter, to avoid the flowers falling messily onto the tennis court. Surrounding the residence was a privet hedge, which was sweet smelling still at the end of June, when lilac had become a memory.

Late spring in Washington was a long, lush and leafy moment. Government workers lunched on the grass of Lafayette Square under the trees, and found it hard to return to their offices. Retired generals asked widows to marry them, instantly regretting it; and the Speaker of the House would bring that body to order

46

with a movement of the gavel that was more langourous than decisive.

In the eighties even the high-minded Henry Adamses felt the compulsion of the season, and made moonlight calls during hot nights in May, sitting with friends on piazzas fanning themselves idly, while drinking Apollinaris water. Adams wrote: 'No European spring had shown him the same intermixture of delicate grace and passionate depravity that marked the Maryland May.'

Afternoon tea at 1607 H Street disappeared after April, as the Adamses took their horses out for four- or five-hour rides in the Maryland or Virginia countryside through the long afternoons, returning at sunset.

If sober people of middle age could be so affected by the Washington spring, what could it have done to Victoria? Gone were the stuffy calls in the afternoon, the ladies' luncheons; instead came invitations of a very different tone. Victoria, who adored the open air all her life, would have received insistent notes on her breakfast tray. They were to gallop in Rock Creek Park immediately, that very morning. Everyone was going, for the dogwood had just come out and Miss West mustn't miss it, it only lasts two weeks . . . There was a party gathering at the Georgetown reservoir that afternoon at three o'clock, this time on foot, because someone thought it would be fun to walk along the towpath of the Old Chesapeake and Ohio Canal. Miss West would like the wild-flowers, the wild blue phlox, which matched her eyes, and the bi-coloured violets, too . . . Mt Vernon! They would take a picnic down the river, and if it rained, they could lunch on the verandah. It was a bit of a ruin, but as no one visited the place it could be rather jolly, and Miss West must smell the boxwood – it was even better in the rain. Please Miss West, you must see Mt Vernon. Would Saturday do?

To go to Mt Vernon, they had to take a little steamer, while Negro spectators at the wharf quietly watched the bustle, as the party assembled. Miss Emily Beale usually arrived late in a flutter of apology; Victoria probably supervised the Legation footmen, who carried the bursting hampers while Monsieur Roustan twirled his dyed moustache flirtatiously. (He was much in love with Victoria, who must have overdone her earlier-mentioned effort to help her father with Franco-British relations.) As they passed the Alexandria docks and swung into the magnificent mainstream of the Potomac, which was heavily wooded on both sides, he often quoted Chateaubriand and said something about Rousseau's noble savage, causing Miss Beale to giggle irreverently and tell the Minister of France that she had just been waiting for that one, as he always gave 'the same lovely French quote' at that particular point on the river.

There was always a secretary of Legation along, inevitably about to dash his brains out for love of Victoria while he searched desperately for a better quote to outdo Roustan, Mrs Cameron would have been deep in conversation with the Senior Senator from Ohio about Blaine's last speech, that masterpiece of selfless eloquence, in which he said nothing of seeking public office but spoke instead of the cruel injustice shown by the British Government to the subjugated Irish. This was a clear indication to the two experts that he was off and running hard for the Presidency, and already had New York locked up.

Sackville-West probably sat in the stern in a deck chair and went to sleep; it was warm in the sun and Victoria would have looked after everything; she always did, and the Moselle would be chilled just as he liked it. He would have awoken as they reached the little boat landing below Mt Vernon from which the party climbed up the hill through the flowering dogwoods to the sacred tomb, where they would have stood assembled in reverent silence for a moment. Monsieur Roustan from sheer force of habit surely started to evoke the memories of Lafayette and Rochambeau, Washington's comrades in war, but noticed in time the look of opaque boredom on the face of the British Minister; so they would have proceeded through the fragrant orange honeysuckle (Hall's Honeysuckle, a speciality of Mt Vernon) to the lovely shabby house for a convivial luncheon on the verandah above the great river which George Washington had loved so much. Later, the party certainly divided to visit the famous gardens and the estate. There is no record of how Victoria behaved on what should have been a most romantic walk.

She was always extremely reticent about her early love affairs, but it is surprising that she never really fell in love in Washington. She was so attractive; as Vita Sackville-West wrote later: 'If ever the phrase, "turn one's heart to water" meant anything, it was when my mother looked at you and smiled.' She had many suitors; she made a list later on for Vita. It comprised twenty-five names, some of whom were to become distinguished and many who were charming. Yet the exuberant girl who was the belle of Washington, the daughter of the hot-blooded Pepita and the sensual young Lionel reached the age of twenty-seven before she fell in love.

Victoria was so innocent when she left the convent that Mrs Mulhall's announcement on the Channel boat meant nothing to her except that illegitimacy must mean something dishonourable, possibly disgraceful. When she did learn the meaning, with it tumbled into her quick mind the kaleidoscope of her short life and the explanation for the snubs to her beloved mother at Arcachon, the friendless life of the children, the snobbishness of the Béons and the loneliness of the convent upbringing. This probably explains her extreme physical fastidiousness. Her lady companion Mademoiselle Louet told her 'the facts of life' in Washington: perhaps until then she did not know what sex was exactly; she subconsciously associated it with pain, sadness, and above all her father and mother's tragedy. It meant danger, and now that she had found security she might instinctively have grown a carapace. The Cinderella aspect of Victoria's life cannot be sufficiently stressed; less than six months before the picnic at Mt Vernon she had been a shivering schoolgirl in England, facing her new high position speaking broken English, with little education and no knowledge of the world.

But the carapace was inflammable and she flirted like mad – see the beautiful and anguished lines from one of Cecil Spring-Rice's love letters:

My dear Miss West,
... I tell you that you are charming, fascinating, heaven knows what. There is no end to your perfections – but you have one great fault, I can neither forgive nor forget – simply that you like other people better than me ... Your speciality is love, you are an accomplished mistress of that art: only it's not art, it's nature. You play with it and manage it, like a seagull the winds; on which he floats but which never carries him away ...

His name was on the list of suitors, on the left-hand corner of which was a tiny pair of initials, 'R.S.'.

'R.S.' was in fact Baron Carl Nils Daniel Bildt, chargé d'affaires of the Swedish Legation in Washington, aged thirty-two when Victoria met him. She called him 'Buggy' because he was so fond of driving his buggy through the flowering streets. She, of course, did not accompany him, although she had a remarkable amount of freedom during that first summer in Washington. On a warm evening, she often drove out before dinner to the higher ground of the Soldier's Home on the edge of the city, where there might be a breeze and where the tall oaks provided shade and refreshment. Sometimes a girl friend was with her, but often she was alone in the back of the carriage. Perhaps Buggy joined her there, perhaps he didn't, but she marked in her diary every year for the next fifty years the date of the eighth of May, the anniversary of the day he first proposed to her in Washington. Bildt left Washington in 1883 to go on to a highly distinguished career in the Swedish diplomatic service, but we have by no means heard the last of him. Men never forgot Victoria, and years later, there was another spring, less frustrating for the handsome Swedish lover.

Faster than Carl Bildt's buggy and even more fun was the droshky and its Russian coachman owned by Greger, the rich young secretary of the Russian Legation, drawn by a big Russian horse. The turnout was a sensation in Washington. How and where Greger proposed is problematical, but he was on the list, and so were several Frenchmen, Son Excellence Théodore Roustan, the Marquis de Löys Chandieu, and the unfortunate young Duc de Blacas, who bore a great name, but was so poor that all he could send Victoria was some cheese of his own make, which appealed to her in contrast to the innumerable boxes of chocolates and bunches of flowers with which beautiful young girls were surfeited when she arrived in America.

The American suitors were numerous. Victoria described Jesse Tyson, the sixty-year-old Baltimore millionaire with whom she and her father stayed. Although a Quaker, his medicine chest contained many bottles of champagne with which the guests were 'dosed' when they showed the slightest sign of fatigue. He naturally seemed terribly old to Victoria. Charles Allen Thorndyke Rice was a most suitable admirer – thirty-one years old, rich, handsome, versatile and cosmopolitan; he came from Boston and was a childhood friend of Henry Cabot Lodge. He met Victoria at one of Mrs Blaine's dinners shortly after she arrived; the other guests were not dull (the President, Henry James, Andrew Carnegie among them) but Victoria must have 'looked at him and smiled'. No luck for Mr Rice nor for Mr Sturgis of Boston, Mr Roach of

New York, Mr Bookwalter of Illinois, Mr Russell of London nor for the dashing Captain Drury, who belonged to one of the most distinguished families in Canada. Of them all, two young Englishmen were exceptional. One was Charles Hardinge, the other was Cecil Spring Rice; both names are familiar to readers of British diplomatic history, both served as young men as secretaries on Sackville-West's staff in Washington, and both loved Victoria.

Charles Hardinge came from a family of soldier-statesmen, who served their country and the Empire. Hardinge of Lahore, Governor General of India and later Field-Marshal was his grandfather; his father was Under-Secretary for War and a Member of Parliament. He himself was to head the Foreign Office during the reign of King Edward VII, and was close to the monarch personally. Aware of the German threat, eager to reform the cumbersome machinery of the Foreign Office, he influenced policy, and Cecil Spring Rice, his rival for Victoria's hand, wrote one of the nicest and most honest sentences about him. 'Hardinge himself is no courtier, but a good business man and perfectly fearless and decided.'

In Washington in the eighties, Hardinge was a junior secretary of the British Legation with an eye for a pretty girl. Victoria turned him down, but they never forgot each other, and they met often later.

Cecil Spring Rice fell in love with America through his friendship with the young Theodore Roosevelt, for whom he was best man at Roosevelt's wedding in London in 1886. He asked the Foreign Office for permission to follow his hero to America. A colleague wrote: 'I hope you may get your exchange, though why choose Washington, which is out of all politics? Of course, it is interesting in a way, and West is a charming chief. But still, it seems so off the line.'

Spring Rice persisted, and joined the Legation as Hardinge left it. His hero worship of Roosevelt and the new, cleaner America for which Roosevelt stood never left him. Imbued with a supreme disgust for political corruption he saw much that revolted him and he did not spare his satire; his sceptical letters are good reading today. He was much happier in Mrs Cameron's drawing room or at the Adamses, than he was on Capitol Hill, but he seems to have been popular with everyone. Always sloppily dressed, it was said that he made a disgraceful figure in a smart frock coat because he was too busy talking to have learned to tie his tie; he was always talking and talking well, his eyes shining behind his eyeglasses. Such people are sometimes described as being too clever by half, but one finds no such criticism in the records of the time. On the contrary, he had a singular gift for lasting friendship and women adored him. He was said to have been more than commonly sensitive to beauty and those who knew him, remember how he would sometimes come back from a party depressed and moping and not fit to speak to until some of his friends, forcing out the confession, would draw from him the declaration, 'They were all such ugly people there.'

The astute reader will already have perceived the pitfall before this brilliant, charming young man of twenty-eight.

My dear Miss West . . .
How perfectly happy I should be, if I could be on terms of intimate friendship and never wish for what I couldn't get! How happy everyone would be, if they thought of what they had and not of what they hadn't! But, we are all a set of fools and never shall be wise till we're dead. I daresay even the philosophical Vicky has her moments of unphilosophical wishes . . . Preach, preach! I'm always at it, do you think I should make a good priest? Lord Tennyson told me he had often had a great longing to be a monk and live without anxiety or care, but after all, it is better to take the lights and shadows together – a great feeling is a great pain or a great pleasure – I had rather have that than nothing. The worst of the pain is better than indifference . . . Now, I am off. Goodbye my tormentor, I forgive you, but can't forget just yet – yours ever . . .

Sir Cecil Spring Rice returned to Washington to serve his country as British Ambassador during the four years of the First World War. To his harrowing mission dedicated to bringing the United States from neutrality to the side of the Allies, he gave all he had; his mind, his experience, his love of our country and his own, his physical strength, dying a month after relinquishing his post, from what his doctor diagnosed as sheer exhaustion. Happily married and with a family, one cannot imagine that he often thought of Victoria, that ghost from thirty years before. Yet, Washington springs were tricky; the magnolias came out at the same time of year and the mockingbird still sang outside the British Embassy. Sitting at Sackville-West's desk in the same

familiar house, he might have had a moment to remember the
young man that he had been, writing:

> ... But seriously, as it is, without holding out the smallest of
> hope here, you have me like a compass always turning to the
> pole, but never nearer it. If I were wise, I should get myself
> unmagnetised and turn East, West, South like a free Briton.
> After all, other people have been the same and other people have
> been cured; but now when the door is open, I can't leave the
> cell. Goodbye you gaol, you prison-door. I could call you names
> for a month on end and then be none the better for it.

Victoria saved few letters from admirers, but kept those from Spring
Rice all her life.

In summer the pace in Washington was leisurely. Government
offices closed at 3 p.m.; a vacation of several months was routine
for senior diplomats, who either went home or rented a house in
some cooler place. Sir Edward Thornton had informed the
Foreign Office during the seventies that it was not prudent to risk
his family's health by staying in dangerous, malarial Washington.
Even in 1882, the President and the Secretary of State left town
in mid-August, not to return until October. The presidential
yacht, *Dispatch*, lay in Newport Harbor while the President dined
at the Cornelius Vanderbilt's summer home, which they referred
to as a cottage. For the dinner of twenty-four people, the flowers
alone cost $1,000. Joined by the Secretary of State, Frelinghuysen,
the President cruised along the New England coast, enjoying the
fishing in those cold but salubrious waters.

The Sackville-Wests stuck it out, and the newspapers mentioned
with surprise and gratification their fortitude. In fact, summer in
Washington has never been a severe ordeal for a young and
beautiful woman, especially one who lived in a high-ceilinged
house, closed and shuttered during the cruel day, opening in the
evening to tennis on the Legation court until darkness fell,
followed by casual dinners at which there were ten men to one
woman, the fans in the ceiling bringing relief. And there were
visits; one by Victoria to her friends the Sturgises at The Glades,
south of Boston, and a trip with her father to Niagara Falls in
September.

All the same, fall was pleasanter. The autumn season was as
relaxed socially as the winter was crowded; by the end of October

Mrs Adams, Mrs Cameron and Miss Beale had drifted back to town and there were long rides in Rock Creek Park, the beeches golden green and the low-growing scarlet sumac bordering the Creek where the horses splashed through the fords. Early spring in the park had been palest yellow-green; now there were the intense yellow of the sugar maple and the hickory tree, the ravishing clear red of the sourwood, the orange persimmon – the strong palette of an American fall. But there was something wistful about the Washington autumn, unlike its clear cut New England counterpart. On soft days it was pleasant to sit on a bench in Lafayette Square, dreaming under the tall willow oaks; even in November there was still a sweet, sad fragrance from the Russian olive bush with its buff-coloured blossoms, speckled all over. Unlike the more dramatic cities to the north, in Washington, a southern town, everything, even the seasons move slowly.

Social Washington sprang to life on 1 January, on which day the *Star* devoted five and a half columns of closely-spaced type to the names of those who were holding New Year's Day receptions, headed by the President. Following the White House reception, it was traditional for the Secretary of State to give luncheon to the whole Diplomatic Corps; to do this today he would have to take a hotel, but in those days the small corps was easily accommodated in the Frelinghuysen's private residence.

It was a festive month. Victoria went to Senator Miller's fancy-dress ball as a Neapolitan fisher maiden and to the diplomatic dinner at the White House, where she and her partner, the Russian Minister, found themselves facing the other guests over a five-foot-long canoe made of white and crimson roses. But the great event of the season was the British Legation ball on 26 January for the Marquess of Lorne, Governor-General of Canada and son-in-law of Queen Victoria.

For months the Sackville-Wests must have been worrying about their guest list, for the Legation could hold 500 comfortably, not more, and nothing made the heart beat faster in social Washington than an invitation to meet British royalty. If only Lord Lorne had chosen the unfashionable summer months for his visit, it would have been safe to invite every official in Washington and every private person who had ever left cards at the Legation, and be sure that three quarters of them would decline; but January!

The ball was a brilliant success, even the acerbic Mrs Adams, who didn't go, admitted that those who did vowed it was very gay. The newspaper accounts fill pages; Victoria, pasting them into her scrapbook, must have been delighted by her triumph. She was a natural decorator, but the big house had its problems. The chief one was to cheer up the hall, sombrely panelled in dark mahogany. As the guests entered, they saw ahead of them a grand staircase which rose straight, only to branch off midway into two curving arms, their voluptuous baroque lines enhanced by every piece of gingerbread that the fertile mind of the Victorian carpenter could devise. Gargoyles leered from the top of the banister heads, and from the first landing the traditional portrait of Queen Victoria looked down, embraced in a huge teakwood frame. The curtains, which had not been replaced since 1873, were of heavy dark blue plush. Victoria brought in two Virginia cedar trees and placed them on each side of the staircase; their triangular height averted the eye from the bad architecture, the ugly banisters garlanded in pine and cedar went unseen; and the portrait of the Queen carried on its frame more piny garlands, enhanced by pink and white carnations, which Victoria liked to stick into her arrangements everywhere, as was the fashion of the time. The guests were greeted by the smell of the evergreens and impressed by the two fine palm trees at the door, and above all by the bright lighting which made the dark hall cheerful on the January night.

On the left of the hall was the entrance to the first drawing room, at which the Marquess of Lorne, wearing the wide sash of the Order of the Thistle, Sackville-West in plain evening dress, and Victoria in shell-pink tulle received the guests. This big room was easier for Victoria than the hall: the red brocade on the walls was becoming and she lowered her lighting, using small lamps with red silk shades. A big crystal chandelier carried candles, but not too many of them, for Victoria wanted to achieve a rich, mysterious warmth in her big red drawing room, a place to which couples could return, breathless from dancing the german, to sink into the intimacy of a padded sofa and idle over a glass of champagne. The furniture was all soft and buttoned and fringed, the central ottoman was surmounted by a cast-iron urn containing as its centrepiece a noble yucca, the cactus so popular then, from it fell jasmine and smilax, spilling over. Heavy red curtains gave into the second drawing room. Then came the crimson and gilt ball

5
North-American Adventures

In February, the following month, the Sackville-Wests returned Lord Lorne's visit. He was the Governor-General of Canada, and this was the first of several visits to winter Ottawa. Victoria sleighed, tobogganed and broke more hearts. The Duc de Blacas, ruined by his father's speculations, was ranching in the west of Canada; meeting her in Ottawa he offered her his hand and his illustrious name, sobbing bitterly when she refused him. Captain Drury, ADC to the Governor-General, was another suitor. Victoria was too naive to understand his flirtatious compliments and in her bewilderment asked Lord Lorne why his ADC always told her that his favourite flower was tulips (two lips). She wrote: 'I was almost stupid with that overwhelming state of perfect innocence.'

Her comments on the Canadian visits continued to be charmingly naive. Later, staying with Lord Lansdowne, the succeeding Governor-General, she wrote of her capacity to light an extinguished gas-jet with her nose.

I used to do this at Ottawa, on cold and frosty nights, by rubbing my feet in the carpet all along the big corridor and coming in contact, at the end, with the gas-burner. It was Lady Lansdowne who made me try it. I was so successful that I gave people a baddish shock when I touched them. It hurt me too.

The return from Canada was followed by a period of serious trouble. Irish acts of terrorism in England were increasingly blamed by the exasperated British Government on the Fenians, the Irish-American nationalists who were the instrument of extremism. There had been the ghastly murders at Phoenix Park, in which Lord Frederick Cavendish, Chief Secretary of Ireland, and the Under-Secretary, Mr Burke, had been assassinated; there had been the bomb at Victoria Station, and the attempted explosions at Charing Cross and Paddington. The money flowed across the Atlantic and the British police, noting the American clockwork and dynamite in American-made bags took photographs which the Home Secretary sent to Queen Victoria. The Queen, in her remarkable letters referred only eight times during the early eighties to the United States; six references concern the Fenians and the intolerable encouragement given them by American newspapers and by leading politicians. Sackville-West remained cool and calm, explaining to Lord Granville that the Irish vote would be decisive in the next presidential elections; typically, he dismissed in a few casual sentences the fact that he and Victoria were evacuated from Washington on the President's orders for ten days in May. Victoria was a more vivid reporter:

> It must have been in 1883 that my father and I escaped being blown up or poisoned at the Legation by the Fenians after the Phoenix Park murders. Papa had much to do with the finding of the murderers in America and every week the Fenian papers were headed by these lines: "The British Minister is not bullet-proof". I received many post-cards saying we were spared because I was a Roman Catholic; but when the President found we were going to be blown up, he sent Papa and me on his yacht with General Sherman and Rachel, his daughter, and we remained on board till all danger was over – What luck! ! And every day that great General took out his map and went through the Georgia campaign with me and gave me graphic descriptions of the fights and the wounded . . .

It is not hard to imagine the drama of those evenings in the saloon of the *Dispatch*; General Sherman moving the silverware around on the table as he relived his march through Georgia. He did this often at Washington dinner parties; but for young, blue-eyed Victoria it was new, it was history, it was marvellously exciting.

Also, Victoria had never been on a yacht before and the *Dispatch* was considered to have been one of the handsomest crafts of her kind in the world. She was built of live oak, her cabins and deck-house were of mahogany and her appointments were considered to be magnificent. She carried ten officers and when they stopped at Fort Monroe, a salute of seventeen guns was fired in honour of

General Sherman, after which the British ensign was run up to the foretopmast head and a salute of fifteen guns fired for the representative of the mother country. They stopped at Jamestown, where 'General Sherman took us to see the church Pocahontas was christened in, and I remember stealing a brick from the Church and using it for years as a paper weight for my ever-littered writing table'.

The party sailed back to Washington safely and a few days later, the Queen's Birthday was celebrated as usual at the Legation.

Of course there was tension and Victoria was highly aware of it, but she was always at her best when facing challenge. She and her father carried on as usual, and August brought them an opportunity to see and be seen by a wide, new section of American society.

Henry Villard, President of the Northern Pacific Railroad, was a German-born entrepreneur of dash and vision. In order to celebrate the linking up of the Pacific Northwest with the Mississippi Valley, he gave a party on the grandest possible scale. The cream of governmental and financial figures from all over the world were invited to be present at the 'Driving of the Last Spike'. The invitations were generous, for they included return steamer fare from Europe, six weeks on Villard's private trains, and an extraordinary opportunity to see the final conquest of America's Western frontier. Villard was hailed as a saviour from Minneapolis to Portland, for his energy had laid the basis for the development of an immense, unpeopled domain; growth and prosperity followed the new transcontinental railroads and the North-West was to be opened to world commerce.

There had been other spikes laid as the railroads were linked from East to West before Victoria arrived in America, famous occasions marked by much fanfare. But the meeting of the Northern Pacific and the Oregon Railway and Navigation Company was probably the most publicized ceremony of them all. Henry Villard was not the man to deny himself the fame that was his due, also he was a worried man; there were rumours that the company was in financial trouble. What better way to restore confidence than to complete the road with a flourish that would be noticed throughout the world? The engraved invitations went out to Queen Victoria and to the Imperial German Government asking them to send representatives ... to the President of the United States; the list read like *Who's Who*.

Four trains linked up in St Paul, Minnesota. The English train of eleven cars included one called the De La Warr, a delicate compliment to Sackville-West, whose ancestor Lord De La Warr had been governor of Virginia in the reign of James I. They stopped at Chicago, where Victoria loved the drive along the Lakeshore, but found the Palmer House a bad and gloomy hotel. The real start was from Minneapolis and St Paul, where the combined party gathered for the first time, staying at the Lafayette Club on Lake Minnetonka, a gigantic structure in Queen Anne style. It was noticed by Nicolas Mohr, a German correspondent, that Professor James Bryce, the English historian, was taking the lead in promoting social mixing between the different national groups. This was the future Lord Bryce, author of *The American Common-wealth* and later Ambassador to the United States. Just as well that he was along, for the party that assembled at Lake Minnetonka was indeed a mixed bag.

There were thirty Germans, some were personal friends of Villard's, others represented German finance and there were famous men of learning, Professors Hofmann, Gneist, von Holst, Zittel who had accepted the invitation because of their special interests; von Holst had written several books on the American legal system, the geologist Zittel wanted to improve his knowledge of the formations of the Rocky Mountains. In the diplomatic party there were besides the ministers of Germany and Great Britain, the chargés d'affaires of Austria-Hungary, Denmark, and Sweden and Norway; the last being Baron Carl Bildt, Victoria's 'Buggy'.

The English party was as large as the German. Beside the Sackville-Wests and that helpful social mixer Professor Bryce, there were the Earl and Countess of Onslow . . . Lord Onslow was later described as haughty, unlike the other English. Lord Justice Bowen, Lord Carrington, the Earl of Dalhousie, Mr H. Gibbs, Governor of the Bank of England, Chief Justice Charles Russell, and a number of members of Parliament 'and lesser title holders' completed Villard's English list. Not a bad one. Former President Ulysses S. Grant arrived, bringing a train of American notables, 'a swarm of politicians, former senators, ambassadors, governors, and members of Congress'. There was the Secretary of the Interior and the Attorney-General, there was the former Secretary of State Evarts, and President Arthur himself found time to join the party for an evening banquet at the Lafayette Club, at which he spoke. Sackville-West responded to the toast 'To our Foreign Guests', which was followed by General Terry of Ft Snelling: 'The Army – Holding the Savages in Check while the Shores of the Continent were United', was the title of his address. The German correspondent, Mohr, was overawed by the grandeur of it all; the comfort of the good beds at the Lafayette Club – the great names, but he covered his story well. To him we owe the descriptions of the wild scenes that took place the next day.

The young cities of Minneapolis and St Paul, full of vigour, vitality and competition had been unable to cooperate on a joint welcome for the Villard party. So there were two parades. First St Paul with its many marching units and floats – Negro troops, Indians, the Fire Department, Irish, French, Bohemians, Free Masons, Germans, cattlemen, fruit growers, mail carriers – a panorama of mid-Western life in the 1880s. An ingenious, typically American touch:

> The *Pioneer Press* had set up a printing press and staff on its float and was turning out a newspaper which contained descriptions of the City of St Paul. As it moved along in the parade, the papers were printed and scattered immediately among the crowds.

Minneapolis followed with a seven-hour parade. The dogged Mohr followed it all, admitting that everything was swimming before his eyes and his hand was lame from taking notes. The party adjourned for a breakfast of champagne and cold delicacies, oysters, buffalo tongue, and prairie chicken. There were more speeches by General Grant, Villard, Evarts. The real part of the trip was about to begin and the reader will not be wearied by more descriptions of speeches; but it must be remembered that they were incessant and repetitive. The Germans admitted that the daily schedule exhausted them and that the trip required great physical stamina; Victoria never mentioned a moment of fatigue. By 4 September they were on the far side of Fargo, travelling across the prairies of Dakota towards the city of wooden huts that was Bismarck, typical of a town that owed its existence to the railroad. The cornerstone of the capitol was laid and the famous Indian Chief Sitting Bull was produced, tame and pathetic, selling his autograph for $1.50. Next came the Badlands, '*pays mauvais à traverser*' as it was originally called by the French, and the party learned why when they left the train to cross it by foot or by carriage, the carriages slipping badly. Just as they neared the exit, they had a sudden, dramatic sight. A woman on horseback flew by them at full gallop, self-assured and bold, a nineteenth-century cowgirl, followed by two cowboys. All three were on their way to watch over the gigantic herds below . . .

As the travellers crossed Montana, they saw occasional buffalo and took potshots at them. Billings, named for Frederick Billings, one of the Villard party, was still a very young mining town. After visiting the opera house Nicolas Mohr wrote that society then was like 'the criminal element in our large cities . . . the revolver is always loaded'. But Henry Villard's enthusiasm had infected the young German, he was much impressed by seeing the huge stretches of fertile land being opened up to civilization, and struck by the fact that Americans in the West talked only of the future – never the present. And they were resourceful; when the engine of the fourth section of the train broke down an extra track was instantly laid around the disabled engine allowing the other traffic to detour around it and rejoin the permanent track in front. The trains were comfortable, well-equipped with excellent chefs who provided good food three times a day and there was no shortage of Pullman porters to make up the beds and serve the passengers. Presumably, as the English party of thirty occupied eleven railway cars, the guests must have brought their personal servants too. Victoria would probably have had two lady's maids with her as was not unusual in Victorian times, and they would have had their hands full caring for her wardrobe on the train.

The small town of Livingston, Montana, just five months old, had its bands and welcoming committee and the population out on the streets to greet the distinguished guests. Before leaving Montana there was an evening with the Crow Indians, who obligingly performed their war dance, a wild sight which the Germans found terrifying. Victoria wrote:

We stopped at Helena to see a War-dance by real Indians. It was really quite dangerous, as the Indians were in an inebriated state and might have made short work of our handful of Britishers . . . one young Indian, who came towards us after the dance and war whooping was over, said to me: "You go. Me

62

go," and wanted to get into my carriage. Buggy and Alan Johnstone were also travelling in our car.

This was not the only danger Victoria encountered. Crossing the Continental Divide in those days must have been highly alarming. The tunnel had not been finished, so a temporary track had been laid across Bozeman Pass. The heavy trains were taken up two cars at a time, climbing at a pitch more than double that allowed by federal regulations and descending so steeply on the other side that a switchback, ascending a hill, was laid in order to stop runaway cars. Bad enough, but worse was to come at Mullen Tunnel, which also was not completed. The process of pulling the cars up two at a time began again, at night. Mohr wrote, 'It was too dark to see, but we guessed that we were being pulled along terrifying cliffs. From time to time we caught sight of a light far down below us.' On the descent there was an accident. The train separated and when the front part stopped the loose rear section came rolling down from behind, smashing one of the English cars, the De La Warr. The roof and a side wall were ripped off, but no one was hurt and the 'Englishmen, with characteristic good humour', according to the German journalist, 'called to Villard that he should not worry'.

The next day the Last Spike Ceremony took place at Deer Lodge, Montana. There were farmers, ranchers, cowboys and miners, there was the thunder of cannon and the sound of the band could hardly be heard over the cheering of the crowd. The two crews, one from the East and one from the West held a contest laying the track, competing to see who would reach the meeting place first. The last spike was driven in, the trains from East and West touched noses like friendly camels, the engineers shook hands and the band played 'Yankee Doodle', 'God Save the Queen', '*Die Wacht am Rhein*' and out of respect 'for friends who were not present, the Marseillaise'. The Crow Indians gathered around enthusiastically; it was a great day.

After crossing the Marent Gulch on a wooden viaduct that was the highest of its kind in the world, and the pride of Villard's heart, the Snake River was the final hazard before reaching Portland and civilization. The Snake was crossed by ferry, from which the same unlucky English car tore loose and nearly rolled into the river, causing Lord Carrington to cut his head. This extremely unpleasant experience was not recorded by Victoria, who was de-lighted by Portland and especially by the Chinese she met there. She dined on Birdnest Soup and Shark's Fins with a Chinese family:

> The young wife had a most delightful little yellow baby of a few months, he had a little cap from which hung a pigtail. I loved him and nursed him and could hardly part with him. They took me afterwards to their Joss House. They examined my clothes with much curiosity.

From Portland the party proceeded to Seattle, where Victoria noted seeing an ox being roasted on the marketplace, on to Vancouver where 'Papa was received with great honours and gun-firing by the British fleet'. The party then split up, some like the Sackville-Wests and Mohr went on to Yellowstone National Park. This was the hard core; the original party was now down to fifty guests from the original 240; the frailer travellers appear to have drifted off, some to the comforts of San Francisco. Mohr wrote that the German Minister and his wife and the British Minister and his daughter were among the remaining fifty who found themselves 'in a wooden hotel, only half finished but of colossal dimensions . . . all alone in the wilderness, a few hundred feet from the hot springs'. Victoria wrote, 'The best part of the journey was camping out in the Yellowstone Park . . .' and de-scribed the unlucky accident that overtook Mr Robert Benson, one of the English travellers, 'who got scalded in the Yellowstone Park sitting on an extinct geyser which woke up suddenly and burnt his Bobo badly. He could not sit down afterwards for a week.'

The irrepressible Victoria did not describe the buggy trip to the Upper Geyser Basin, a dangerous, rugged adventure. Mohr recommended waiting a few years before taking it:

> You won't believe how much dust and dirt we have swallowed, or how many bumps and bangs we have endured in the buggies or what dubious and dangerous paths we have crossed in order to reach the Upper Geyser Basin . . . We were shaken up, covered with dirt, harried by danger, and even dumped out of the buggy.

At last they reached the geysers and found them a strange and magical sight. They camped out, eating dinner in the tent by the light of a single candle.

From outside came the light and warmth of a huge campfire. Our entire party gathered around it ... the mood of the party got more and more exciting. Somebody started singing a German song ... which sent one German song after another into the dark night ... around the fire were the drivers and their assistants, all adventurous-looking fellows ... The daughter of the British Ambassador [*sic*] asked for "*Die Wacht am Rhein*" and of course her request was fulfilled. Such a cheerful chord was struck and the mood lasted till quite late in the night.

In the morning they washed in the brook, had breakfast and continued what Mohr called 'our awful journey' to the Upper Basin where they saw the magnificent drama of Old Faithful. Mohr felt that the national sense of vanity of the Americans was strengthened by having recently discovered such a unique wonder as Yellowstone Park.

At last Victoria and her father returned quietly to Washington. Unlike the introspective German, she would not have given a thought to the effect of the phenomenon of Yellowstone on American vanity, but she would have minded very much that kind Mr Villard had to rush home before the expedition was over to face the very financial crisis which he had hoped the expedition would help him avoid. Northern Pacific stock slid as rumour about the railroad's precarious state spread. The next year Henry Villard resigned as President of the Northern Pacific, and never achieved financial prominence again. He had given Victoria a great deal. It had been a foolhardy adventure to balance precariously over the cliffs of Yellowstone, then virtually *terra incognita*; it had been terrifying to be in the car De La Warr on the Great Divide as the rear half of the train gathered speed to roll down and crush the English car, it must have taken courage to dress for dinner and play the charming hostess a few hours after the car had slipped to the very edge of the ferry boat crossing the Snake River, throwing everybody about in the slide that was just barely reversed. The Indian episode would have frightened most young women, and probably did Victoria at the time; but in retrospect she looked on it lightly and ended the fragment from the *Book of Reminiscences* that recalled the happiest days in her life with 'You go. Me go ...'

6
Final Years at the Legation

Flora was seventeen and Amalia fifteen when they arrived in Washington in December 1883 to join their father and their sister Victoria. The press noted that they were thoroughly English-looking, which conflicts with later descriptions of Amalia as 'another Spanish beauty', and that they were fond of outdoor exercise, especially their walks with their father. But as they were too young to enter society the reporters, while friendly, devoted little space to them; at the Legation Ball in January 1884 they were mentioned as sitting in the drawing room, one on each side of their governess, dressed in white albatross cloth. For the next year they dropped out of the press, but in January 1885 Victoria organized a magnificent coming-out ball for Flora, the debutante, and from then on the Misses West were publicly inseparable, especially after Amalia entered society at another big ball. Amalia was described as the clever woman of the family, Victoria as the beauty, Flora as shy and reticent.

Years later Mrs Cameron said, 'Washington thought the arrival of the two younger girls rather too much', which suggests that society was shocked by the appearance of more illegitimate daughters at the British Legation; having already charitably swallowed Victoria two years before. But there is no evidence whatever that Amalia and Flora suffered more than the normal fate of younger sisters whose older sibling had become the belle of the city. Of course they must have envied Victoria her popularity; they would not have been human otherwise, but the record shows that in fact they had a remarkably good time during their Washington years.

1884 was a campaign year. The Sackville-Wests watched the contest between the magnetic Blaine, nominated by the Republicans for the presidency, and the solid, hard-working Democrat, Grover Cleveland. As a reform mayor of Buffalo and reform

Governor of New York, Cleveland had a reputation as honest as Blaine's was clouded; but the election was so close that it was three days before the results could be known. Blaine lost the Irish vote and New York State as the result of the unfortunate 'rum, Romanism and rebellion' speech of one of his supporters; which was taken as a slur on Catholics. It was a nasty election, during which the Republicans in their zeal had turned up an illegitimate son of Cleveland's, but this scandal could not begin to offset the damage done to Blaine by the loss of the Irish-American vote.

Cleveland was a sober man, remote and ungenial. No one questioned his integrity nor his devotion to duty, but imagination was not one of his qualities. A bachelor of fifty-two when he was inaugurated, he married Frances Folsom, the twenty-two-year-old daughter of his law partner the next year. President Arthur slipped quietly out of Washington in March, respected but unmourned by the mercurial public; although not forgotten by Sackville-West, who gave a farewell dinner for Arthur just before he left, attended by all three daughters.

It was a diplomat's business to get to know the new administration as soon as possible and Victoria and her father were soon close friends with the most attractive and important couple in the Cabinet: the Secretary of the Navy William C. Whitney and his remarkable wife, Flora.

The Secretary was an outstanding public official; during his four years in office he revived and modernized the navy. The Cabinet was full of able men; Thomas Francis Bayard at the State Department was high-minded, hard-working and competent, as was the Secretary of War, William Endicott; and there were other excellent public servants. But the unbending President and his new wife needed help in the ways of society and the lavish Whitneys made things fun in what was otherwise an overly sober and serious minded administration. They were a phenomenon in Washington society, very rich but also very elegant, and their parties while extremely grand were warm occasions; Flora Payne Whitney knew how to mix people and her receptions were different from those Washington society were accustomed to at the homes of millionaires. Their dinners were famous for the high quality of the food and wine but they were never pompous. The Whitneys moved easily from their big house in town to 'Grasslands', their country place near what is now the National Cathedral. President Cleveland, delighted to have Mrs Whitney take his wife under her wing, established himself around the corner at 'Oak View', an area still called Cleveland Park. The Sackville-Wests were frequent visitors at both houses. Then there were the summer houseparties; the Whitneys ultimately owned ten residences but during the Washington years Lenox, Massachusetts was their summer home and Victoria stayed there often. She and Mrs Whitney were ideally suited to be friends: both were charming, both loved novelty and both were trend-setters; others followed where they led.

Aided and abetted by Victoria, Mrs Whitney organized paper chases that were like fox hunts except that the horsemen followed a carefully laid trail of paper instead of the scent of the fox; these chases were fast and dangerous and many a handsome secretary of legation would arrive at the office the next day with his arm in a sling, but in compensation there had been the thrill of the end of the run with Mrs Whitney and Mrs Cleveland and the Misses West sitting on top of their coaches cheering the riders and offering congratulations and sympathy. Even the Cabinet took part and the *Star* criticized the President in an editorial for permitting busy men to waste their time racing about the countryside on horses after bits of paper, but Cleveland was wise enough not to mind this, knowing that the Whitneys gave some style to an otherwise pedestrian administration. Another novelty was the dancing class, organized by Mrs Whitney, Victoria and Mrs John McLean (the former Miss Emily Beale) in order to teach the men of Washington the latest steps; the dancing class took place at the Legation ballroom or the Whitney or McLean ballroom and became a Washington institution; aging envoys extraordinary strained to 'do the graceful' and soon what had started as a class became a full-fledged series of balls.

The Whitneys brought luxury without vulgarity to Washington. They were much loved; and after the christening of their baby Dorothy at St John's 700 friends trooped into the house to offer their good wishes. A reception for 700 was nothing for Mrs Whitney, who, it has been estimated, entertained 60,000 people during her Washington years.

This was also the period of Victoria's greatest social activity, frequently innovative. She had outlawed the sending of bouquets by impecunious young men to young girls; she broke diplomatic tradition by ejecting from the Legation party-crashers who had come uninvited to a concert, thereby rejoicing the hearts of more timid hostesses and establishing a precedent; she introduced the *bal masqué* to Washington, inviting the guests to come in dominoes and masks, and on that evening protocol vanished from the protocol-conscious town. For Flora's debutante ball she organized classes in the Scottish reel and made it a Highland Fling party. Always an original decorator, her arrangements were increasingly imaginative. At a dance in 1886 the favours given out were tiny willow baskets, tied with ribbon, at one edge a nest of humming birds. For another occasion 'there were balls of clipped white paper, rolled in tissue paper, and as each lady tossed her ball at her partner in the dance it burst open and the floor was white with its contents and every lady went home with some of the bits of paper in the folds of her ball dress'.

In the summer of 1886 the British Minister remained at his post. He had been rewarded for his hard work and was now Sir Lionel West, KCMG. The Misses West were taken to England by their companion, Mademoiselle Louet. In London Victoria met her younger brother Henry, whom she had seen off to school in 1880; now he was to go out to South Africa to join Max, and she took him to the stores to buy his outfit. The girls returned to Washington in the early autumn.

The 'Fisheries Question' had been a serious concern to West for years. The chronic friction between England and America over the claims of American vessels to fish in Canadian waters had the news-papers in a fervour of indignation, talking of war with Great Britain to defend the rights of the United States. It was settled during the winter of 1887-8 by a treaty negotiated on the British side by Joseph Chamberlain. For the British statesman it was a highly successful mission personally, for at the Legation he met Victoria's charming friend Miss Mary Endicott, daughter of the Secretary of War, and the widowed Chamberlain and the young American girl fell in love and became engaged. Miss Endicott could hardly wait to announce the news to Victoria in a happy letter.

March 1888, found West and Victoria in New England, looking for a house for the summer. This was the first time that they had taken a vacation house and Beverly, Massachusetts, was a natural choice. The swimming and sailing off the North Shore of Boston were good, and many of their acquaintances spent their summers there. The Henry Cabot Lodges were nearby and the Camerons usually took a cottage as well as other friends from the Washington official and diplomatic community. But before relaxing for the holidays there was an important and difficult family occasion to surmount. Flora had become engaged to Gabriel Salanson, a young French diplomat in Washington, and was to be married in Paris in June. The three sisters left for Europe in April to prepare for the wedding, and were seen off at the station by the whole Diplomatic Corps.

Victoria must have felt extremely apprehensive about the approaching wedding as she sailed for France. As usual in that family, everything was on her shoulders. Papa would only arrive in Paris a few days before the wedding, the English relations were not coming over and she had no one to consult except the girls' old guardian, the Vicomte de Béon. The bridegroom, Gabriel Salanson was pleasant enough but lacking in moral courage. He had announced to his bourgeois family that he had fallen in love with the second daughter of the British Minister but he had not dared to tell them that she was illegitimate. Now, in France a couple had to be married in a civil ceremony preceding the religious one, and awkwardly enough the Civil Code necessitated the use of the phrase 'legitimate, daughter'. Victoria, Gabriel, Béon and the faithful Mademoiselle Louet held a council of war and decided that the safest strategy to employ was for everyone to cough to prevent the fatal words from being heard when the judge pronounced them. Four violent fits of simultaneous coughing should do it – they were as much worried about the presence of Lord Lytton, the British Ambassador, as they were about the Salanson family; as Lord Lytton would have been perfectly familiar with the story of his colleague's illegitimate brood. In any case, the comical and rather pathetic little conspiracy worked, and the young Salansons were married on 15 June and left for their honeymoon in Switzerland.

Victoria, Amalia and their father went for a short visit to London where they found Mrs Bloomfield Moore, she who had given Victoria the pearls in Washington in 1881. For the last few years she had been living in Europe, entertaining lavishly in London and in her Italian villa, where Robert Browning was a frequent guest. Victoria and her father dined with Mrs Moore to meet the great poet and she treasured a card on which he had written, over his signature: 'Miss West. *J'ai vu trop tard la parfaite beauté.* June 30th, 1888.' He was to die the next year.

The Wests moved into their rented house in Beverly, Massachusetts in July. It was a pleasant enough little cottage in good weather, perched on a rock with a fine view of the sea. But it must have been dreary in the rain; rented New England summer cottages were puritanically stark in Victorian times. The sitting room held some rather shabby wicker furniture, a rocking chair and some uncomfortable straight chairs, and the lamps were most inadequate to read by. It was the sort of house in which not a towel dried when the weather was damp, and sometimes when the swirling fog had embraced Beverly Cove for several days at a time everything, from the straw matting to the sagging mattresses on the beds smelled of mildew.

In mid-September the girls left their father in Beverly while they crossed the state to pay visits at Lenox, in the Berkshire Hills. September was the season for Lenox, the big houses were crammed with guests; there were coaching parties through the mountains and tennis parties, golf tournaments and every night a dinner party.

On 13 September, West sat alone in the damp cottage by the fogbound coast; it was probably a relief to him not to be obliged to attend Mrs Whitney's dinner and musicale in honour of Victoria that was taking place at the Berkshires that night, but it was a dreary day and he must have been bored. There wasn't much news in the papers; Cleveland had been renominated by the Democrats in June and Benjamin Harrison, Governor of Indiana was the Republican candidate. It was bound to be a close election, the chief issue would be free trade versus protectionism; Cleveland stood firmly and courageously for the former. Another issue had been the Canadian fisheries.

When the diplomatic bag from Washington arrived in Beverly, West read his letters with unusual care. One letter he thought worth answering at length, although in Washington it would not have deserved his attention and he would have handed it to a secretary of legation for a routine, noncommittal answer. Instead, having perused it with his sad, blue eyes, he took up his pen.

The writer, who signed himself Charles F. Murchison of Pomona, California, sounded honest, sincere and worried. Born an Englishman, now a naturalized American citizen he was uncertain who would best stand up for England of the two candidates in the coming election and respectfully inquired of the British Minister his opinion.

> I am unable to understand for whom I should cast my ballot, when, but one month ago, I was sure Mr Cleveland was the man. If Cleveland was pursuing a new policy towards Canada, temporarily only and for the sake of obtaining popularity and the continuation of his office for four years more, but intends to cease his policy when his reelection in November is secured, and again favor England's interests, then I should have no further doubt, but go forward and vote for him . . . As you . . . know whether Mr Cleveland's policy is temporary only and whether he will, as soon as he secures another four years in the presidency, suspend it for one of friendship and free trade, I apply to you privately and confidentially for information which shall in turn be treated as entirely secret.

Lionel West had been in the Diplomatic Service for over forty years, serving England faithfully and competently. It is inconceivable that he could have done what he did. Breaking the inviolate rule that a representative of another country should remain neutral and without publicly expressed opinion concerning the domestic affairs of the country to which he is accredited he wrote an honest answer, to the effect that Cleveland was the best choice for after the elections he would be reasonable regarding Great Britain. He marked his letter 'Private' and sent it off that same day. He had written:

> Sir,
> I am in receipt of your letter of the 4th instant and beg to say that I fully appreciate the difficulty in which you find yourself in casting your vote. You are probably aware that any political party which openly favoured the Mother-Country at the present moment would lose popularity and the party in power is fully aware of this fact. The party, however, is, I believe, still desirous of maintaining friendly relations with Great Britain. . . . It is impossible to predict the course which President Cleveland may pursue in the matter of retaliation should he be elected, but there is every reason to believe that, while upholding the position he has taken, he will manifest a spirit of conciliation in dealing with the question involved in his message . . .

The importance of this simple and honest letter may not be immediately apparent but professional diplomats are trained to smell traps and there never was a simpler trap than the one into which West had fallen. There was no Charles F. Murchison, the writer was a Republican called George Osgoodby, who now had written evidence that the British Minister had reason to be confident that once the elections were over Cleveland and the Democratic Party would act favourably towards Great Britain. Yet in the preceding month the President had repudiated his Secretary of State's Fisheries treaty in his message, thus covering his exposed flank, the political danger of appearing to be influenced by the British Government, thereby disconcerting the Republicans and leaving free trade as the only dangerous campaign issue.

West's letter, of 13 September, was turned over to the Republican managers who held it back gleefully until ten days before the election.

While the time bomb ticked away the Wests remained in New England, oblivious. On 1 October 1888, West's brother Mortimer died without issue at the age of sixty-eight, and Lionel West became Baron Sackville, lord of the great house and estate of Knole, at Sevenoaks, Kent. This had long been expected and there was no thought that he would not continue his diplomatic career. The family went into mourning but on 22 October Victoria and Amalia made a countryhouse visit to the John B. Trevors at their place up the Hudson, Glenview. The son of the house wrote,

> Victoria was one of the most fascinating girls I ever met and Amalia was a typical Spanish beauty but lacked the extraordinary intelligence and charm of her older sister, Victoria . . . While Victoria and Amalia were staying at Glenview, the ground was blown from under the feet of Sackville-West by the exposure of his foolish letter to a man who pretended to be a naturalized American of British descent asking advice on how he should vote in the coming presidential election. Victoria was terribly upset and bemoaned the fact because she said that her father never would have answered that letter if she had been with him. I think Victoria was clever enough really to have kept her father on the rails . . .

The bomb went off on 21 October with the publication of Lord Sackville's letter to Murchison by the *Los Angeles Times* and distribution to the Associated Press, the next day the chief organ of the Republican party, the *New York Tribune* carried it followed by the *New York Sun*. The Republican timing was perfect and the reaction as violent as their managers could have hoped. At last, cackled a thousand voices, the administration had been caught in its truckling to Great Britain. The frantic Democrats screamed that it didn't matter whether Sackville was a fool or a knave, he must go. Cleveland received letters of this kind from his supporters: 'Now kick out Lord Sackville with your biggest boot of best leather, and you've got 'em. HESITATION IS DEATH!' On 25 October Blaine gave the first of three speeches that he was to make in the next ten days. They were all similar in theme, but this was an important speech as it was to a huge Irish-American audience in Madison Square Garden. Still the best orator of his time, Blaine fired salvo after salvo and the audience groaned and cried as the golden voice rose and fell.

> For the past four months the Democrats have been denying and the Republicans affirming that the first and last constant wish of England was that Mr Cleveland's administration [groans] that Mr Cleveland's administration should be sustained by the full force and effect of English public opinion. And just when they had begun to make an impression . . . upon the American people . . . we have the letter of the British Minister himself [groans]. I know you do not like to hear about it [cries] – We have the letter of the British Minister himself.

Both the American and British Governments were thrown off balance. Sackville had expressed his regrets to Bayard immediately after the *New York Tribune* article containing his letter, but the next day he gave a foolish interview to the same paper in which he spoke resentfully of American political tricks and the action of Congress, and by implication the good faith of the President. When he called again at the State Department Bayard expressed his amazement and it was too late for Sackville's explanation that the reporter had garbled his remarks to mollify the President. In any case Cleveland was in a difficult position. A fair and decent man, he surely would have liked time to straighten out the facts of the case – the name George Osgoodby was not known – and it was many years before the story was told in full. But Cleveland didn't have time to allow Sackville a chance to clear up the affair; the election was now only a few days off and the Irish vote could swing the balance between victory and defeat. The British Minister's recall was demanded. In London, the Prime Minister and Foreign Secretary, Lord Salisbury, treated the demand with a calmness which infuriated both the President and his Secretary of State, who then sent Sackville his passports. Lord Salisbury, cool and loyal, could do nothing now but order Michael Herbert, senior secretary of the British Legation, to take over as chargé d'affaires. Salisbury's view of the discreditable incident is contained in a note to Edward John Phelps, the American Minister in London.

> Private communications made by an Ambassador in good faith have never, I believe, before been made the subject of international complaint ... It is sufficient ... to say that there was nothing in Lord Sackville's conduct to justify so striking a departure from the circumspect and deliberate procedure by which in such cases it is the usage of friendly states to mark their consideration for each other.

The British press were on the whole critical of Sackville for his stupidity, but here and there, even in America, there was sympathy and support for him.

> Are there not many sensible Americans, and especially sensible American newspapers, of both parties making fools of themselves? For three or four days they have been howling over a silly, inconsequential letter written by a kind-hearted diplomatist, innocent of the wiles and trickeries of American party leaders ... After Tuesday next there will not be a sensible American who will attach the slightest importance to the silly unimportant letter which Lord Sackville was heedless enough to write.

Poor Victoria cut out this clipping and underlined 'kind-hearted' in ink when she pasted it into her scrapbook, adding it to others suggesting that Cleveland had been forced into taking a very abrupt and undignified stand and that Sackville did not deserve such treatment. Even Blaine in a speech the day before the election said coldly of Cleveland that he had deliberately weighed Lord Sackville against the Irish vote and dismissed him.

The election was a close one, won by Benjamin Harrison. The President awaited the returns in the White House library with his wife and a few friends. At midnight Secretary Whitney, crossing from the telegraph room down the corridor, announced, 'Well, it's all up'.

In the aftermath of the elections of 1888 there was virtually no public blame of Lord Sackville for the Democratic defeat. Cleveland's failure was laid entirely on the tariff issue. It seems conceivable that the President's strong, perhaps brutal handling of Sackville neutralized what could have been a very damaging issue in a close election. By treating the British Minister so roughly he may have turned the Murchison affair into a plus. In any case, it certainly did not lose him the election.

It would have been too soon for the traumatized group at the British Legation to consider any general question. They could not have taken in anything beyond the immediate practical question of departure in disgrace, and disgrace it was. Later, there would be time, and in his privately published *My Mission to the United States*, Lord Sackville told his version of the story. In it there is nothing new; but wounded, hurt and furious with himself as Sackville must have been at his indiscretion, bitter as he was with the trickery of the American politicians who had cost him his job, he still found the humour to copy a farcical letter which he received from a Mr John B. Dorris, GREAT INTER-OCEAN SHOWS, THREE-RING CIRCUS, MENAGERIE AND WORLD'S MUSEUM, COLOSSAL HIPPODROME AND NEW WILD WEST.

My Lord,
Having read the newspapers carefully in all things appertaining to your now famous letter to Mr Murchison . . . I respectfully address you these lines, hoping that they will receive your Lordship's attention. In view of the fact that you are now, without exception, the most prominent man in American politics, and that your Lordship will soon be recalled to your home duties, I, in my capacity as manager of the greatest museum in the world, respectfully beg to make your Lordship the following offer so that you may be placed in position to properly place yourself before the American people previous to your departure . . . Two thousand dollars per week.

There were fine letters of encouragement from distinguished Americans. John Hay wrote from Cleveland on 1 November:

My dear Lord Sackville,
I shall not be in Washington in time to say goodbye in person, and I therefore take this means of bidding you farewell. Without saying many words in regard to a disagreeable subject, I wish at least to express my regret that we are to lose you in Washington, and my shame and disgust at the unexampled meanness and cowardice with which you have been treated by the present Administration. Mrs Hay joins me in regards to your daughters and I am, etc.

John Hay, private secretary to Abraham Lincoln, historian, later Ambassador to Great Britain and Secretary of State, was one of the most admired men in the country. His letter must have pleased Lord Sackville and Victoria.

There were only three weeks before departure. The *Star* which had loved Victoria since her first appearance at the New Year's White House reception in 1881 did its best for her. Her years in Washington were reviewed, lovingly, in the manner of an obituary for a much-admired public figure.

It is said by those who have known her longest and most intimately that she has never made a mistake in all the delicate social duties that she has been required to perform in seven years at the British Legation . . . Every day quantities of flowers are left at the Legation for the young ladies . . . After the issue of the President's ultimatum, which settled their diplomatic fate with this government, gifts and costly presents began to arrive every day . . .

Straining for news of farewell dinner parties the *Star* reporter was not able to report very many. On 7 November Judge and Mrs Bancroft Davis were the hosts at a large dinner attended by Lord Sackville and his daughters. Mr Davis had been Under-Secretary of State under Blaine and his wife had been a member of the Ladies' Committee. The next engagements were on the last two nights in Washington, 21 and 22 November. On the first evening the French Minister took a box at the theatre for his party, and Mrs Whitney did the same thing the next night.

Lord Sackville and the Misses Sackville-West spent the last evening of their stay with Mrs Whitney in her box at Albaugh's theater. At the close of the performance, the ladies held quite a levee in the foyer of the house, their many friends pressing forward to bid them good bye. The hour of their departure from the city was kept within the circle of their intimate friends, as Lord Sackville feared an unkind demonstration at the station. The word was passed among the few . . .

Victoria had kept herself busy organizing the sale of the Legation effects. This was routine in Washington; Thornton had done it before leaving and usually a mass of sightseers appeared at any Legation sale, staring with awe, fingering the objects, and sometimes buying very little. The Sackville sale went well, possibly because of the recent notoriety of the family or because of Victoria's highly publicized fame as a decorator. Pitifully, the favours she had brought back from France that summer for her mid-winter ball went for good prices, as did the bric à-brac from her own sitting room. 'A brass hot water kettle caused lively competition, and was captured at a figure that exceeded its value many dollars . . . The stable . . . such a crowd had never before invaded the ordinarily quiet precincts . . .' the brougham, the landau, the victoria, the buggy, all went for good prices as did the horse blankets and the sleigh robes. 'This was probably due to the fact that each was ornamented with the Sackville monogram . . . A sleigh, which was dear at $15, was captured for $22.'

During the hiatus between dismissal and departure, Joseph Chamberlain returned to Washington to marry Mary Endicott. It was a small wedding, attended by the President and Mrs Cleveland and members of the Cabinet. Although Victoria had introduced Mr Chamberlain to his bride, Lord Sackville and his daughters were not invited. This does not sound like Mary Endicott, but she would have had to give in to her parents' prudent desire to avoid a confrontation between the President and the Sackville-Wests.

Ironically, when the newly-married Chamberlains left Washington on 23 November they departed on the same train as Lord Sackville and his daughters, and they all sailed on the same steamer for Europe. It was a sad little scene at the station, in sharp contrast to the departure of the three West girls in April, when the entire Diplomatic Corps had turned out to see them off. Faithful Monsieur Roustan was there, and Mrs Whitney (who wouldn't have given a pin for the opinion of the Clevelands on such matters),

Mrs Cameron, Mary Leiter and her father, the Chinese Minister and his suite, and a handful of acquaintances. Victoria and Amalia carried bouquets of roses. 'As the train rounded the curve they waved their yellow roses from the vestibule of the front car as long as they were in sight . . .'

7

Winter in France, Spring in England

Because of complications arising from his brother's will, Lord
Sackville could not take possession of Knole immediately, and the
winter of 1888–9 was spent in France. Leaving Victoria and Amalia
in Paris, their father crossed the Channel to see about his business
affairs, and Victoria began a diary which she kept from then on,
writing in French.

Had she written a diary that survived from the Washington
years, its style might not have been unlike that of the *Book of
Reminiscences*, bubbling and enthusiastic, disarming in its simple
pleasure in her own success, the record of seven extraordinary
years marked by comments like the one she made on being told
that she and her father were to be evacuated from Washington on
the President's orders during the Fenian menace of 1883: 'What
fun!'

It was a sadder girl who took up her diary in Paris in December
1888. She had kept her nerve in Washington after the Murchison
incident, arranged for the sale of effects, smiled when she had to
smile and transported her father and Amalia across the ocean,
probably making delightful conversation on shipboard with the
honeymooning Joseph Chamberlains who had not dared to invite
er to their wedding.

Now reaction set in; she was hurt and despondent, possibly
angry with her father for his blunder, more likely protective of
him and furious with the strange American politics that had
forced his recall. In any case, she was shaken as she faced the
future. Washington had seemed so safe; the horror of her mother's
death and the convent years must have blurred into a nightmare
memory; Papa was so proud of her diligent efforts to help him at
the Legation and of her success as his hostess. Papa was sure to
go on to another, bigger diplomatic assignment, and she would

accompany him, with Knole as a pleasant background for the future. Now nothing was secure and the diary reflected her depression. The first entries were short, numb:

4 December 1888, Paris
We left America after the Murchison incident. I am very worried about the future. Bad crossing.
8 December 1888, Paris
Papa has gone to London on business. I feel ill with worry. The Queen and Lord Salisbury have been very kind to him. He writes me that Knole will bring in £11,000 in two years ... Everyone in our Embassy here have been extremely kind; they are giving a dinner for us ...

Victoria clung to the kind Lady Lytton, wife of the Ambassador, who let her go to see her whenever she liked, and it must have been a relief during that bleak December to lunch and dine at the beautiful British Embassy on the rue Faubourg St Honoré. To cheer up her melancholy father she visited galleries with him by day and went to parties with him by night, but these efforts were mechanically described; even her '*toilettes*' seemed to bore her.

Early in January 1889, Victoria and her father joined Amalia in the South of France for the winter. Their life was filled with luncheons, dinners and picnics; their friends were cosmopolitan – German, English and French aristocrats and a few Americans, including the ubiquitous Mrs Bloomfield Moore whom Victoria liked, but who embarrassed her by offering her a present of £10,000, which Victoria declined. Almost every night there were cotillions and quadrilles, and they went to Monte Carlo to play roulette. She made an effort to describe the fairy-tale-like beauty of Monte Carlo's lights at night, but a more genuine note was struck when she spoke of the weariness induced by 'the endless bodies'. Even the attentions of the Prince of Wales failed to excite her, although she was appreciative of his kindness to her. They met first at a dinner in February after which he invited her to go to the smoking room for cigarettes. She refused to smoke,

however I had to join him and I took Miss Stonor with me. He is kindness itself. He wrote his name on my dinner place card which I gave him in order that I would remember to send him a picture of myself, which I intend to delay doing as long as possible.

A week later the Prince was calling across the dinner table to her to ask when he would be invited to Knole, and the next night he looked everywhere for her in order that she could be his partner dancing the quadrille of honour at a ball. He was charming to her, and insisted that she brought him luck at baccarat. They went to Nice together with a party of his ADCs and some other friends, and during the long day he talked to her at great length, and she felt that he took a real interest in her and wanted to help her. Other attentions followed, recorded by Victoria gratefully, methodically, but astonishingly unenthusiastically considering what a great honour it was to be befriended by the Prince of Wales. She was well aware of her ambiguous social position in England, and to be received at Marlborough House was a coveted privilege. Victoria at nearly twenty-seven was still astonishingly unworldly. She wrote that someone had said to her that he was sure that whoever had the good luck of marrying her would find her a charming wife: 'So pretty and not in the least *fast*. (Oh, to be fast! As it is, I certainly am not.)'

What did 'fast' mean to Victoria? She wrote the word in English. unable to translate it. Probably to her it meant to be flirtatious, sophisticated, dashing, worldly and admired. The Riviera was full of examples; one that comes to mind is the Duchess of Manchester, who was travelling with her faithful lover, the Marquess of Hartington. Victoria mentioned the couple twice that winter.

Outwardly Victoria was having a brilliant winter season, inwardly she was still miserable. If only her father could have gone on to another job, she would have had a job too as his official hostess, but Aunt Mary Derby wrote that there was no hope of that. Her only prospect was marriage – dreaded marriage. She could not have confided her depression to her father, who was becoming increasingly withdrawn and remote. His mind as he walked the windy Croisette at Cannes would have been on his broken career, and probably he was already contemplating his book, *My Mission to the United States*, in which he hoped to explain and excuse the Murchison incident. The only recorded intimate conversation with her sisters was an unpleasant one. Flora and Amalia cornered her to find out if she was going to marry a suitor referred to in her diary as L.C. and told her that if she was not, she should stop flirting so outrageously with him. Flora added as a parting shot that if she did marry him, she would be unhappy.

Victoria had indeed been a flirt and the sisters would have been justified in giving their gratuitous advice several times in Washington, but in the matter of L.C., they were unfair. She took him very seriously and made herself wretched over him. The first diary entry mentioning him was dated 1 February 1889, Cannes. His name was the Marquis de Löys Chandieu, and he fell head over heels in love. Tender, passionate, very rich, he came from an old Protestant family of the French nobility; except for his religion, he was eminently suitable. The guileless diary shows Victoria wavering: there was a good day when she went to Mass and was inspired to feel that after all she could bear to have her children Protestants, thereby putting L.C. into a state of paradise; he came rushing, his arms full of mimosa and roses. Then there were bad days; on 22 March she sat alone in the rain, reflecting on the marriage that she did not want to make. It was unlike her to be self-analytical, but that unhappy winter she had lost confidence in herself and her judgement. She wrote that she wished to be free, but how could she be free? Also, she felt that she was spoiled and frivolous and not serious enough. On bad days L.C. would be reduced to tears, and falling on one knee protest once more how happy he would make her. For these difficult scenes she invented a buffer in the form of a huge piece of embroidery, curtain-sized, which irritated everyone when she dragged it about, but she found it useful when L.C. came to call.

The sisters returned to tease her; kind friends inquired discreetly if they were to hear a happy announcement. Mrs Bloomfield Moore surged forward again, offering £1,000 as a wedding present, and was refused once more. Victoria wrote miserably, 'Oh, what am I to do about L.C.?'

Paris at the end of April brought no decision; but it did bring distraction and Victoria began to sound more like herself. All the world had come to see the great 'Paris Exhibition' of that year and she watched the President of France drive by on his way to open it. The city was full of friends from Washington. Lucy Frelinghuysen and she visited the dressmakers together, and her old suitor Jesse Brown took her up the Eiffel Tower, which at night was a great sight, all lighted up. She saw much of the dear William C. Whitneys; they went to the Café de Madrid in the Bois to take tea; they dined at Armenonville; they went to a ball at the British Embassy where Victoria wore a pink tulle dress and danced the cotillion with the Duke of Vallombrosa who was so attentive to her that by the end of the week L.C. was making jealous scenes.

One beautiful May night they danced at the Gustave de Roths-childs' and came home in broad daylight, and went the next evening to the opera to hear Emma Eames and Jean de Reszke. Victoria's sparkle was returning. She wrote a long entry about her *toilette* at the opera, and a few days later described with delight meeting at another ball the Duc de Blacas, her old admirer from Ottawa days. L.C. was proud of her when the Prince of Wales singled her out at the Princesse de Sagan's reception before all Paris.

Altogether, it was a lovely month of May, and the introspective passages disappeared from the diary.

When it came time to leave for England at the end of June, she minded leaving Paris badly and wrote in her diary how sad she was to go. Her last day was spoiled by a headache, and there is not a line of anticipatory pleasure, although arrival in England was to bring reunion with beloved Aunt Mary Derby, who was to give a very grand dinner for them the night they landed, 1 July. The Prince of Wales had followed up his kindness in the South of France with a promise in Paris that Princess Alexandra and he would be waiting to receive her, and above all there was Knole – which she had never seen.

Paris must have seemed a safe little island. Admiration, flirtation, an easy life requiring no immediate decisions, no hideous respon-sibilities. But England meant making up her mind; even Aunt Mary had been asking about what she meant to do about L.C., and he himself was in London. They went down to Knole together two days later, chaperoned by her American friends Mr and Mrs Cheston; an impromptu visit, lunching on the way:

3 July 1889, London
. . . I went at once to see the housekeeper, Mrs Knox, who seems very nice and obliging; the pictures and the tapestries impressed me, and the perfect order in which both the house and the gardens are maintained is remarkable. We had tea and brought back some pretty flowers. The house is so big that one could get lost in it.

This unimaginative description disappointed her daughter Vita when she read it later, but the outsider can guess at some of the reasons for its flatness. It was too much to expect that Victoria could describe the mystery and beauty of Knole after one hasty afternoon there. In the first place, her mind would have been on her own problems. Would she live there as Papa's daughter, mistress of the house, or would she be married and coming to stay, as the Marquise de Löys Chandieu? She would have been told about the seven courtyards and the fifty-two staircases, and the treasures would have come as no surprise. But, just as many people are strangely disappointed by their first view of Versailles about which they have read so much, so she may have been a little intimidated by that cold north front, and felt diminished by the long walk through the confusing galleries and rooms. If so, she would have fallen back on the practical side, which was something she could understand, and it would have been a relief for Papa's sake to find everything so neat, the housekeeper so friendly, and the gardens in perfect order. 'The house is incredibly large – one could lose oneself in it.' This cliché is such a natural one, coming from a confused and uncertain young woman, overwhelmed by her situation and not a natural descriptive writer like her daughter.

It was much easier to write breathless details of the crowded London life into which she then plunged:

Lunched with Aunt Mary and went on to a garden party at Marlborough House which was very beautiful. I was so happy to see my old friends from Cannes again. I saw the whole Royal Family and the Shah, who is very grumpy. He carried an enormous emerald on his tummy ... The Queen [Victoria] looks very red and very common. The Princess of Wales is ravishing, but her dress is out of date. Everyone wore far too many bustles. All the same, it was a most imposing sight. That evening I went to a great turnout given by the Sassoons at the Empire Theatre in honour of the Shah of Persia. The whole theatre was a wonderful sight – nothing but marvellous looking women with brilliant diamonds. The Duchess of Rutland is a superb woman ... I never saw so many fine jewels.

The Prince of Wales was as good as his word and she managed to get Amalia in on every invitation that she could. The Princess of Wales was kind and flattering; and at a party at Hatfield particularly spoke to Victoria's father about her beauty.

16 July 1889
Having been ill, I unfortunately missed the Duke of Devonshire's beautiful ball to which the Prince had gotten us
invitations.

17 July 1889
I couldn't get up until it was time to go to Mrs Oppenheimer's
concert for the Prince and Princess. They spoke to me very
kindly when they came in; the Princess in black with masses of
pearls and a diamond tiara. Melba sang marvellously ... the
house was decorated with 20,000 roses. I came home so tired,
but at least I was able to take Amalia.

22 July 1889
The ball tonight was at Grosvenor House ... the Prince sent
for me to join him for supper ... The Duke of Westminster
wore the Order of the Garter – it is a funny-looking thing.

25 July 1889
On coming in, I found an invitation from Lady Dudley, whom
the Prince had asked to invite us. At the ball I saw C.H., he
became so pale that one could hardly see him ... [This was
Charlie Hardinge, who had loved her in Washington when he
was on her father's staff.]

The season was over at the end of July. Victoria, who was
always faithful in her religious observances, attended Mass at
Brompton Oratory and left with her father on a country-house
visit to Mr Edgar Drummond's near Southampton. There she
found a letter waiting from Lady Derby saying that she was
pleased with her niece and enclosing a cheque for £20. The loving,
but worldly aunt had every reason to be proud of the illegitimate
niece whom she had taken under her wing; for she had been an
unqualified success during her first London season. Even Aunt
Bessie, the Duchess of Bedford, thawed and invited her niece to a
party. The diary shows her as still remarkably modest and despite
the excitement of all the glamorous new people she was meeting,
she did not forget her first English friend, Mrs Mulhall, the lady
who had removed her from the convent. Victoria wrote to the
Prince of Wales, asking for and obtaining a ticket for Mrs Mulhall

for one of the concerts in honour of the Shah. She must have been please to receive Lady Derby's accolade and £20 was a generous present. What the prescient Aunt Mary could not have foreseen was what was about to take place the day her letter arrived, 30 July 1889. Victoria went for a walk with her host, Mr Drummond, and came back to the house to meet the assembled party. Among the guests was her first cousin, Lionel Sackville-West. She wrote in the *Book of Reminiscences*:

> I knew Charlie and Bertie, Cecily and Mary, but I had never met Lionel – I remember feeling I was looking my best that night. I was wearing a tight-fitting bodice and skirt of a pale yellow striped satin dress. Yellow suited me, being rather dark – and I had in my hair a wreath of 'ears of wheat a la Cérès'.
>
> Lionel never took his eyes off me during that dinner. I felt much disturbed, as he attracted me immensely. And I was delighted when the next day, he came to fetch me for a walk. It was not long before he told me how much he cared for me.

8

Mistress of Knole

Five years younger than Victoria, Lionel was the son of William Edward Sackville-West, hence her first cousin.

The history of the title was an intricate one. The first Sackville arrived in England with William the Conqueror. His descendant, Thomas Sackville, was Lord Treasurer to Queen Elizabeth and created Lord Buckhurst of Buckhurst in the county of Sussex and first Earl of Dorset. Lionel Sackville, seventh Earl of Dorset became the first Duke of Dorset, a title that died out with the death of the fifth Duke. Lady Elizabeth Sackville, daughter of the third Duke, married John West, fifth Earl De la Warr, and the family name became Sackville-West. The first Baron Sackville was the uncle of both Victoria and Lionel.

Lionel was a simple young man, sensual, unambitious, unreflective and very good-looking; tall, dark, with the famous Sackville hooded eyes. Since childhood he must have known that he was likely to become third Baron Sackville and heir to Knole, and that what was expected of him was marriage to an appropriate girl of good family and some money of her own. Instead, he fell in love with his older first cousin, whose foreign accent made him laugh, and whose charm and beauty were of a sort to which he was wholly unaccustomed. The early diary entries are full of laughter as the young couple met again at the De la Warr family home, Buckhurst in Sussex:

> I sang for Lionel and thought I would die laughing when I heard Cantelupe (the oldest son of the Earl De la Warr) imitating me ... Was a long time on the lake with Lionel ... yesterday I laughed until I nearly died, because Lionel had organized a game with some bottles ... I caught them and broke them; he banged against the wall. He does make me laugh ...

Victoria hadn't sounded so happy since before she left America. She always had a simple and childlike sense of humour. But she wasn't yet ready to fall in love, attracted as she was by the new young cousin who was besotted with her, and while he went off on the Duchess of Bedford's yacht, she settled down with her father at Knole in August. Two weeks later Lionel was back again:

> In the evening, we had decided to see the showrooms by moonlight, but there was very little moonlight – that will be for another time . . .

6 September 1889, Knole
We lunched at Chevening with Lord and Lady Stanhope . . . In the evening, Lionel finally opened his heart in the King's bedroom – "God help me, Vicky, I love you so!" He made my heart ache seeing him so tremendously emotional and upset.

7 September 1889, Knole
. . . I talked to Lionel after dinner in the smoking room. I was very frank and very loyal towards him. *Toujours loyale!* It is one of the mottoes of the family. Lionel is berserk.

The next few days were much the same; protestations of love on Lionel's part, regrets on Victoria's part that she was making him so unhappy. He left at last for Weimar to study German for his Foreign Office examinations with nothing decided. Victoria settled down to a quiet autumn with her father, interrupted twice by the arrival of other suitors. The clever, sensitive Cecil Spring Rice came down to make his last useless declaration, and before leaving he told Victoria that she would never be as happy as she would be if she stayed at Knole and married her cousin Lionel. She commented, 'If only he knew that Lionel asks for nothing better than to marry me.'

Löys Chandieu followed Spring Rice and was told by Victoria about Lionel.

> He won't give me up, so here I am between L.C. and Lionel . . . L.C. begs me not to abandon him, although at the same time he advises me to hold onto my beautiful castle at Knole. He has been most unselfish . . . Poor Lionel writes me desperate letters.

Lionel returned from Weimar and on 11 December he proposed again in the King's Bedroom. This time there was moonlight. They would have climbed the Great Staircase, and thus far they would have had gas lighting, but Lionel must have carried a candlestick for the long walk down two long hushed galleries and quiet rooms; intermittently the moonlight would have shone a pale ray on a hand or a face in the portrait of one of their ancestors in his Elizabethan ruff or Cavalier brocade. The King's Bedroom would have been dark and mysterious until Lionel drew back the curtains, then the silver furniture and the high canopied bed with its silver and gold hangings, the silver sconces and firedogs, the silver mirrors and the tripods must have come to life, without the almost vulgar brilliance that sun lends to masses of silver, but gently and gracefully. The garden below the closed windows must have looked white in the moonlight, although there was no snow that night.

This time Victoria accepted Lionel and wrote underneath the day's entry in her diary the family motto – JOUR DE MA VIE.

Two days later the inconsolable Löys Chandieu returned and the diary showed Victoria's state of mind:

16 December 1889, Knole
L.C. is getting more and more desperate, although he is trying heroically to pull himself together. It gives me atrocious pain and yet he thinks that my meeting Lionel was providential as a way to assure the future of my brothers and to legitimize my own name. I had never realized how profoundly and sincerely he loved me.

17 December 1889, Knole
We went to see Penshurst ... that brought back the time Charlie Hardinge was so in love with me and wanted to marry me and here I am marrying his cousin. For love? I really don't know. They say that women change their minds so often. Men also ... I am very tired of fighting against life and what does the future hold for me? I have the satisfaction of being perfectly loyal towards L.C. and L. ...

18 December 1889, Knole
I went to bed at nine o'clock perfectly broken with exhaustion

by the struggle of the preceding days. L.C. left this morning under a torrential rain storm. Poor fellow, he looks so sad . . .

A few days later Victoria and her father left to spend Christmas at Knowsley, Lord and Lady Derby's great house near Liverpool.

The entries tell the story of Victoria's emotional life that autumn as she saw it, and they were totally honest. She was still innocent, still incapable of loving anyone to her full capacity, still uncertain. Without realizing it she was clinging to the only security she knew: her father, and her father and Knole had become inextricably intertwined. Clever Spring Rice had seen it at once and given her wise advice in his parting words.

It was astonishing how quickly Victoria had taken to Knole. Lord Sackville and she had moved in on 24 August 1889, a day of pouring rain. Amalia was in Bad Homburg; later she begged to be allowed to spend the winter in Cannes and Victoria persuaded her father to give his permission. Flora, expecting a baby, was in Paris with her husband. The boys were in Africa, so the father and the daughter were alone that wet August day.

The administration of the great house must have seemed as alarming a prospect as the Legation had been eight years before, perhaps more so, but Victoria's diary entry written the evening they arrived was a happy one, describing her successful first interview with the chef, and what fun it had been to install herself in Archbishop Cranmer's Tudor bedroom. Next to it was a pretty sitting room full of flowers, and in the drawing room she found a splendid new toy, an 'orchestrina' (player piano).

The next day she went to Mass in the poor little Catholic Church that she was to learn to know so well and then, with the help of the housekeeper, Mrs Knox, began to delve into cupboards looking for pretty china. Within three days she had discovered masses of Chelsea porcelain and dug up a book which showed that the 'Golden Anchor' mark on it meant that it was very valuable. Pleased as a child, she took to the attic where she found a fine Gainsborough drawing of a beautiful ancestress. There was an afternoon in the plate room marvelling over the silver and the gold and gold-plate, a morning going into a dusty trunk containing old lace. A week later she was discussing the price of farm land with Glasier, the agent, and going over the housekeeping books. 'Not much fun, but I really am obliged to take care of everything.'

At Knole many of the people on the estate passed on their positions from father to son – Jeffrey the house carpenter was one of these, and it must have been strange to him to have a beautiful foreign-speaking young lady giving him his orders. But Victoria had a knack for getting on with people immediately; within three weeks she was writing of Mrs Findlay, the wife of the keeper, as if she had always known her. Mrs Findlay had been very ill, and Victoria worried about her and went to see her whenever she could. The Findlays were among the many people who served Knole with loving pride, taking their responsibilities extremely seriously.

Stubbs, the head gardener, had twenty men working for him, between the pleasure gardens and the two walled kitchen gardens, which were each of two acres. Victoria was particularly fond of the Stubbs family. There was nothing patronizing about all this; class and convention mattered in those days and it was comforting and reassuring to the Knole estate families to have their young mistress care. Mortimer Sackville, the previous owner, had been a misanthropic and unpopular figure, according to the gossip of the time, and it must have been warming to the fifty or so families on the estate to have the lovely Victoria and her quiet, gruff father walking about together, arm in arm, asking the right questions of the right people. Lord Sackville would have known by instinct the questions to ask, although his whole adult life had been lived out of England. It is easy to imagine him showing Victoria that enchanting fantasy, the bird house, and saying to Findlay, 'By the way, what happened to those Chinese pheasants that Lord Amherst brought back from Peking in 1816, golden, weren't they?' And Findlay happily telling him that they had bred and that there were still golden Chinese pheasants on the estate.

Knole, only thirty miles south of London, was a self-contained world. The home farm supplied milk, butter, cream and eggs for the big house, under a farm bailiff with eight or nine men and two dairy maids for lighter duties. The foresters, six or seven strong, were responsible for cutting timber and planting new trees. The carpenter's shop, with three men and an apprentice under Jeffrey took care of the household repairs, except for those that were undertaken by the painters and the plasterers. At the sawmill two men had the job of sawing logs into given lengths for various fireplaces at the house. All had to be planed smooth, not out of consideration for the odd man, who would wheel them into the house in his barrow, not for the benefit of the housemaids who would clean and shine the fireplaces at 6 a.m. and lay the fires, nor for the footmen whose duty it was to keep the fires going by day – but just in case Victoria, the lady of the house, or one of the guests might decide to put fuel on the fire, and had forgotten to put on the black velvet mitten which always lay in readiness on top of each wood basket.

Findlay, the keeper, had five or six men under him. To the famous fallow deer in the park, Lord Sackville added a more unusual species, Japanese deer. He also grew very fond of two Demoiselle cranes which used to follow him around the place like devoted spaniels; they were called Romeo and Juliet. Everyone at Knole seemed to catch cold all the time; when poor Juliet did so, it was fatal and Victoria sobbed when she died. There was a pair of tiny cattle from Afghanistan, each no higher than a fallow deer, and there were a great many dogs: a favourite deerhound, Diana, had fourteen puppies that winter to the intense excitement of everyone, but it was too much for her and when Findlay came to the house to report her death, it was he who was in tears and had to be comforted by Victoria. The Victorians were always openly sentimental about their pets.

Some of the game from the place went up to London to be sold, and bunches of Knole camelias could be found at Covent Garden market, but there was an abundance of fruit all the year round for the house. Hot-house grapes, peaches, nectarines and melons, flowers in profusion. The flowers were done throughout the rooms every morning by the gardeners, although sometimes the footmen did the arrangements for the dining-room table, as they were thought to be less clumsy with their hands; and often Victoria, who loved arranging flowers, did them herself.

There was a brewery, an entity in itself, as were the laundry, the stables and the forge, where four blacksmiths were employed.

Inside the house there were twenty-four servants, reasonably modest in an era in which Lord Bath at Longleat, another great Elizabethan house, had more than forty. Alice Butler, who began life as a scullery maid, wrote:

Only twice in four years was I allowed to view the dining room, which seemed miles from the kitchen. Everything looked so beautiful, silver and glass gleaming; it was a far cry from my family's kitchen table . . . There was a terrific hierarchy in the servant world, but somehow it never occurred to us that this was other than it should be. We all belonged to the same family and there was a sense of pride in serving in the Big House . . . The word servant, in the minds of many people, is still confused with servility. No one was servile, and in England, everyone was in some kind of service – government, civil, military, naval, Church or just serving an ideal or good cause. Frankly, I never felt inferior – just a cog in the wheel to help whoever was at the top to do whatever I was incapable of doing – to keep the country going. Christmas was lovely, with a party for the tenants, another for the children . . . and best of all I was allowed to go through the front of the house and help pour tea for the children, and encourage the timid ones to pull the crackers for fancy hats and whistles . . . The kitchen people were always invited into the servants' hall for dinner Christmas day, and allowed to get out of uniform. Black shoes and stockings were always a pleasure to shed . . . The Lady herself saw each of us that day . . .

The detailed description of the working of the servants' hierarchy is fascinating. The butler was always called 'Sir' by the underservants, in the evening his white waistcoat, tie and tails were laid out for him by the hallboy. The valet also had his shoes cleaned and clothes pressed by the hallboy, but no one but he was permitted to touch the master's clothes. The three footmen had separate and responsible jobs: the head footman was closer to the Lady, he filled the footwarmer with hot water for her carriage and tucked the rug around her; all three carried trays, served at table and cleaned silver – nothing was used twice without being cleaned – cleaned with jeweller's rouge, a disagreeable dark-red powder which had to be rubbed in with the fingers and left the footmen's nails and hands stained. In the mornings they wore a kind of clerical pepper-and-salt suit, white shirts, stiff collars and black ties, for lunch and dinner they wore the liveries of the house, brass-buttoned tail coats, striped waistcoats, stiff shirts, wing collars, white bow ties and white gloves. They were all about six feet tall.

The odd man and the hallboy had hard jobs and served the upper servants as well as the master of the house. The eight housemaids too worked very hard, up at 5.30 a.m. with grates to polish and, for the juniors, floors, on hands and knees. There were no vacuum cleaners. They used longhandled stiff brooms for the carpets. The heaviest job was carrying up the hot water cans of brass to the bedrooms. Until 1932 there were few bathrooms at Knole and the water cans had to shine, as did the washstands. There were clean sheets every day on the guest beds, and a special housemaid called the linen maid gave out the immense amounts of linen required for use in the great house on Monday mornings. The lady's maid was entirely devoted to the personal service of the mistress of the house and held a high position in the hierarchy, but the gods were the butler, the housekeeper and the chef, who at Knole was French. The departments, as they were called, were very separate one from another, but it was a meritocracy. Barbara Tate, who is still at Knole, employed in an important administrative capacity by the National Trust, wrote to the author about her memories of earlier days:

> The butler and housekeeper reigned supreme and the younger members of the staff had their training for higher positions by waiting upon them. Then in a year or two, they would work their way up. Some of those early days were hard, but it was a good building of character, the handling of precious things, the mixing with some of the best people in the land, goes with one all one's life through.

So the hallboy, who started his day long before dawn getting the fire going in the servants' hall and steward's room could hope one day to attain the glorious position of Mr Hicks, the butler, who was well-tipped by guests for his superior knowledge:

> He was a mine of information, knew the times of all arrival and departure trains to and from London, times of departures from Victoria to Paris, the Blue Train from the Gare de Lyon to the South of France, all theatre and opera times of performances in London . . .

Alice Butler ended her remarkable memories: 'Left to me, we would doubtless be in the Stone Age, but I am very pleased to have been part of that way of life, before we outpriced ourselves . . .'

The salaries of the indoor servants varied, in late Victorian times, from £12 to £30 a year. The chef as the most highly paid sometimes got more.

There were incessant visitors from the moment that Lord Sackville and Victoria moved into Knole; some were local neighbours whose calls Victoria returned meticulously. The Ladies Pratt rather alarmed her; there were the eight of them, tall and plain and shy and hard to talk to. Miss Boscawen was much cosier; she knew all the local gossip and enjoyed recounting it. Later, in moments of crisis Victoria used to rush off to Miss Boscawen the moment she came down from London to tell her the latest news, just as her grandmother Catalina would have gone to the neighbours in the narrow streets of Malaga. It must have surprised this Jane Austen-like character to share the secrets of the highest circles of London society, but half the fun of knowing Victoria was in her enduring rejection of English reticence.

Nearby lived the Comte and Comtesse de Baillet, a Belgian couple who were especially congenial to Lord Sackville because of Monsieur de Baillet's excellent wine cellar, and to Victoria because she could speak French in their house. There were a great many others with whom she kept up; the two most imposing and important houses after Knole were Penshurst and Chevening, with whose owners she was friendly. Besides the local visitors a great many people came down from London to see the house; one week she noted wearily that she had taken people around the showrooms every single afternoon and that her legs ached, as well they must have, for at Knole the guide must cover four acres of masonry, go up and down staircases, across courtyards, from passage to gallery to state room to yet another gallery, like the medieval town that Vita Sackville-West called it. It had none of the homogeneity of the later English country houses through which it was possible to walk in straight lines, following the mathematical precepts of the classical architects who had inspired their builders. Well worth it for Victoria; from her diary the uneducated girl learned fast from the more knowledgeable visitors, and her pride in Knole grew as the sophisticated men and women she had known in Paris exclaimed over the treasures.

Mrs Sassoon said that she had never seen such tapestries as

the ones in the chapel . . . They told Papa today that we could get exhorbitant sums for the Gainsboroughs, but we don't want to sell.

Once again, she learned fast. The first book she read at Knole, beginning the night she moved in, was the remarkable diary of Lady Anne Clifford, the great Cumberland heiress who had married the third Earl of Dorset and lived at Knole during the reign of James I, knowing some happiness, but more unhappiness, and writing a chronicle of daily life in the early seventeenth century that was absorbing reading. Victoria had never been taught English history but it was on the walls all around her and made extraordinarily easy to learn as each Sackville was the prototype of his period. 'JOUR DE MA VIE', for instance, the family motto, leapt out at her from the coat of arms in the stained glass windows. It came from the romantic young man, Thomas West, who fought in the Battle of Crécy during the Hundred Years War. On that great day, in 1346, the English victory over the French was completed when Baron West picked up the French King's crown from the battlefield and handed it to the Black Prince, Edward, Prince of Wales, with the courtly remark, '*Jour de ma vie*'.

Herbrand de Sackville had come from Normandy in the time of William the Conqueror, but during medieval times Knole belonged to the Church, became Crown property under Henry VIII and passed to Queen Elizabeth who gave it to her cousin Thomas Sackville. The house was begun before he was born, but the main block was completed before he died. The Tudor pile of grey Kentish stone suits this austere figure in the portrait, black robed, with a long, thin face and wise, rather intimidating eyes. Ambassador, Lord Treasurer, Lord High Steward, Councillor to his sovereign, he was also a poet and was the writer of the first English tragedy. He was as much an Elizabethan as his grandson Edward was a Cavalier; closely connected to Charles I and Henrietta Maria. When the Civil War began, Edward, fourth Earl of Dorset raised a troop at his own expense and joined the King at York. Knole was later invaded by the Roundheads, and his older son taken prisoner. The younger son, Edward was later taken prisoner and murdered at Abingdon. After the execution of the King, their father back at Knole made and kept a vow that he would never again stir out of his house. He died in 1652.

Then came the magnificent Charles, the Restoration earl, the patron of poets, host of Pope and Dryden, Prior and Killigrew. He looks jovial and a little pompous, painted by Kneller. But as young Lord Buckhurst, he had been a ringleader in the reaction against the grim years of Puritanism that had just passed, and was one of the merriest men in London and the lover of Nell Gwynn. Horace Walpole called him 'the first gentleman of the voluptuous court of Charles II'.

The eighteenth century produced the first Duke of Dorset, to whom George I gave the title, and whom he covered with honours. Lord Steward of Ireland, Lord Warden, Lord Lieutenant of Kent, Knight of the Garter; the list is long and he was representative of the great landowners of the time. But a much more sympathetic and romantic figure is the third Duke, who belonged to the end of the century, a more delicate age. 'I have always looked upon him as the most dangerous of men,' said the lovely Duchess of Devonshire, 'for with that beauty of his, he is so unaffected, and has a simplicity and persuasion in his manner that makes one account very easily for the number of women he has had in love with him.' Ambassador to France, he was the friend of Marie Antoinette and the lover of the Italian dancer, the Baccelli, who caused a great scandal by dancing at the Paris Opera with his Garter as a hair ribbon. The Duke brought her back to Knole and established her with her servants in one of the towers, from which she would descend to walk in the garden with him, followed by a Chinese page. There had always been a black page at Knole since the time of Lady Anne Clifford, invariably known by the name of John Morocco, but in the late eighteenth century a Chinese page came to take his place and he was painted in his robes and red shoes by Sir Joshua Reynolds.

Victoria read the memoirs of the French painter Madame Vigée Lebrun, who came to Knole when the third Duke was still alive. But by now Baccelli had been banished and he was married, all too respectably. The Duchess warned her French guest as they sat down for the first time for dinner, 'You will find us very dull, for we never speak at table'. The son of this marriage, the fourth Duke, died very young leaving little trace at Knole; the title, as has been said, died with him and the succession went, through Victoria's grandmother to the Buckhurst branch of the family, with the family names hyphenated into Sackville-West and the title of the heir Baron Sackville.

Victoria probably learned as much from her conversations with Mrs Knox, the housekeeper, as she did from her studies of books and certainly more than she would have from talking to her taciturn father. Mrs Knox would have known the history of Knole backwards and forwards and would have enjoyed teaching her young mistress as they rearranged the house together.

20 September 1889

We dined with —— [unreadable]. I was very bored. Papa was very happy because of the good wine. They were all very bowing and scraping before me ['bowing' and 'scraping' in English]. I was lovely, this evening, I think in my pretty dress of rose silk, garnished with white ribbons. Papa is so proud of me. All the servants gather to see me when I am dressed to go out to dinner.

This passage will reek of snobbishness and conceit to the modern reader, but it was class and convention again; Victoria was adding up her assets in a practical manner. Papa was proud of her (that was the most important), and Knole was proud of her in the form of its devoted servants to whom it was delightful to see a beautiful young mistress after the gloomy years with the former Lord Sackville. That was as it should be, just as the family banner should fly from the tower over the Green Court, as the bowls of lavender-fresh potpourri should be placed on the window sills according to Lady Betty Germain's seventeenth-century recipe, as the silver furniture in the King's bedroom should shine, so it was fitting that the daughter of the house should be an ornament to it.

Lord Sackville's lumbago had been bothering him, and Victoria persuaded him to cancel some country-house visits that they had been planning to make in November. She loved taking care of him, and prepared his bath herself to be sure it was hot enough, but not too hot. Sometimes she thought him cross and what she called 'agressif' in company, and the lumbago depressed him, but she found him charming when they dined alone together. Others might have found the only example she gave of his dinner conversation eccentric:

14 November 1889, Knole
I went to see Mrs Jeffrey, the wife of the house carpenter. I am
going to try to get to know all the families on the place and hope
to see that they are comfortable. They look happy to see me
when I arrive . . . Papa told me something extraordinary tonight
which really amazed me; that lots of people think I am the
daughter of the Queen of Württemberg (Olga). Papa says that
she did love him very much, but that to say that I am her child
is a pure lie.

How could this conversation have started? It is easy to imagine
the cosiness of the family dining room on a foggy November
evening, the curtains drawn, the fire burning, the oil lamp. The
servants would have withdrawn, leaving Lionel with his port and
Victoria opposite him, her cheeks flushed with the warmth of the
fire after the cold walk to Mrs Jeffrey's cottage. Did she draw him
out, hoping that he would forget his lumbago in reminiscence of
long ago? 'Tell me about Württemberg, Papa, you never have
described that particular post.' 'Ah, Württemberg. Yes, quite.
Stuttgart was a pleasant little capital in the fifties and I got to know
a good many people. One was Queen Olga. By the way, Victoria, it
isn't true that etc.' Impossible to guess. In any case Victoria seems
to have been undisturbed by the unexpected revelation, for the
next night in order to amuse her father she had Glasier bring her
the family jewels which she wore for dinner, noting with annoyance that the heirloom diamond necklace was a bit skimpy –
'*maigre*' is the word she uses – but that the tiara was lovely.

They had a very happy time together; Victoria thought that it
distracted him when she went about the house singing '*Plaisir
d'amour*', and although it annoyed her that she couldn't teach him
to pay her gallant attentions like Lord Stanhope, their neighbour at
Chevening who used to wrap a rug around her knees in the train
coming down from London, she accepted the fact that Papa
would never be gallant and she was grateful for his gruff, shy concern for her when she was laid up in bed as she was for a day or two
every month.

Victoria suffered from adolescence until late middle age from
acute discomfort during her menstrual periods; she was really ill
during the first day and generally weak for several days, and the
specialists she saw later could do nothing to help her. While in bed

she read. *The Mystery of a Hansom Cab*, Thackeray's *The Virginians*, the *Memoirs of the Princess de Ligne*, *Mare au Diable* by George Sand, a novel by Guy de Maupassant and one by Alphonse Daudet, Conan Doyle's *Sign of the Four*, and the *Travels of Sir Henry Stanley* were her list for that winter.

But her health, except for those horrid days, was superb at Knole and the headaches she had suffered from in France disappeared. Country life seemed to suit her and the tone of the diary is the reverse of the aimless, mechanical entries of the winter before recording her endless engagements in the South of France:

24 November 1889, Knole
Lots of visitors today. Mr Staal [the Russian Ambassador] called me 'the lovely chatelaine' and kept saying 'What riches, what riches.' They really said every platitude one could imagine. I love Knole . . . *Quel roman est ma vie!* What is my destiny? L writes that he can hardly bear not to see me.

'*Quel roman est ma vie!*' [My life is just like a novel] was one of Victoria's favourite phrases, and she had surely more reason than most young upper-class Englishwomen to apply it. Certainly her distress over L.C. was genuine; certainly she was not yet in love with Lionel. But perhaps subconsciously she had already decided on her own destiny. She loved Knole and she didn't want to leave Papa. By marrying Lionel she could keep Knole and Papa, and she could legitimize her name, which was the key phrase. Although she had one more bad patch to go through before her ultimate decision, the diary showed me that she was approaching safe harbour, whether she realized it or not. An unhappy girl would not have gone about Knole singing '*Plaisir d'amour*' just to distract her father: it would have been unbearable to sing that particularly sentimental song.

Christmas with Aunt Mary at Knowsley was a wretched time. Shaken by the sadness of L.C.'s departure a few days before and by his tragic letters, she wrote: 'I feel so sad, so lost this evening. I usually am so interested in everything when I come to a new country house . . .' Lionel wrote unselfishly that if she was still uncertain, she must forget her promise to marry him. Aunt Mary was tactful and asked no questions until near the end of the visit. When she did, Victoria told her that she could not marry L.C. because she could not leave her father to which her aunt replied that she was quite right, as her father couldn't do without her; adding comfortingly that probably she would find someone else to marry later. There was no mention of Lionel. Poor Victoria could hardly wait to leave Knowsley, with its kind relations, gently inquisitive. She made an effort as usual:

> Visited the kitchens; the cook told me that he feeds more than two hundred people a day in this season. Tonight I wore my point d'esprit dress and seven diamond stars in my hair. . . . Papa adores the shooting . . . 998 pieces of game killed today, seven guns . . . I am so tired of getting up at eight o'clock in the morning, I went to rest between five and seven. The table was so pretty this evening covered with white cotton wool to simulate snow and masses of holly and mistletoe . . . I put on my white dress embroidered with silver and wore in my hair a diamond swallow.

January and February were tranquil, healing months, spent at Knole. Victoria wrote of long walks with her father in the bare park, of a hunt ball where she was proud of Papa as he was cheered on his arrival: 'Hip, hip, hurrah for Lord Sackville!' There were happy evenings playing halma; she always let Papa win because it gave him such pleasure. Her American friend Mollie Cheston came to stay, and Victoria confided in this trustworthy friend that her decision was made. She went up to London to buy jewels with Lionel, and wrote how handsome he was in his frock coat.

In March the family was informed of the engagement and it was formally announced in the newspapers. The family reaction was predictably adverse. Their reasons were obvious; Lionel was five years younger than Victoria, she was a Catholic, he a Protestant, and they were first cousins. The ghosts of Pepita, the 'Spanish adventuress' of gypsy blood must have been in everyone's thoughts. Eventually the family came around and Victoria was touched by their increasingly warm reactions; by now she was falling in love and wrote that she could think of nothing but her engagement. She had been worrying about Flora and writing to her nearly every day, but happy news came on 13 March that a son had been born to the Salansons and all was well.

In April there was a long visit to Lionel's family in Wales; the diary entries are too long to transcribe, but they form a very moving and poignant description of first love. It had a seismic effect on Victoria, who had waited so long to know what it was like. Lionel could hardly keep his hands off her and they staked out a claim to the smoking room, where they certainly did no more than 'spoon', but every kiss, every caress was artlessly recorded, every passage recounts Lionel's perfections and her own happiness. For one whole morning she didn't see him, as he had gone to talk to the keeper and she had gone to the cathedral with his sister Mary; it seemed an eternity until reunion. His family were kind to her; her future father-in-law, Uncle G., made a half-hearted effort to postpone the wedding in order that Lionel could concentrate on his Foreign Office examinations which were to be in August, but there was no question of deferment.

As Victoria wrote, she was living in a dream, and nothing could interfere with her happiness, even the religious question. Her priest suggested that perhaps Cardinal Manning could arrange a dispensation; Lionel went to see the Cardinal who was kind, but unable to help. When she went to buy her trousseau in Paris, she had a horrid evening with the Bonapartes, old friends since Washington days. After dinner her hostess told her that she would be eternally damned, if she had Protestant children, and Victoria was shaken to the point of tears; but recorded calmly that she was going to avoid going near Catholics in order not to have any more scenes like this. Her sisters were equally disagreeable to her about the religious question, but she rose above the squabbles and concentrated on Flora's adorable baby, Lionel, who had deep blue eyes just like his Aunt Victoria.

It was a golden time. The wedding took place on 17 June 1890 at Knole, in the Chapel. Victoria had closed her diary entry the night before – 'More and more presents . . . this evening I had trouble fighting the reporters off. JOUR DE MA VIE!'

In the morning she received a telegram: 'JOUR DE MA VIE, all of my love. Lionel.'

It was a family wedding with the exception of Béon, who had come over from Paris, 'Bonny' the faithful French companion from the Washington years, Mr Walsh, Lionel's best man, and Mr and Mrs Glasier. Victoria noted that she looked well in her dress of very thick satin and veil of Brussels lace, that the clergyman Mr Doyle made an appropriate little speech, that Papa and Aunt Mary were very emotional, that although the dining room was very pretty with all the silver out and the cake a perfect model of Knole made of sugar, the guests were rather stiff and Béon and the Salansons had a row. She never missed much as a hostess. Her going-away dress was of grey with green velvet and black lace, from Rouff in Paris, and she wore a little hat with lilies of the valley and green knots. The servants threw rice, the local school children threw bouquets of roses and all of Sevenoaks was hung with flags and the street crowded with well-wishers. They arrived at Keston, a house belonging to Aunt Mary at 6.30. Victoria wrote: 'Our little *tête-à-tête* dinner was very nice. I went to bed early being tired. Lionel came to find me at 10.30. He was so sweet, so loving with me, so gentle. I feel how much I love him.'

Diaries and letters of the Victorian era describing honeymoons are sometimes dull reading. Sightseeing expeditions are dutifully described, the weather is recorded meticulously, unexpected meetings with friends from home at the *table d'hote* of the hotel shine through as the happiest moments of the journey. Occasionally a bride writes frankly, as in the case of Lady Airlie in the late eighties:

> One's honeymoon is chiefly passed in feeling dreadfully ill. I, who never feel ill as a rule, did nothing but faint ... I was nearly frightened to death and suffered *tortures!*

Victoria and Lionel's story is very different; an artless, almost childishly told tale of sheer physical rapture. The reader of the diary feels like a voyeur turning the pages written in the fine convent hand, deciphering the simple code invented by Victoria to record the number of times a day they made love, and their declarations of love to each other. She doesn't pretend to describe their sightseeing; although they made a tour of the *châteaux* of the Loire all we hear of it is that they stayed so long in bed one morning in Tours that they nearly missed their train. In Paris they found that they had booked at a very poor hotel and had a horrid little room, but it didn't matter; they went to bed immediately on arrival, as 'Baby' (Victoria's name for Lionel's penis) was what she called 'in chronic condition'. They were so ecstatically happy together that they didn't have the least desire to see anyone else; although they did dine with the Salansons several times in Paris at restaurants, and Victoria couldn't resist a little shopping. From the Loire they had continued to Bordeaux and Arcachon for one nostalgic day in order that Lionel could see Pepita's villa, but

Victoria makes the briefest mention of it; the month's diary entries are concentrated on her innocent, touching discovery of physical love and her gratitude to Lionel for giving it to her.

It was hardly surprising that the daughter of Pepita and the Lionel Sackville-West of thirty years before should have been so passionate a woman, nor that the young husband of the same blood should be so sensual, but in Victoria's case the blazing-up of banked fires was indeed intense.

They returned to Knole on 26 July to be given a tremendous reception at Sevenoaks and to find Lord Sackville, Amalia and Bonny waiting for them. Although Lionel was due to take his Foreign Office examinations within a fortnight the honeymoon life continued.

30 July 1890, Knole
Lionel went out to kill his first deer. I went with Amalia to visit Miss Boscawen then we played Spillikins. I call Lionel 'Tio'.

31 July 1890
Tio has gone out again to kill deer. Miss Boscawen came to see us and told L. that he was looking badly. I told Tio that this was because of e.g.! [making love].

2 August 1890
Baby very naughty this morning while I was pretending to sleep . . .

4 August 1890
Tio went riding. Yesterday I began my embroidery for him – a souvenir of the Château of Blois – this will be a fire screen. I worked a lot this afternoon sitting with him on the lawn in front of the house; all the same I was able to play with Baby. Went to the kitchen garden and ordered grapes to be sent to Mary and fruits to the Childrens' Hospital.

News came that Lionel had failed his Foreign Office examinations, predictably. Victoria dismissed this in a line, commenting what a relief it was that he would not have to get up so early in the morning. Had he passed, it would have meant a heart-rending separation from Papa and from Knole. Lionel was probably relieved himself; it is hard to imagine him rising slowly in the diplomatic service, slogging away at the drudgery inevitable in the early posts. He was twenty-three years old, heir to Knole, and very much in love with a beautiful wife who took all the dreary administrative chores of running a great estate on her shoulders. Of Lord Sackville's reaction there is no record; Lionel's father wrote sympathetically that it had been worth making the try for the Foreign Service; only Cecily, Lionel's sister, had the courage to attack Victoria during a visit to Bangor, asking what career her brother was going to take up. This infuriated Victoria, who went to bed in a bad humour.

But the only real cloud on the autumn sky in 1890 was the perennial question of what to do with Amalia. She was miserably conscious that she was in the way, that even her father was bored be being left alone with her when Victoria and Lionel went on country-house visits. She told Victoria how sad she felt: 'loved by no one'. Victoria tried to console her, but wrote that the trouble was that Amalia didn't understand how to make herself loved. At this distance it is impossible to judge the unfortunate twenty-two-year-old girl; it was inevitable that she should be jealous of Victoria and that she should irritate Lionel, who said after two difficult days during which Amalia sat morosely at meals, speaking to nobody, that he felt like shaking her. Flora was no help, writing from Paris that she and Salanson had no room and that it was easier for her to find a husband in England, to which Victoria replied that it was impossible. In fact, in the next few years several prospective husbands appeared, but in each case something happened at the last moment to cause the engagement to fall through. It is unusual to have three sisters of Latin blood get on as badly as did Victoria, Flora and Amalia, and the correspondence from the two younger sisters to the rich oldest sister is full of demands for money and whining complaints. But in the first autumn of her married life Victoria may have been callous; she was still living in a dream. Her diary entries continue the honeymoon:

20 August 1890
Tio is getting more passionate every day.

13 September 1890
Baby was very naughty this morning, we kept Mrs Knox waiting for forty minutes – awful of us.

16 September 1890
Tio got up even later than usual this morning; he simply can't leave me and often returns about 11 o'clock so that we can have caresses that never end.

18 September 1890
Tio was perfectly mad tonight – he kissed me passionately even in front of Amalia and Bertie, which ended in the most delicious love making. He really is a stallion – 4 times.

28 November 1890
Delirium. Afterwards Tio said, "Was it nice, Vicky?"

Visitors came and went, interruptions to the love making. On 3 December they had a nasty scare. It was in the morning, and 'Baby' was being particularly active when the lovers heard the terrible sound of the great bell that tolled for fire at Knole. Victoria ran downstairs in her nightdress without even a shawl over her shoulders, Lionel joined her, dressed, in two minutes. The fire had started in the dining-room fireplace; and Amalia and Lionel's sister Mary who were having breakfast there acted with great presence of mind. They ordered the butler to sound what Victoria called '*la grosse cloche*' – it sounds even more alarming in French – and then the two girls hauled down the portraits of Shakespeare and Ben Jonson from the dining-room walls. Soon every man on the estate and the firemen from Sevenoaks were with them to work the pumps and the firehoses; but it was in fact Jeffrey, the house carpenter who saved his beloved Knole. Seeing that the panelling was smoking, he unhesitatingly took an axe to the floorboards, as a surgeon in emergency might have operated on the vital part of a body that only he had cherished and known. The fire controlled, Victoria and Lionel could relax, and while she did not mention anyone saying a kind word of thanks to Amalia, she wrote of Papa and of his great calm. She did not say whether he wandered in followed by the remaining, faithful crane Romeo, but it is easy to imagine him, never raising his voice and possibly carrying in his hand a volume of *Decline and Fall of the Roman Empire*. He read through Gibbon every other year; the story would have suited his melancholy spirits.

It had been rather a lonely time for Lord Sackville; and a

worrying one. Victoria was too euphoric in 1890 to concern herself overly with economic matters; she probably didn't realize what the imports of cheap American corn were doing to the rents of English landowners, and when the great Gainsborough picture of the Baccelli had had to be sold in September, she wrote as if it was an isolated incident and not the beginning of a painful decline in their fortunes. It woke her up when her father came to her to announce that their planned trip abroad that winter should be put off, 'but he leaves me free to decide'.

After going over the accounts she did indeed decide, the trip was off. She was sad not to go to Italy, but somehow through her new economies she was able to afford three more fine horses for Lionel, which seems odd as Lord Sackville had expressly pointed out to her the already ruinous costs of the stable; but Tio loved to hunt and making him happy was Victoria's delight. '*Quel roman est ma vie!*'

9

Entertaining at Knole

Christmas at Knole must have been a happy time. The children from the estate came to tea and were so over-excited by the beauty of the tree and the glory of the occasion that Victoria had to ask the assistant-plumber to serve as nursery maid – she was always good at finding unexpected people to help her out at any given time. Tio helped her to hand out the presents from the tree, then carried her off to the library in a burst of passion.

They had no guests that Christmas, but in January they started to entertain:

12 January 1891, Knole
We had our first big dinner, which was very successful. Received in the Colonnade Room, full of pretty plants, lighted with big and small lamps. On the dining room table, the big vermeuil "chandelier", champagne coolers full of cyclamens, vermeuil plates. Used Crown Derby and Sèvres services. Lord and Lady Stanhope, Lady Emily, Mr and Mrs Davison, Miss Boscawen, Mr Du Bose, Mr Walsh and seven Wests. The band from Sevenoaks played during dinner. Lionel said that he was proud of me.

Those were country neighbours, but from Saturday to Monday there were weekend houseparties; sometimes old friends from America like Mrs Cameron, the Chestons, the Joseph Chamberlains, to whom Victoria bore no malice; in fact, she wrote that Chamberlain reminded her of William Pitt. There were friends from the Continent, there were connoisseurs with letters of introduction who wanted to see the collections, there was a lot of family. Victoria saw a good deal of Daisy Cornwallis-West, a beautiful young cousin who was to marry the Prince of Pless and live a semi-royal life in his great castle in Germany. The parties were not large by Edwardian standards – a dozen people at most – and the winter days sound idyllic, shooting, skating, tobogganing, feeding the deer, and playing gentle, old-fashioned games in the evening. Dumb crambo, charades and card tricks were favourites, and there was one game they particularly enjoyed in which the players wore masks made from newspapers; one put newspapers in front of people's faces, two holes cut out for the eyes, and the other guests attempted to guess the identity of the players. Thought reading had come into fashion, and a game described by Victoria as 'such a good one' was called Knights of the Infanta. Ten years later, she noted with annoyance that the guests had begun to insist on playing bridge so that she had to arrange a room for it; in contrast the early nineties at Knole sound deliciously old-fashioned and countrified. The winter weather was often cruel, but after the guests had left (they took the 11.30 train from Sevenoaks on Monday mornings, in their leisurely way, and Victoria described the tedium of the last half hour making conversation while they waited for the carriages and the bus for the visitors' servants to draw up to the door) she would sigh with relief. She was very happy and very busy; one day she and the housekeeper, Mrs Knox, collected all the blue and white porcelain in the house and made the Colonnade Room a Chinese drawing room, filled with green plants from the hot houses; then there was the daily walk with Lionel to the farm and the stables and a discussion with Papa about whether or not it would be possible to plant fresh asparagus in the kitchen garden, and if so, where; there was her new bathroom to work on, its walls entirely covered with stamps pasted on with her own loving hands. She was mad about them; the next year she made a screen, six feet high, of four panels, each carrying 1,500 postage stamps. And how they read aloud – the next winter Lionel read to her *Plain Tales from the Hills*, *Lorna Doone*, *Adam Bede* and *Vanity Fair*. Becky Sharp fascinated her as a character.

Occasionally, during the winter they would go up to London for a night at the Chestons and a day of shopping; Victoria could never resist jewels, and while they couldn't afford to buy important ones, the loving Tio would insist on giving her a trinket, and they would spend hours in Bond Street discussing the resetting of the heirloom jewels. But there was so much to do at Knole; she couldn't wait to get back. In February Papa put in electric bells, which was exciting enough, but in April came the telephone, 'our great amusement'; one extension in Papa's bedroom. The year 1891 was fairly early for the telephone in England, and as there was still no central exchange Lord Sackville could only have called through to his friends who also had telephones. One was Lord Salisbury at Hatfield; a scientific innovator, who had laid on his own telephone lines some years before. Visitors used to be electrified by the sound of the great Prime Minister's voice, testing. 'Hey diddle diddle, the cat and the fiddle . . .' was one of the nursery rhymes he always used.

There is no record of an electrician at Knole in those early years; Jeffrey, the house carpenter, and Victoria coped together and very dangerous it must have been. But what fun they had! Soon they were doing over Black Boy's Passage (named for John Morocco, the page boy), in order to make more guest rooms. By 4 April 1890, Victoria was eating strawberries out of the kitchen garden as she walked through it, and in the first week in May the lilacs were out and she wrote that two of the greatest joys of her spring house-parties were taking the guests to walk down the '*allée des lilas*' and showing them the state rooms by moonlight. It must have been heavenly to arrive at Knole as a guest during the spring or summer. From the unpretentious gates, the carriage would have wound its way through the beeches of the park, which was all valleys and hills as the drive curved serenely towards the hollow in which lay the stern monastic north front of the house. Some of the beeches were enormous; there was one in particular called the King's Beech, around the bole of which a seat had been built, a pleasant spot on which to rest, the ladies spreading their muslin skirts around them. The stronger among the guests would have walked to Masthead for the great view below it over the Weald of Kent; Victoria and her friend Mollie Cheston did this one day, two exuberant women, swinging down the rides, arm in arm, so exhilarated by the spring woods that they sang all the way:

> I had not heard the Blue Bells ring,
> Nor had I heard the Crocus croak,
> But yet I knew full well twas Spring,
> The instant I awoke . . .

For the less energetic there was the walk to the Bird House, and tea was sometimes taken in this charming Gothic folly. But the centre of life in the spring and summer was the lovely garden side of the house, and it is possible to speculate on the thoughts of an imaginary visitor lying on a deck chair under the hornbeam on the right side of the lawn, waiting for Victoria to return. If it was his first visit to Knole, he would have been exhausted, for much as she complained about the fatigue of showing the house, she was in fact so proud of it that she was a relentless guide.

A visitor would have tried to draw a mental map – was he looking up at the window of the Venetian Ambassador's bedroom, which he had so much admired, or was it the Spangled Room? And those three galleries – God, how his feet hurt, but surely he couldn't have forgotten the Cartoon Gallery with the red Genoa velvet on the walls and the Meytens cartoons – but where was the Leicester gallery, that forbidding long dark vista with the family portraits? Just off the ballroom? Or was that the Brown gallery – he had climbed a flight of stairs to reach it – but he had been climbing stairs and crossing medieval courtyards all day. He was lost, tired and annoyed, for he had even forgotten the ten pictures that had expressly been pointed out to him by Victoria; she had said, 'Papa is lending these pictures to the Exhibition in London'. What were they? And he was famous for his photographic memory. Ah, yes – now he had it: '*Miss Linley and her brother* by Gainsborough; the three children by Hoppner; two pictures of cupids by Poussin; cupids by Parmigiano; *The Chinese Boy* by Reynolds; an *Infant Samuel* by Reynolds, the Cranfields by Meytens', and she had said that she was sorry that she couldn't show him the Baccelli by Gainsborough that had been sold, but had shown him the drawing. And there were the others that were not going up to the Exhibition – Victoria had pointed out Holbein's great *Sir Thomas More*; the little *Head of a Woman* by Rembrandt, which she knew would have to be sold one day, and which she especially liked; the *Young Man* by Frans Hals and *The Holy Family* by Perugino, the two Wouvermans, very much in fashion at the time. She had spoken of the tapestries from the Chapel, soon to be sold to America, and of the carpet from the Cartoon Gallery and the one from the King's Room. What a woman she was. That scent of heliotrope, for instance. Or was it lilac? No, white heliotrope, she had said so herself and before conducting him to his rest in the garden had been thoughtful enough to tell him the name of the shop where he could buy it for his wife in Paris – just off the rue St Honoré in Paris.

He relaxed, looking drowsily from his deckchair in the sun at the brown roofs, the casual, wandering walls of grey Kentish stone, the irregular windows; the seemingly unplanned lawns and beds of the garden around him. There were white pigeons circling above him; he knew that Lionel, when finding no better sport, used to shoot them from the window of the King's Bedroom. Was he looking at the King's Bedroom? It no longer mattered; for the visitor had by now forgotten his museum feet and his cerebral gymnastics. Knole, as seen from the garden side, was a house of tranquility. It began to soothe and to rest him.

It was hard to realize that it had been built more or less at one time; nothing seemed ordered, done in one neat piece. The house had caught and held its basic form from Tudor times on, but gave the effect of having grown organically and naturally as a village might as the population increased. This chapter of English history in the Kentish countryside, this gentle marriage of protective, heraldic stone leopards over the great Green Court on the north, to the sun-filled garden in which the visitor lay made the classical order of the other great houses which he had admired seem foreign in contrast. Sleepy, lilac-lulled, he all but closed his eyes. Still, he was not quite asleep, for although he was alone, there were other people in the garden . . . They did not worry him, he felt the sense of their continuity. Mixing up his dates, as sightseers do; in happy semi-dream, he imagined the Sackville children from the Hoppner portrait running across the lawn on their way to where the groom stood waiting with the ponies; he imagined lonely Lady Anne pacing through the seventeenth-century afternoon, followed by her grave chaplain, both of them straining their ears for the sound of My Lord's long-awaited carriage; and he imagined the Restoration earl emerging from the house, arm-in-arm with Dryden and deep in discourse as they went to walk in the Wilderness. The Wilderness was only a step from the garden front where the visitor lay. One of the loveliest parts of Knole, it is wild and wooded, romantic and Arcadian, unregulated to the eye, yet beautifully planned. In it the daffodils and bluebells of spring were followed by rich rhododendron, beech and oak and shiny-leafed ilex shaded the summer paths. Had he had the energy – and Victoria preferred people to have energy – he would have been exploring the Wilderness by himself at this very moment. But there she was – he heard the famous, seductive, low voice calling him. She must have remembered that he had not yet seen the little deer that had been born that morning. '*Voyons, vous n'avez pas encore vu mon petit cerf* – Lionel, you come too – where are you, Lionel? Oh, good, shall we all go, quickly – there is plenty of time before we dress . . .' He found the broken accent compelling, and he ran to meet her.

During the nineties there were three possible sets to which Victoria and Lionel might have belonged. The Souls were a coterie of intellectual members of the aristocracy: George Curzon, Arthur Balfour, George Wyndham, Herbert Asquith were among the men whose political influence was considerable, whose charm was great, and who concealed their erudition as they played the same after-dinner games that were played at Knole, dumb crambo and charades and the rest, for the style of the Souls, both the men and the women of the group was a gay, teasing one in conversation. Their luncheon tables sparkled and their love affairs were discreet, sometimes sexual, sometimes merely flirtatious friendships that were accompanied by letters that are embarrassing to read today, for the Souls were as full of extravagance in their written expression of sentiment as they were casual and bantering in their talk. A woman friend wrote to Lady Desborough: 'My blessed sweet, what can I say to you? You make me cover my face with my hands and thank God I have such a friend!' A man wrote to her, 'It really is such a privilege to have lived in the same century with you . . .'

Lionel would simply have been bored by the hyperbole and suspicious of the brilliance of the Souls, Victoria would have known that she would never have fitted in; although she may have envied the gaiety of their luncheon tables and once wrote in the diary of the dullness of conversation at Knole.

9 April 1891
L. says that I talk a lot, and I do as I am always trying to keep the conversation going at meals, which I dread. I think there is so little small talk in England.

The Souls were an exclusive lot, filled with contempt for the set around the Prince of Wales, with their open love affairs and their lack of culture. Lady Warwick, who had been one of its queens, said of this group,

Of course the Marlborough House Set had glamour; indeed glamour was its principal asset . . . We resented the introduction of the Jews into the social set of the Prince of Wales . . . as a class, we did not like brains. As for money, our only understanding of it lay in the spending, not in the making of it. But society's prejudice was not limited to Jews, it extended to artists, writers, musicians, lawyers. We acknowledged that it was necessary that pictures should be painted, books written, the law administered; we even acknowledged that there was a certain class whose job it might be to do these things. But we did not see why their achievements entitled them to our recognition . . . On rare occasions, if a book made a sufficient stir, we might read it, or better still, get somebody to tell us about it, and so save us the trouble. We responded to Opera, especially of the type which provided a stimulus for the emotions.

We considered that the heads of historic houses who read serious works, encouraged scientists and the like very, very, dull and they had only the scantiest contact with us. We wished to know as little of them as possible, and our wishes were our law.

We were good mothers in those days, but preferred to keep our children young, for the younger generation, we knew, would date us. Time was the one thing we could not control; and consequently it had power to inspire us with fear. Many of the women who were my friends died when youth had left them – not of any particular disease, but of a lack of desire to go on living.

These acid lines ring horribly true, but they were written much later by a unique Edwardian, looking back. The lovely Lady Brooke, later Lady Warwick, had given the Prince of Wales nine passionate years, during the last of which she had been the only woman of her time to become a social reformer and an effective one. A practical humanitarian, she didn't just sigh over the conditions of the miners' children; she did something about it.

It is odd that Victoria was not more attracted to the Prince of Wales. He had befriended her in Cannes in 1889, when she had arrived from America, lonely and shaken, and she owed many of her invitations to him during her first London season that year. Certainly, he would not have behaved offensively to her, for he never paid court to young girls or newly married women, and the seventeen letters that he wrote to her in his own hand are kind and trouble-taking. He continued to befriend and to be interested in her welfare; he made sure that she was received by Princess Alexandra and that she and Lionel would continue to be invited to great occasions at Marlborough House during the season. He was warmly congratulatory on the occasion of her engagement, delighted when the baby was born, grateful and personal in his response to a letter of condolence from her when the Duke of Clarence died, pleased by her congratulations on his having won the Derby, eager to come to Knole. And they had much in common – the Knole guest book contains many names from the great Jewish families to which British society objected – Sassoon, Rothschild, Oppenheimer, the Prince's friends. She deeply admired Princess Alexandra and wrote of her warmly; grateful for her gracious kindness. And, always filled with eager curiosity and love of life, Victoria wrote from a big shooting party at Lord Ilchester's that she was frankly impressed by the conversation of 'fast' people, calling it '*épatant*'. This word can be translated as astounding, marvellous, flabbergasting; it is clear that in the early nineties Victoria was still unworldly. Sometimes, to her own surprise, she got on well with someone really fast – Lady Brooke came to Knole in 1891 and later Victoria and Lionel went to one of her huge houseparties for the Prince of Wales.

But the young Sackville-Wests by no means fitted into the third category of upper-class English; those aristocrats who lived in their country houses all the year around, bestirring themselves to come up to London for the season when there was a daughter to bring out, but otherwise hardly moving from their counties. June and July found Lionel and Victoria in London going to parties every night – balls at Holland House, Stafford House, Devonshire House – and Victoria noted proudly their number of dinner invitations, which averaged between sixty and seventy for the two-month period. Then, in the autumn they went from houseparty to houseparty for the shooting; Lionel slaughtering thousands of pieces of game and Victoria meticulously noting the bag each day. While the men shot, she spent her time with the ladies; noting politely, 'such an interesting talk with Mrs X. or Lady Y.,' but she never became intimate with any of these women. Admired, decorative and popular as the young couple were, they were not an integral part of any set.

Pepita dancing 'El Olé', 1854

Juan Antonio de Oliva

Amalia

Pepita and Victoria

Henry as a boy

ABOVE The Minister
(*centre*) and his staff on
the steps of the British
Legation

RIGHT Victoria
in Washington

Amalia in the carriage with Victoria at the
window, Beverly, Massachusetts

Sitting room, Beverly, Massachusetts

Knole from the air

Lionel, about 1890

Victoria grooms her
spectacular hair

Victoria at Knole

Luncheon for the
Prince and Princess
of Wales, Knole,
10 July 1898

Amalia in a carriage, Knole

Tea at Knole;
Vita sitting on the ground

ABOVE Lord Sackville,
Lionel and Victoria
at Knole

RIGHT Victoria, 1900

Victoria and Vita

Lord Sackville at Knole

Return to Knole after
the illegitimacy case

The Misses Scott and Walter
Scott leaving the trial

Lionel arriving for Scott hearing

Sir John Murray Scott (Seery)

ABOVE LEFT Lionel in uniform

ABOVE RIGHT Olive Rubens

RIGHT Vita

Victoria with grandson Ben Nicolson

Sir Edwin Lutyens

It can only be a guess, but it is possible to imagine several reasons for Victoria to have been as frightened of the Marlborough House set as she was of the Souls. Their flagrant love affairs would have shocked her still naive soul, and in her practical way, she would have realized that to keep going in that group required an outlay of expense that was beyond the Sackvilles, even had they wanted it. Then, society in the sense of large numbers of dressed up people gathered together in the name of pleasure intimidated her when she was young and bored her later on, so that although her training was such that it would not have occurred to her to decline an invitation to a great London house; what she preferred all her life were small gatherings of sympathetic friends, especially admiring friends who made her the centre of attention. Again and again, the freest and frankest diary entries are written from Knole:

22 May 1890, Knole
Every day the same thing, walking and sticking stamps on, reading, playing the piano, making love.

27 June 1890, Knole
What a heavenly husband I have and how different our love and union is from that of other couples.

It was always a relief to get back to Knole and Papa. Through the gate – into the Green Court, up to her own flower-filled bedroom – security again. She was safe at Knole, with her two adoring and dominated men. Her fear of loss was still acute – when Lionel went up to London without her and returned late on account of fog she panicked, when a newspaper story described the death by accident of a foreign prince her first thought was, 'Tio, it might have been Tio'.

It is also possible to conjecture that another reason why she shied away from 'the fast people' who in one way fascinated her, foreign to England and unassimilated as she remained and hence naturally drawn to King Edward's cosmopolitan friends, was that she preferred to keep Tio on the fringes of their glamorous society. He was five years younger than she and extremely handsome and attractive. There are ways of losing men other than having them disappear in the London fog or being killed in an accident.

The years 1890 to 1892 brought special happiness. The dispensation from Rome came at last and she and Lionel were married in the sacristy of the Catholic church at Sevenoaks. This meant that she could no longer be reproached for having been married in the chapel at Knole. That Rome permitted this was surprising, as any children would be brought up as Protestants, but the ceremony gave her comfort. And in July 1891, she was told that she was pregnant. From the beginning Lionel and she spoke of the child as Vita – evidently determined not to be disappointed should their first child be a girl.

That winter Tio hardly left her side during the long months of waiting for the baby, and her father was equally devoted in his shy, reticent way. She invented an occupation for herself during the last weeks, which was to bring the old-fashioned guidebook to Knole up to date. Although she was very heavy, she dragged herself about the four acres of building making notes. When her father and she had moved in the house was already open one afternoon a week; the far-sighted Victoria realized that the time would come when money would have to be made from paying visitors. Two years later she inserted a notice in the newspapers that Knole would be open three afternoons a week. Her only arguments with her father were about money; she was responsible for the household books and periodically he would reduce her to tears with his demands for economy. There was a particularly bad scene the autumn before Vita was born: Victoria went to Lionel sobbing about how cross Papa was, and while it is impossible to imagine Lord Sackville apologizing, the poor man did the next best thing, which was to agree that when Vicky was able to travel, they would all take a splendid trip to Italy followed by a visit to Egypt which would be done '*en prince*', houseboat up the Nile and the rest of it. It was not suggested that the trip would include Amalia, indeed there is little mention of her that winter. She must have been at Knole, presumably at her sister's side, but there is no record of it. During these years Amalia acquired suitors three times, known as Amalia's sparks. First, there was Mr Eliot, then a Mr Jackson, and finally a Mr Tobin from California. Both Lord Sackville and Lionel disliked the first two so much that their visits to Knole must have been untenable, and they faded off the scene. Mr Tobin was approved of, but his family at home insisted that he should return to marry an American; so he, too, disappeared. There must have been other reasons – no young Californian in the nineties would have been so lacking in independence that he would have broken his engagement so abruptly on orders from his family. What is mystifying is why the other suitors were given such lack of encouragement, unattractive as they may have been. All Pepita's children suffered from their lonely, rootless childhoods and the stigma of their illegitimacy, but of the girls, Amalia suffered the most. Victoria possessed immense charm, beauty and resilient courage. Flora had a certain toughness. Amalia, poor Amalia, what did she have? It is extraordinary that her father and elder sister didn't leap at the possibility of getting rid of her; it would be interesting to know more.

The baby, Victoria Mary Sackville-West, known to her parents as Vita, was born at Knole at 4.15 a.m. on 9 March 1892. The pains had started at noon the day before, and Victoria's first order was that her father should not be informed, as he was so frightened for her. She had a very bad time, and writhed in the arms of Lionel and Mrs Paterson, the nurse, imploring them to kill her. At the end she was screaming for chloroform, raging at Lionel because he was unable to open the bottle. She was horribly torn during the delivery, and the next days were extremely uncomfortable, but the reader who turns once more to the *Book of Reminiscences* (see Appendix) will find an enchanting description of her emotions.

That a young couple should have adored their baby was to be expected, but what seems remarkable in the daily descriptions, beginning on 10 March, of Vita's perfections – the adorable hands, the blue eyes 'of the same blue as Lord Derby's' of the masses of hair – is that there is not one line suggesting disappointment in the sex of the baby. Victoria was now thirty, and while she might have several more children, if Vita was to be an only child, Knole would, on Lionel's death, pass to his brother. Yet the reiterated note in the intimate diary that her mother kept was of pride in Vita, joy in Vita, gratitude that they should be blessed with such a daughter.

During the summer Victoria persuaded herself that the trip to Italy and Cairo must be undertaken, if only for the sake of her father. 'Poor old Papa, he becomes so unhappy sometimes, and I want him to be distracted. He is miserable when he is all alone.' She felt guilty because he had been worried by an unpleasant lawsuit with Béon – in fact, she had handled this with perfect competence by herself, both Lionels flaccid and ready to be led by her. But the money problem kept cropping up – the estate agent, Glasier, had been down to lunch again; his principal reason for the visit was to persuade Lord Sackville to sell '*beaucoup de Gainsboroughs et Sir Joshuas*'.

She thought it was too unfair; especially as she herself was so wildly happy. 'I love him, I love him,' she wrote in a passionate entry about Lionel during an interminable absence – two whole days – from Knole that he was obliged to make in June. No, Papa must be cheered up, and the money problem must wait.

Money is mentioned so often in these pages; Lord Sackville's situation was roughly this: in the nineties his gross income was about £12,000, of which £1,300 was his pension from the Foreign Office and the rest from the Knole estate. His expenses were about £3,000 per annum to Victoria for the housebooks, and about £6,000 for keeping up Knole. This left him £3,000 out of which he had to support the two boys in Africa, very unsuccessful in their farming efforts, help the Salansons and their child, and take care of Amalia. By 1907, the Knole gross income had risen to £13,500, but by now it was taxed (£2,000), and the expenses that year were £8,300 on the estate. Victoria had brought the household books down to £2,000 (this must have been an heroic effort, as they were entertaining generously that year) but Lord Sackville found himself overdrawn by £1,000. To make figures of the period vivid today, writers often suggest multiplying the sum in question by nine or ten – in other words Lord Sackville was overdrawn by nine or ten thousand of today's pounds. Another measuring stick is that if one takes the internal purchasing power of the pound at 100 pence in 1889, its value in February 1976, was approximately 6 pence. If one took 1907–10 as 100 pence, the corresponding figure in 1976 would be 7 pence.

Dismissing Glasier and his gloomy conversation from their minds, the party set off just before Christmas for Genoa. Lord Sackville, Lionel, Victoria, Vita and her nurse, Mrs Brown, and two servants. Vita and her nurse went on to Cannes to stay with Bonny, while the others proceeded to Rome. Victoria's diary is a conscientious and conventional report of Victorian travel. They swooned over *The Dying Gladiator*, they visited church after church, Baedeker's guide in hand, they experimented with Italian wines and found them excellent. A typical entry:

31 December 1892, Rome
Tio was so loving that we got up very late to go to see the

Vatican Museum; the *Apollo Belvedere* impressed Tio tremendously, although he generally doesn't like statues . . . We saw the
same Demosthenes as the one we have at Knole and visited the
Sistine Chapel (a bit disappointing) and came in starving at 2 p.m.
Then went out in the carriage to visit the Villa Borghese . . . walked
on the Pincio, what a view of Rome! No news of Vita today.

Cairo and the trip up the Nile were equally classic. They lunched
with Lord Kitchener, danced at Lord Cromer's, went to see *Aïda*
at the opera and watched a review of the Black Watch on the polo
grounds. There are long lists of other English visitors and descriptions of *toilettes*, but now and then Victoria made observations that
were fresh and intelligent; not very original, but she was beginning
to be struck by things and by people that the girl of four years
before would not have mentioned. She even embarked on politics
and described how exciting it was when the eighteen-year-old
Khedive chose a minister of whom the British Government did not
approve. The next day the Khedive caved in and the crisis was
over, so the Sackville-Wests were able to fulfil an engagement to
go into the desert to visit the Blunts. This was a long and exhausting day, but Victoria describes it with more gusto than she does
any expedition undertaken during the three-month trip. It was
interesting that she did so. The Blunts were the first intellectuals
to have appealed to her, and very different from the English she
had met in Cairo. Wilfrid Blunt was an anti-imperialist, almost
unique for his race and his class. Very pro-Arab, he was a famous
traveller, writer, and scholar.

They returned to Knole in April, having picked up Vita on the
way, and took up their regular routine. August found them in
Scotland for the shooting, with Lord Sackville remaining at Knole
with his two grandchildren, little Lionel Salanson and Vita.
Always good with small children, he wrote a charming letter to
Victoria describing Vita determinedly crossing the Green Court
alone – she was just eighteen months old – followed by a footman
and watched with bated breath by her grandfather. Except for the
usual money worries – Max had asked for and was given another
loan – the year ended happily. Vita was beginning to talk and every
word was noted down by her mother. She must have been a
precocious child, for by the next spring, she was calling herself
Vita Sackville-West and by the end of the summer Victoria wrote,

'We are trying to teach her to sing like me, "Tom, Tom the Pa-i-per's son!".' And a favourite game was playing house, Victoria and Vita on the floor together, pulling cushions and chairs about. These were years of contentment at Knole. The house-parties were frequent and Victoria was always trying out new innovative decorations just as she had done at the Legation. She was especially proud of one of her inventions, 'Two Bacchanalian little vines, dwarfed but bearing grapes of natural size, which stood in gold wine coolers on either side of the door of the banqueting hall.' She first tried them out one weekend in June 1894, for a party consisting of the Duchess of Bedford, Lord and Lady Erne, the Cantelupes, Mr and Mrs Percy Wyndham, the Harry Oppenheimers, and Captain Dawson, and the little vines were such a success that they became a specialty of Knole. It was Victoria's habit to dine at one long table in the banqueting hall, but to lunch at several small round tables. This was not only more informal, but made the seating arrangements easier in case some of the guests who had been invited to come down only for luncheon were delayed or didn't show up at all, as occasionally happened when motor cars came in.

During these years Victoria was genuinely not interested in flirting. Lionel was still a passionate lover; 'He seized me so hard in the train going to Dover that he dented his hat . . .' [Surely it must have been a hard hat – hence, a truly vehement embrace] and Knole and the child absorbed her remaining time and energy. There was the day when she lost Vita, who chose to return to her nursery from the Colonnade Room by walking alone around the gardens and through the house – it was like looking for a small child in a rambling town. There was the day that she found a pin in Vita's bed; there were the happy moments when, waking in the morning on return from a trip, she heard the scratching sound on the bedroom door: *'Petite Maman . . .'*

It was a full life, and her administrative responsibilities were considerable. Death duties were a haunting thought, for Lord Sackville was now an old man. Using all her charm she attacked the Chancellor of the Exchequer, Sir Michael Hicks-Beach about the unfairness of the law directly after meeting him at a houseparty. It was a tough and protracted campaign conducted by letter and in person, but she pulled it off, and was able to write the simple words in her diary on 17 April 1896:

Last night Sir Michael Hicks-Beach proposed in his budget to abolish death duties on pictures and heirlooms. This will save Knole. He has written to me telling me that it was I, who made him understand the injustice of the law, when we met at the Wimbornes.

This was an incredible feat, yet how modestly recounted. What a mixture Victoria was. The same woman who had persuaded a Chancellor of the Exchequer to change his budget at a period in English history when the public mood was beginning to resent the privileges of the rich tossed off the achievement. Yet, she could be petty and wilful about things that hardly mattered.

Lord Salisbury had always been a family friend, and it was natural for him to reply affirmatively to Lord Sackville's request that Lionel should join the British Embassy at Moscow as honorary attaché for the coronation ceremonies of Emperor Nicholas and Empress Alexandra in May 1896. This would be a wonderful sight to see, and Victoria described her preparations for it at Knole:

21 April 1896, Knole
I showed all my *toilettes* for Russia to the neighbours today. They were arranged like a shop all around the Colonnade Room.

The neighbours, who were presumably the Misses Boscawen, Miss Herries (another Jane Austen-like figure, very close to Victoria), possibly Lady Amherst and the Ladies Pratt were no doubt suitably impressed by this childish gesture which has in it a touch of Catalina's love of showoff, but when the Sackville-Wests arrived in Moscow, Victoria had an immediate row with Lady O'Connor, the wife of the British Ambassador, who felt that some of the *toilettes* were unsuitable for the Russian court and could not be worn. This would have been disappointing to any beautiful young woman, but Victoria's diaries from Russia were really too full of complaints. Curiously, she wrote in English during the visit – perhaps under the impression that spying Russian servants would read that language less easily than they would French, and her English was extremely fluent, but the content was so vain and self-indulgent that the historic scene never comes alive. She listed the people she met, commented superficially on the magnificence of the royal palaces in Moscow and St Petersburg, and remarked on the fine jewels worn by the Imperial family and the distinguished guests from all over the world, but a less self-centred diarist might have described what it was like to talk to the great Chinese Viceroy, Li Hung Chang, or the Amir of Afghanistan in his diamond-studded turban as they sat having tea, waiting for the coronation service to begin. Instead she wrote pages about Lady O'Connor's objections to her wearing a toque, and how horrid it was to have to put on a bonnet instead.

Once she was genuinely roused. On 18 May half a million loyal subjects of the Tsar gathered on Khodynka Field, just outside Moscow, to receive coronation mugs filled with free beer, and loaves of bread. The Diplomatic Corps and foreign visitors, including the Sackville-Wests, were to watch the scene from reviewing stands. Bad handling by the authorities permitted a rush for the presents to become a panic, and hundreds of people were killed. Mothers found themselves standing on the bodies of their suffocated children as they themselves fought vainly to escape. The foreigners were removed before they could see more than that something had gone badly wrong, but when Victoria learned about the dreadful massacre she was appalled and shocked that the Emperor and Empress should attend the great ball at the French Embassy that night.

She wrote of the ball,

> It was very well done, especially noticeable were the magnificent flowers and the Gobelins lent by the French government. I went to supper with Monsieur Chacon, and met Princess Yousoupoff.

Susan McCook, a young American girl, met Lady Sackville at a dinner party the night after the massacre. She too had been at Khodynka Field, and her memory of that day and night was still vivid eighty-one years later:

> We all knew that something terrible had happened at the Fête Populaire in the morning, but we didn't know the extent of the horror. We set off for the French Embassy ball from our Embassy in a carriage with drawn blinds – the Military Attaché had drawn them pretending that there was dust, but I knew there was no dust so I peeked out and saw a long line of wagons carrying the dead bodies for burial. When we got to the ball I

ran into Richard Harding-Davis [the American correspondent] and I stood with him on the staircase hall to watch the Imperial party come up the stairs. It was awful – I said to Harding-Davis, "But the Empress looks dead – like a ghost!" He told me that she had been on her feet visiting the wounded in the hospitals since morning, and that it had been a terrible decision whether or not to go to the ball; but the French Ambassador had put fearful pressure on them. Paris had sent the furniture as well as the Gobelin tapestries and the flowers, and the Russian government didn't dare to risk offending the French. You see, the Entente [Alliance] had just been made and was vital to Russian foreign policy.

Oh, what a ghastly evening, I can still see those white faces under the tiaras – the Grand Duchess Serge was the most beautiful of them all. I didn't feel much like dancing although all my beaux were there, and I was glad when Papa ordered the carriage to go home.

Two weeks later Victoria wrote in the diary, much brightened up:

We danced after dinner. Sir Nicholas [the British Ambassador] told me that the Czar had noticed me at Court, as the prettiest woman in Moscow, and asked who I was. Several people told me that the Czar had noticed me again at the French Embassy.

Lionel and Victoria returned to England laden with purchases from Fabergé, the fashionable court jeweller, and were delighted with the interest everyone expressed in the trip.

It was the last fling before she entered one of the most painful times she was ever to know. Some people have lives that can be charted as flatly as railway lines from birth to death and others live from drama to drama. Do these last have some curious attraction for excitement, or is it just luck? Here was Victoria, thirty-four years old, having had enough excitement for a lifetime and now apparently on a safe plateau; admired and cherished to a point where she was becoming spoiled, the wife of an adoring husband, the mother of a beloved little girl, the mistress of Knole – surely, if anyone was in calm waters it was she. Instead, her world was about to rock and crash about her.

10

'The Romance of the Sackville Peerage'

During the Arcachon years of Victoria's early childhood Lionel
Sackville-West had been, according to his lights, generous and
affectionate to his mistress. Pepita had accepted her social ostracism
and her loneliness, in return he had indulged her whims, shrugging
off with indifference her embarrassing habits of choosing royal
persons as godparents for the children, all of whom were represented by proxy, and her pathetic fake title, 'Comtesse West'. One
whim in which he had indulged her through a mixture of indolence
and pity was that with the exception of Max, the oldest boy, who
had been registered at birth as the son of Oliva, and Victoria, who
was registered as the daughter of an unknown father, the other
children were legally registered as his children, under the name of
Sackville-West. This indulgence was paid for dearly. It was the
cause of a notorious law case known popularly as 'The Romance of
the Sackville Peerage', which would bring him an embittered old
age, turn the children into warring adversaries, cost the family
£40,000 (approximately £400,000 today) in lawyers' fees, and
desperately hurt his beloved child Victoria. How could Sackville-
West have made this careless gesture? The answer seemed to lie in
three words from his sad, cold trial evidence: 'I loved Pepita.' For
to Pepita, reaching for respectability, it was important that as
many children as possible should be legally Sackville-Wests; as her
Spanish husband Oliva lived until 1888, this was as much a fiction
as the coronet on the gates of the Villa Pepa and it must have
seemed as unimportant as the coronet to Lionel.

When Pepita died and the children were dispersed, little Henry
was only three years old. The poignant, childish letters earlier
quoted showed how miserable he was and Victoria's answers
showed her concern. She kept up her loving interest and her first
thought on learning of their illegitimacy was to warn Henry before

he left for boarding school, lest a stranger should shock him with the news. She saw him off from England for Africa in 1886, and encouraged her father to set him up as a farmer with £3,500. A charming letter from him in 1890 illustrates their relationship.

> I am very glad to hear that you are engaged and will be even more glad to hear of Amalia's engagement. You will then all be safe, and there will only remain me for Father to deal with. Victoria, when you come to think of it, a father could not have done more for his children than Father has done for us; how kind he has always been towards us. *Remember we are his illegitimate children.* [Author's emphasis.] What pluck he displayed in taking you all over the place so as to enable you to marry well; he could not have done more for us two than to send us far away, we never would have got on in England had we mixed with young men of good families, who would only have jeered at us on account of our illegitimacy; he thoroughly tried to educate us both in classic and farming matters, and started Max, and now he is helping me too. He is a grand old man, that is what I think of him.

There were other warm letters, especially one when Vita was born. Then, beginning in 1893 and continuing until 1896 the tone changed and the letters written to Lord Sackville took on a self-pitying note; one asking for money in 1893 was typical:

> It has been a hard lot for us boys, especially for me who has felt and still feels that my presence would not be at all appreciated in England among my own relations. It is a cruel blow to my pride, however I will endure it for your sake until the bitter end.

Lord Sackville, encouraged by Victoria, sent out more remittances, occasionally Victoria added a small sum of her own for which Henry thanked her affectionately. At last he appeared in Europe in the spring of 1896, and there were uncomfortable meetings in Paris with Victoria and in London with Lord Sackville. Victoria felt that he had lost interest in anything but extracting more money and wrote sadly in her diary that he had forgotten his brotherly feelings for her and was upsetting their father each time they met. She continued to write appeasing letters; then they all separated for the summer, which Henry unfortunately spent with the Salansons.

No one was prepared for the horror of what happened next. Lionel and Victoria were staying with Lord and Lady Iveagh for a shooting party on 30 October when they received word from Lord Sackville that Henry had informed his father that he had proofs and papers showing that he was his legitimate son; hence heir to the title and to Knole, and he threatened legal action. Lord Sackville added that Amalia had completely disappeared, presumably to join Henry. The Sackville-Wests took the first train for London and rushed to Knole, to find Lord Sackville distraught. The diary entry the next day is short and touching.

> 31 October 1896, Knole
> I went around and around the kitchen garden with Papa trying to divert him.

During the next ten days Henry kept up his bombardment. There were more insolent letters to his father, a telegram: 'If I don't hear from you regret taking steps Monday.' Each member of the family received a letter: The Earl De la Warr, the Dowager Countess De la Warr, the Duchess of Bedford, the Countess of Galloway, the Countess of Derby. Later, in court, the counsel for Lord Sackville was asked by the President of the court, what the point of these letters had been. Sir Robert Finlay replied simply:

> Well, your Lordship sees the tenor of that; it is a letter stating that unless pressure is brought to bear to have him proved legitimate, he will make declarations which will drag the honour of an ancient family into the dust.

It does not take very much imagination to conceive of the effect of Henry's letter on these persons, who must have been particularly irritated by the fact that although none of them had ever met him, the letter started in each case as though the writer was a familiar nephew or cousin. 'My dear Aunt Bessie', and so on.

Victoria had her hands full that month of November. Her first priority was to shield her father, confused, miserable and hurt; he seemed to her destroyed, ten years older and hopelessly vague. Although one of her friends, Violet Spender-Clay, was getting married and Vita was to be a bridesmaid, Lionel and Victoria cut the wedding and spent one whole long weekend in London with their solicitors, who advised that counteraction must be taken immediately. Lord Sackville was only sixty-nine, but he seemed much older, and it was imperative that he write down every single detail of his life with Pepita, every fact of how and when he had registered the children as legitimate, if indeed he had so done, every memory he had of the existence of her legal Spanish husband, Oliva, every episode of the nineteen years of the liaison, hours and places, times and meetings, witnesses, names of servants, everything. Then if he died they would have something to fight back with, and the legal name for it was to be 'action for perpetuation of testimony'. This cold phrase meant little to Victoria, but she trusted the solicitors, Meynell and Pemberton, and went to her father to tell him what he had to do. This must have been agony. The eager, sensual young Lionel of the 1850s was now a cold, embittered, remote old man; if he had spoken of Pepita since her death in 1871, there is no record of it. Vita Sackville-West remembered as a little girl a curious scene at Knole. She and her mother scampered down a corridor into Lord Sackville's room, laughing. Victoria's lovely long hair was down her back and the child was hanging on to it, playing a game. Vita remembered her grandfather springing up: 'Victoria, never, never, let me see the child do that again.' Her mother had looked frightened, and had pulled her out of the room. If it had been painful for Lord Sackville to recall another lovely young woman, another laughing child; how difficult to open all the old wounds now, and to dictate grimly to a smooth-faced, tactful young clerk at Meynell and Pemberton things that he had almost forgotten.

Fortunately, he was given some time, and his actual testimony was written a few months later, but, oh, how sad it was. Everybody behaved typically during that month of November. The Vicomte de Béon, the former guardian of the children, came to Henry's side as did Flora and Amalia, and Béon and Salanson could hardly wait to give evidence to Henry's solicitors that neither of them had had the faintest idea that Flora had been illegitimate when she married Salanson in 1888. Victoria countered this by immediately producing from her retirement 'Bonny', the lady companion who had been with her for seven years in Washington, who had been present during the conversations about how the marriage was to be pulled off without the British Ambassador and the other distinguished guests hearing the word 'legitimate daughter', which had been solved somewhat ludicrously by a concerted coughing fit. Dear old Bonny (Mademoiselle Louet) was a very good witness, for she had forgotten none of her conversations with the ambitious Salanson.

Amalia behaved like the White Rabbit in *Alice in Wonderland*, scuttling about. Now you saw her, now you didn't. Poor Lord Sackville, who must have already felt like King Lear, could not have been amused when he received letters from her asking for money to live alone in London, and in the same week was told by the Knole servants that when he and Lionel and Victoria were in London, she had arrived at the house, crept in by a side door, and had said that she needed no service; she was just spending a quiet day looking up some old papers.

It was typical of Victorian convention that life at Knole went on as though nothing had happened. Visitors came to meals and were taken around the house by Victoria; there were weekend parties. Only the neighbours received her confidences; Miss Boscawen and Miss Herries and Lady Amherst were appalled and sympathetic, Miss Herries in her indignation went so far as to say that in her opinion, the only thing to do with the faithless Amalia was to send her off to live with Henry; and then she would find out what he was like. As for the Salansons – and Béon – the ladies of Kent threw up their hands, speechless.

The man who stood to lose the most, Lionel, was the calmest of the family. Reading his practical letters to the lawyers, written in his beautiful, neat hand, it is impossible not to be impressed with Lionel. Speed was essential and money was of secondary importance. It was crucial for Meynell and Pemberton to get their representatives out to Spain to collect what evidence they could for the suit for perpetuation of testimony before Henry's agents were on the scene. They acted fast, for those days, and on 10 December 1896 Mr John G. Littlechild, a private inquiry agent, formerly Chief Inspector of the C.I.D., Scotland Yard, arrived in Madrid. That same day he went to the church of San Millan, accompanied by an interpreter in order to examine the register of marriages for 1851. There it was, in black and white, the certificate of marriage of Pepita Duran and Juan Antonio de Oliva, signed by both of them. Mr Littlechild obtained a copy of the certificate and, returning to the church a few days later with a Mr Harrison, an English lawyer practising in Madrid, showed the original to him and together they had the copy notarized.

Mr Littlechild was joined within a week by Mr John Brain, a

junior member of the firm of Meynell and Pemberton. Together, these two enterprising men had before the end of the year obtained the signed declarations of three witnesses to the marriage. Isabel Hernandez, sister to Oliva; a brother, Augustin de Oliva and Manuel Pedrosa, who had been a close friend of the bridegroom's. But, there had been a warning, which the Englishmen took seriously, that Henry might cause trouble, and it seemed essential that the depositions should be made before a court of law. Gibraltar, being nearer than England, was chosen and all the witnesses were taken there. In the Supreme Court, before the Attorney-General of Gibraltar, representing the Attorney-General of England, a motley group gathered. There were figures from Pepita's early Malaga life, such as her aunt, Micaela, there were representatives of her theatrical days in Madrid, there were Catalina and Lopez's disreputable friends, shady and nervous, there was a smuggler or two, there were the awed peasants who had watched the luxury and expense of Catalina's rise following Pepita's success abroad, there were endless cousins and neighbours and hangers on. Henry had in fact been at work and the lawyers wrote to Lionel in London that the threats and bribes offered by Henry's agents nearly had serious results:

> These gentlemen do not rest for a moment offering money and threatening them all – I feared that they would at one moment succeed in carrying out their plans for the witnesses.

Poor Mr Brain – it was a long way from the Inns of Court:

> Micaela, for instance, cannot sign her name and this will cause some delay as she will only permit one of her sons-in-law to sign for her, we are sending for the son-in-law.

But, from the point of view of the action for perpetuation of testimony, these squalid and exhausting weeks of washing dirty linen had been worth it. Should Henry attempt on the death of his father to continue to insist that Oliva and Pepita had never been married, there were a great many Spanish words taken under oath to say that they had been. Unfortunately, the case did not end there. Five years later Mr Brain was back in Madrid, writing hopelessly to his senior partner:

131

Hotel de Rusia, 29 December 1902
Dear Mr Pemberton,
I am writing this in bed before the translation is begun. I can't get up to write because there is no one to light the fire. Please forgive the pencil . . . I am in the position of a Spanish Procurador who has arrived in London to investigate a crime which has baffled the public Prosecutor and Scotland Yard for more than a year . . . I can only go on from day to day what seems expedient without regard to the length of time occupied. Please send some more foolscap envelopes like the one I am sending by this post, also some paper fasteners, and "relief" pens.

What had happend to reduce the energetic Mr Brain to this pitiful state? The events of the intervening years will be recapitulated as briefly as possible.

During the time that the mole-like Sackville solicitors were collecting their evidence in Spain, Henry's solicitors were doing the same thing at Bordeaux and Arcachon. It was unsatisfactory, for, as has been already recounted, the good-natured people of Arcachon thought that Pepita and Sackville-West had been married. Only a handful of snobbish English residents disagreed.

Henry, like many frightened men in a tight corner, changed his tune. The next year, 1898, he wrote a frantic letter to Victoria asking for help. Blaming everything on the malign influence of Flora and Salanson, he asked her to forget the deplorable events of the preceding year and to 'give me your hand, as you used to do, remembering that I am your brother'. It must have been an impossible letter to answer; fortunately there was no time to do so, as he immediately appeared at Knole, sending his card in to his father with a request to see him. Lord Sackville, Victoria and Vita were alone. Lord Sackville told the porter, Lipscombe, to say that he was out. Henry returned to Sevenoaks, just at the gates of the park, and wrote to his father threatening to shoot himself. His father replied that he could not see him after all that had happened and requested that Henry should go to see the solicitor, Mr Pemberton. Henry returned to Knole.

5 October 1898, Knole
. . . Henry turned up again at 5 o'clock . . . I took Vita away. I saw Henry forcing his way across the Court. Papa rang for the footman and told him to help Lipscombe turn out Henry. The

second footman came too and they stopped Henry in front of the second gateway. He talked in a loud voice, saying that he was the rightful heir here and that Papa had been married to Mama. Then he burst into hysterical tears. When we saw that he was forcing his way into the house, Papa gave the order to fetch the police. Henry stayed talking to the servants and left just before the police arrived.

There followed a series of more desperate letters – Henry knew how to touch the chord that moved his family the most:

I don't want your riches – or to live like you – I just want to disappear and live quietly on the continent, and to get married; it is useless to tell you that I regret having taken action against you.

Suicide was always threatened.

Lord Sackville gave in, resumed the allowance, and an icy letter to Henry saying that he never wished to see him again was followed almost immediately by a raise in the allowance, which Henry wrote was inadequate, in view of his situation. Victoria wrote, 'Lionel is doing his best to keep cool. Henry says he wants an honourable situation "like a footman", added Tio.'

Flora was getting a divorce – another worry for Papa.

14 November 1898, Knole
I sent £25 to Flora who sounds in great distress. Papa cannot possibly send her any more.

The English family underestimated Henry. He seemed to disappear, mouthing his regrets for having taken action against them. Instead, he returned to Spain and in 1902 Mr Brain was back in Madrid, attempting to disentangle a curious case indeed, with which the Crown Prosecutor of Madrid had been struggling for months. Henry had been in Madrid, dealing with a certain Enrique Rophon and two other men, Manuel Anton and Jose Sanchez, all three were known to have received money from him – in Rophon's case considerable sums. Henry then instituted a proceeding known as a *denunciar*, calling the attention of the Spanish courts to the falsification of documents concerning the marriage of his mother, Pepita, to Juan Antonio de Oliva. Could he prove that the documents were bogus, Henry would be able to bring the case back to the English courts. He was playing for high stakes – Knole and the title – but it is impossible to discover where his money came from. The Sackvilles were pouring it out – borrowing it – but Henry? The only possible guess is, and it is purely speculative, that he had convinced some person or persons to back him; in the event that he won, it would have been a good investment, but there is no evidence to support this supposition.

In order to be married in Spain in 1851, five documents had been necessary:

(1) the application for a licence, registered at the Municipal Court,
(2) the entry in the same book requesting a publication of the banns,
(3) the licence, issued by the Municipal Court to the priest who was to perform the ceremony,
(4) the entry in the register kept at the church recording the celebration of the marriage, and
(5) the entry in the Civil Register of Marriage.

Mr Brain could prove that the crucial marriage entry, (4) had been seen, examined and copied by representatives of his firm in 1896, and that there had been no sign of tampering with it. But, in 1902 the entry had been scratched out of the church registry, and then rewritten, without varying the sense. The application (1) seemed to have disappeared. Evidently, the other items had been too difficult to get at, but in the summer of 1901 Henry and his fellow-conspirator Rophon would not have found it difficult to bribe Sanchez, the attendant at the church, and his assistant Anton, who had every opportunity to falsify the San Millan records, to provide grounds for the litigation or *denunciar*.

All three men, Rophon, Sanchez and Anton were tried on suspicion of illegal tampering with official records, but the jury divided evenly on the question of their guilt, which, under Spanish law of the day, meant that they were acquitted. Mr Brain had a terrible year; he was assisted by Spanish lawyers whose knowledge and good will were essential to him, but he was little accustomed to midnight rendezvous with shady witnesses in ill-lighted taverns, to whispered surmise concerning men in disguise who had been slipping into the Church of San Millan, to the mutterings of Ricardo Dorremocea, a former clerk in the office of archives of the church.

Lord Sackville died quietly at Knole in 1908, and the next year Lionel wrote to Victoria from Scotland that Meynell and Pemberton had informed him that Henry had put in his petition to go to court. Lionel's letter was a model of brevity. 'D—— Henry. I am leaving tonight. We did rather well today.' And then he listed the number of game shot.

It was the waiting that must have been the worst for Victoria. She prepared to shut up Knole, as was legally necessary until its ownership was finally determined. The bitterness of the last walks around the garden and the good-byes to the worried people on the estate could only have added to her pain. She was torn and desperately unhappy. She who had adored her mother and deeply loved her father was going to have to sit in court and listen to their most intimate secrets recounted by highly-paid men who were engaged to help her fight for her husband and for Knole: her home, the only home she had ever had. She must reiterate her own illegitimacy, the subject from which she had always shrunk, and she would be in a glare of world-wide publicity. Everyone would hear about the cruelty of her little brother Henry, about the disloyalty of Flora and Amalia; she would have to relive the humiliations of childhood and know that every scullery maid and every duchess was savouring the story in the press. Max had been an unexpected comfort these last years; furious with Henry, totally loyal to her, his fine letters from Africa had come in a steady stream of reassurance. He had been ill, and the solicitors had sent a man out to get his evidence which he gave clearly and well. But Max, the only strong one beside Victoria of Pepita's children, was thousands of miles away. Vita Sackville-West wrote,

> She was torn between the most intimate ties that can humanly exist: her mother, her father, her brother, her husband, her home . . . and to all of us Knole meant as much as any human being.

It was the scandal of the day. The case opened on 1 February 1910 in the High Court of Justice, and was covered as completely by the American press as it was by the British. Seven New York dailies, the august *Transcript* of Boston, three papers in Philadelphia, and small-town papers from Watertown, New York to the West Coast carried the story day after day for the six days of the proceedings. The President of the Court was The Right Hon. Sir

John Bigham, the Petitioner in the matter of the Legitimacy Declaration Act was Ernest Henri Jean Baptiste West or Sackville-West, v. The Attorney-General, Lord Sackville and others cited. The Right Hon. Sir Edward Clarke, was Henry's counsel, instructed by Messrs Nussey and Fellowes, the Sackville counsel was The Right Hon. Sir Robert Finlay, instructed by Messrs Meynell and Pemberton.

It must be remembered that this was not a jury case. The evidence, gathered over a period of thirteen years by the solicitors representing the litigants, would be presented to the President of the Court, who after hearing it and summing up the facts, would render judgement. Most of the evidence would be read, from those long ago depositions taken from 1896 on. Victoria, sitting in court, was never called to the witness stand; instead she listened to them reading the story of her life. The hardest part must have been listening to her father's wandering evidence. She had tried so hard to pin him down, but he had been hopelessly forgetful:

> If I made a declaration that Pepita was my wife it was done simply and solely to save the reputation of Pepita at her earnest request. I will not swear that I did not. I don't recollect.

He couldn't remember having gone to the Mairie to register the birth of Amalia ... he didn't remember the birth of Amalia. 'I don't think I ever introduced Pepita to anyone ...'

It didn't matter. By the third day it was apparent to everyone that Sir Robert Finlay's drumbeat of testimony from the people who had been sure that Lionel had never married Pepita, much as he would have liked to have done so, made Henry's evidence flimsy indeed. Lord Saumarez, an early colleague of Lionel's, was a distinguished man, Mrs Cameron and Mrs Cheston and the other witnesses for the defence were impressive people, but the case was really over when the quiet Littlechild, ex-Chief Inspector of Scotland Yard, described in his plain way the examination of the marriage registry in 1896 and the testimony of Oliva's sister Isabel, witness to the ceremony, given at the same time. It had been she who had held her brother in her arms when he died in 1888.

On the third day, Henry, displaying the courage of a cornered rat, took the offensive. To the stupefaction of the court, Sir Edward Clarke introduced a letter from his client, just received, in which

Henry requested his counsel to ask the President to adjourn the trial in order that a series of further documents should be brought from Spain. The letter was signed, with a rather pathetic flourish, 'Sackville'. The documents were obscure and not material, the expense and inconvenience of adjournment were obvious. It was an impossible position for Clarke, who was dismissed from the case by his client, as was Mr Harold Morris, junior counsel.

HENRY: They have all left me. If your Lordship will give me time, I will go on with the case myself. I know I shall lose it, but I will have a good try.

THE PRESIDENT: Very well, then, Mr West, I shall proceed with the examination of your witnesses tomorrow.

HENRY: I shall have no solicitor or counsel, my Lord, and in fact I am a stranger in London because I have been for the last few months abroad with my wife who has been very ill – nearly dying – and I do not know whether I shall be able to get a solicitor or counsel, but if I do not, I shall do my duty and go on with this case . . .

The court adjourned until the following morning at 10.30.

The next two days, the fourth and the fifth of the case, were splendid examples of British justice. The President of the Court, who must have been driven mad by Henry's conduct, did everything he possibly could to be kind to him. He assured Henry that if his cross-examination of witnesses satisfied him that adjournment was necessary to the cause of justice he would consider it, and when Henry's cross-examination turned out to be confusing, wavering and delaying to the proceedings, he was patient to a point when at moments he almost seemed to be taking Henry's case for him. Sir Robert Finlay was equally fair. But, at last the moment came when the following exchange took place:

THE PRESIDENT: I am afraid Mr West, I should do a very great injustice if I granted you this adjournment which you are asking for . . . and therefore I refuse your request.

THE PETITIONER: Then I can do nothing more, my Lord. I am done.

On the sixth and last day the President concluded his long and well-reasoned judgement:

The foregoing evidence satisfies me that Pepita was the lawful wife of Juan Antonio de Oliva during the whole period of her connection with Mr Sackville-West, and that Juan Antonio de Oliva survived her. I therefore dismiss the Petition with costs.

So failed the assault on Knole. What happened to the assailants? Henry presumably paid Sir Edward Clarke's fees. Why had that great advocate of the English bar, in his day the greatest of them all, ever taken the case? The answer was probably a sad and simple one: Clarke's ambition was primarily political; he failed to achieve the success he sought and by the time of the Sackville case his practice had been declining for years. Younger barristers, F. E. Smith and Edward Carson, were now the stars of the English Bar. He needed to make a legal comeback, and the Sackville case was a guarantee of publicity. This can be the only explanation – for although by reading the brief submitted to him by Henry's solicitors, it must have been apparent to Sir Edward that his case was impossibly weak; although there was no chance that he would have an opportunity to use his wonderful voice before a jury, although his still incomparable lucidity, his dazzling gifts would be stifled and useless in view of the nature of the material with which he must deal, he took the case.

Flora may have helped Henry with his legal expenses, although where she got the money is unexplained. An unattractive letter showed that she was counting her chickens before they were hatched. It was written in French, and was undated. She told Henry that she could provide 100,000 francs if he needed them, and 50,000 more later if necessary:

> I would be too happy to help you crush them, wipe them out, which I haven't the least doubt will be done. Don't forget to find me a very elegant motor car in London, to take me backwards and forwards from the court. P.S. Don't forget to send me some postcards of Knole.

Flora's life became rather hard to follow – at one time she was on the stage as a music-hall actress; and there were later references to a good many men in her life, of various ages and kinds. Both she and Amalia had been left legacies by their father. In Amalia's case the original sum had been £1,300, but Victoria gave up her share to her, making the capital £2,500, besides which Lionel and

Victoria gave her an annual allowance of £100, so she received £270 per annum. Amalia left Knole in 1896, and little Vita only remembered a vinegary spinster aunt, but a happier later description came in a letter to the author, from Sir Sacheverell Sitwell:

> She quite often came to stay at Renishaw when I was a child, before 1914. I remember her as very Spanish and very charming. And then, after a long interval, probably in 1926 or 1927, when Georgia and I were married, we stayed the night at the Lord Warden Hotel in Dover, and there she was with her husband, Monsieur Martin, who was Chef du Protocole of the French Foreign Office ... M. Martin was a very distinguished old Frenchman with beautiful manners. I remember her telling me that she had come to live in the hotel because it was near Knole, which had been her home, and thinking it was very pathetic. I have no idea what happened to her, but cannot think that she was a bad character. On the contrary, to my mind she was immensely pathetic and the victim of circumstances over which she had no control.

Years before, in the summer of 1897, Lord Sackville, Lionel and Victoria had gone up to London to face giving the testimony that has been described above, and which was eventually read during the case of 1910. Victoria, out of her mind with rage at Henry, made several startling entries in her diary. She had been badly disturbed by Pemberton having told her that Henry wanted to 'put Papa in the box at any cost'. She wrote in her diary on 26 July 1897: 'Henry is the image of Comte de B ——.' (The Vicomte de Béon became the Comte de Béon.)

On 6 August, after an unpleasant interview with Salanson at which Henry was not present, she wrote: 'Papa does not believe that Henry is his son.'

Out of all this pain, it is impossible to guess what was the solace that Victoria sought. Better to believe that horrible Henry, who was causing her father such anguish, was in fact the child of the traitorous Béon, who had been entrusted with their guardianship, and was now on the side of this brother?

This would have meant that beloved Mama had betrayed Papa. But, perhaps anything was better than to believe that Henry was a Sackville. The unprovable point was never mentioned again, and Henry disappeared forever from the story when he died in 1914 by his own hand.

The official return of the Sackvilles and Vita to Knole following the case was a glorious occasion. The horses were taken out of the traces of the carriage, which was pulled through Sevenoaks by the local fire brigade right up through the park to Knole, with cheering crowds all the way and bouquets presented at intervals by the local children. When the last of the speeches was over, the family settled down quietly to a peaceful dinner together; they had come home.

11
Seery

They had come home, to what? During the years preceding the case, 1896–1910, a good deal had happened to Victoria, Lionel and Vita. Vita was a clever, secretive girl who wrote long historical novels, which she sometimes showed to an admiring mother. Victoria worried only that she wrote too much and was happy to see that at eighteen her daughter was becoming extremely handsome, with a special style of her own. She was not alarmed by Vita's intellectual gifts as was Lionel, who wrote gloomily to Victoria, 'I shouldn't be surprised if Vita ended by marrying a Soul.'

To Lionel, the Souls were a coterie who spoke a language he didn't understand. They talked of books and poets and general subjects; they had private jokes that were alien to him; and although they were well-born and had had the usual upbringing of the English upper classes to Lionel they might as well have been foreigners.

Victoria's diaries showed how conventional the conversation must have been at the Knole dinner table. All major public events were carefully noted, and especially every victory and defeat of the Boer War, during which she was predictably pro-Chamberlain and pro-war. She wrote that her pride in the Diamond Jubilee of 1897 was great, as was her sorrow over the death of Queen Victoria in 1901. Election results were never analysed, but produced comments on the success or defeat of the candidates she knew personally – the great Liberal sweep of 1906, a landmark election, was covered by one line: 'Imagine Winston Churchill getting in with such a majority.'

There were two Victoria Sackvilles during these years. The private woman miserable over the case and her father's depression and failing health was a different person from the triumphant public beauty who attended Mrs Oppenheimer's ball in Jubilee Year:

> All the ladies were supposed to be dressed as flowers. I was a wistaria. My dress was made like a basket with high handles over the shoulders. I had a straw basket on my head on which I sewed many diamonds. I could see that it was *very* much admired.

The historic fancy dress ball at Devonshire House that same season has been mentioned in many memoirs of the time. Victoria danced before the Prince and Princess of Wales in Lady Warwick's well-rehearsed quadrille, dressed as the eighteenth-century Duchess of Dorset in a flowered blue silk dress that had been kept at Knole since the Duchess's time. The week of the ball was spent struggling with her testimony for the solicitors, but to the outer world she was the frivolous Mrs Sackville-West, who was doing up Knole as if she didn't have a care in the world, buying new carpets and curtains, planning to replace the ugly stained glass in the chapel, going through all the china with a London expert and writing gleefully, 'We only found two pieces of modern china'. Another day: 'Thomas, the Bond Street jeweller came down to look at the silver. He said that we had not the largest, but the *best* collection of silver in England.'

What could have been more successful than the visit of the Prince and Princess of Wales and a large party to Knole on 10 July 1898?

> They left at six o'clock, I went to the station with Vita, Papa and Tio to say goodbye. Everybody told me how well everything had been done. That if we were millionaires we could not have done it better. I walked so much today that the silk around the bottom of the skirt of my new grey dress is worn down to the threads. The Prince had wanted to invite Lady Warwick and also his new friend Mrs Keppel, but I told him that I preferred to ask some of the County ladies . . . especially as the Princess was coming. He acquiesced and was very nice about it.

How curious, Pepita's daughter telling off the Prince of Wales and getting away with it! Very few of the great ladies of the period would have even thought of daring to change the list suggested by the Prince, but Victoria admired Princess Alexandra and she never lacked moral courage.

It is time to stand off and look at Victoria as she entered the twentieth century. Approaching forty, she was at the height of her beauty – a bit plump by modern tastes, but not for those of her time. The success and admiration were spoiling her – the rather tiresome entries from Russia had showed this already in 1896. But how hard not to be spoiled. She was so often the centre of attention. For example, Lady Diana Manners was a little girl when Victoria and Lionel went to stay at Belvoir Castle, her family home, and she was kept up to be introduced to the guests and to see Victoria's jewels. Many years later as Lady Diana Cooper she still remembered the fascination of a live tortoise whose shiny shell carried Victoria's monogram in diamonds and the wonder of the great Sackville jewels.

Vita wrote:

> My mother was adorable at that time in her life. She was tiresome, of course, and wayward and capricious, and thoroughly spoiled; but her charm and real inward gaiety enabled her to carry it all off. One forgave her everything when one heard her laugh and saw how frankly she was enjoying herself. As a child can be maddening at one moment and irresistable the next, so could my mother be maddening and irresistable by turns. For, like a child, she neither analysed nor controlled her moods, they simple blew across her . . . She never thought much; she merely lived. Whatever she was, she was there with all her heart; there were no half-measures . . .
>
> Really, nobody could have failed to love her as she was then, in her middle youth, so gay, so vital, so amused, so absolutely herself with all her faults, all her tiresomeness, and all her charm.

This is an excellent, as well as a generous description. Vita could not have remembered the Knole of the nineties – she was born in 1892 – with the clarity with which she remembered the Knole of the following decade. In the nineties it had been a very grand house, but also a cosy house in which people amused themselves after dinner with simple parlour games. Her mother and father had taken walks every day – generally to visit Lionel's farm, and looked forward with eagerness to the moments of being alone together when guests were absent. In the 1900s Knole was an even grander house, but it was less cosy. It was inevitable that fashions would change – that bridge and baccarat would replace parlour games, that the glowing, expansive Victoria would invite more and more new names over Sunday, and that, in a period when upper-class eating habits became richer and richer, so would the food at Knole. 'That particular dish of the . . . Chevron chef was famous: an ortalan within the quail, a truffle within the ortalan, and paté de foie gras within the truffle.' Chevron is Knole in Vita Sackville-West's novel *The Edwardians*.

Victoria never stopped her innovations. It took her and Jeffrey a year to install electric light, tearing through the Elizabethan panelling and searching London for fittings, but it was done by 1902 and other, less up-to-date owners of great houses came to her for advice as to how they could emulate her achievement. She loved helping people, giving her strength to those who needed it, whether it was a question of doing over a house or patching up a broken marriage; she adored being called on, pouring out the positiveness of her own zest for life and joy in living. It was her strength as much as her charm that drew people to her, and she gave it generously. She loved dramatizing – transforming the commonplace – and of course when she could help and at the same time be the centre of attention she was at her happiest. What she could not accept was polite indifference.

The diaries from 1899 on were full of pain that had nothing to do with the approaching case. Through the entries, increasingly guarded, hard to reconcile with the earlier Victoria's unselfconscious outpourings, the figure of Lionel becomes elusive. There was no open break, as she accepted his first infidelities. Joan Camden entered his life about 1899, followed a few years later by Constance Hatch.

Victoria was to blame for several reasons. She was bored by Lionel's interests; the Yeomanry and the Kent County Council meant nothing to her. Incorrigibly possessive and demanding, it annoyed her that he should leave her in the mornings for a com-mittee meeting, and insist on being prompt; time meant nothing to Victoria. She would beg him to stay and gossip beside her bed; he, looking at his watch would say, resignedly, 'Dear, I really have to go,' and walk out of the room quietly. He never lost his temper; it would have suited Victoria far better had he done so. A good blazing row would have cleared the air and appeased her Spanish nature, but rows were as repugnant to Lionel as they were natural to Victoria. His politeness was intolerable to her and her frustration the more complete, as she must have realized that the scenes that used to bring him to his knees now bored him. One night Vita and he arrived late from London to find her hysterical with anxiety, but he met her tears without apology. In the old days he would have carried her off to bed and all would have been well in the morning, but bed was another problem, for Victoria was inexorably against having another child. As early as 1895 Lionel wanted one, and to give an heir to Knole should normally have been Victoria's greatest desire. But she was terrified of a second pregnancy, and although Lionel slept with her from time to time as late as 1901, their relations must have been inhibited by her fear. They took 'precautions' which, in those primitive days probably meant that the pleasure was diminished for Lionel. He was five years younger than she, extremely virile, extremely attractive to women. Why did Victoria, so brave and so much in love with him, dread childbirth so much that she took the risk of losing her husband to another, more understanding woman?

Lady Camden was a delightful companion for Lionel. Married to the Lord Lieutenant of the County of Kent, she understood and appreciated the importance of Lionel's commitments to the county, and was probably as interested in the Yeomanry and the Council as he was. She would have understood that one had to be on time for committees, and that women must be kept waiting if men are busy. An excellent golf player, a keen sailor – it was no wonder that Lionel found it agreeable to play the odd round with her when his county duties were finished, and it was pleasant to spend a few weeks a year on Lord Camden's yacht. The first mention of her came in Victoria's diary for 11 December 1901:

The Camdens came to dine at the flat. He was very cantakerous. We went on to the theatre and had supper at the Carlton. I feel so sorry for poor little Joan Camden; how different my darling husband is to me. I love him all the more when I see such a striking contrast.

12 December 1901

. . . Joan lunched with us. I went back to Knole this afternoon. Lionel stayed and dined with the Camdens.

Another entry tells us that 'Tio is having a mild flirtation with Joan Camden. Dear Boy! I have such implicit confidence in my darling husband; how I love and worship him.' How hypocritical this will sound to the reader today. But it was Victoria's only defence. The Spanish side of her surely made her long to take Lady Camden's No. 5 iron and knock her head off, then throw a lamp at Lionel as he returned from one of his health-filled cruises on the Camden yacht; she had known about the affair for some time. But she was playing the English game. In Edwardian times class and convention demanded that one didn't make a fuss about marital infidelity provided that the surface relationship remained intact. There was the couple who had been on the point of divorce when the Duchess of Devonshire sent for them and told them that divorce was vulgar and intolerable and an affront to society. So they remained together and didn't speak to each other for twenty years: appearances were saved.

Victoria's urbane diary entries about Joan Camden, followed by her acceptance of Lionel's next friend, Lady Constance Hatch, must be seen against this background. Occasionally there is a very sad diary entry. The early candour returned when she wrote ruefully that the Camdens had failed to turn up for lunch at Knole one day and she found herself alone with Lionel, trying to amuse him and failing. It made her head ache, for she had tried so hard to entertain him, and for the first ten years of their married life, there had been no treat so great as to be alone together. Suddenly, she burst out in the diary: '*Cela me fait tant souffrir.*'

But there were few entries to suggest her unhappiness about Lionel. On the contrary, there were far too many protestations of their mutual love to be natural. Even to her diary she would not admit that they were drifting apart; her dignity was her armour. They were always genuinely united on three vital things: the upbringing and care of Vita, the care of Lord Sackville during his last years, and the fight for Knole. However, the strain told; in 1904, a brilliant year at Knole to the outer world, Victoria was privately visiting a doctor for her nerves and while she recorded the parties faithfully, her writing was poor and sometimes the entries were chaotic. She had been writing in English since 1899 in a large and legible hand and rarely returned to French again, but when she was under strain she went back to the fine, tight convent script of her youth.

One result of Lionel's increasing absences was that she began to make new friends, clever and gifted men and women. John Singer Sargent painted her and although the picture was a failure, destroyed by the artist, the charming drawing that he did for Vita remained. Through Sargent's friend Mrs Hunter, she met other artists, Auguste Rodin, John Lavery, Jacques-Emile Blanche, writers like Max Beerbohm, opera singers such as Patti and Melba. Although she preferred the company of men to that of women, she was always fascinated by anyone who had had a successful career, and listened spellbound one evening to Patti as she sat on a sofa with her, hearing the artist tell about her life.

When the famous French diplomat Paul Cambon talked to her for two hours about foreign affairs – she felt that she was back in Washington. She found the explorer, Nansen, 'rather revolutionary' but fascinating. In 1900 she met the American financier J. P. Morgan and was immediately attracted by him, noting that she even liked his gigantic nose, the butt of the cartoonists. Later she was to see a great deal of Morgan and also of Rodin, and to make friends of men as different as Kitchener and Kipling, Garvin, the editor and writer, the industrialists Gordon Selfridge and Lord Leverhulme. This new world was a very different one from that of Lionel and his shooting parties, and with her quick mind and her charm, she fitted in among these clever people easily. Rudyard Kipling wrote later to a friend, speaking of her: 'On mature reflection *the* most wonderful person I have ever met.'

But to restore her pride, to flatter her ego, she required one man to whom she was everything, and in 1899 she found him.

Sir John Murray Scott was fifty when Victoria met him fleetingly in 1897. Two years later they saw each other again at a luncheon party and he took her afterwards to Hertford House to visit the Hertford-Wallace treasures which were, thanks to Sir John, about to pass to the nation. He was the son of a Scottish doctor who had practised in Boulogne, and his story was almost as much a fairy tale as Victoria's had been. The fourth Marquess of Hertford, collector and francophile, had left his possessions to a mysterious man called Sir Richard Wallace, thought by some to be his son. Sir Richard was as much a collector as Lord Hertford, and equally pro-French. He took on John Murray Scott as secretary and reposed his entire confidence in him, as did Lady Wallace. When Sir Richard died, he left everything to his widow, and everything was a great deal. During the troubles in France following the war of 1870, a large part of the collection had been moved to Hertford House in London, but the rest of it remained in Paris in an apartment at 2 rue Laffitte and at Bagatelle, the lovely little 'folly' in the Bois de Boulogne which had originally been built for Marie Antoinette's brother-in-law, the Comte d'Artois. There were also properties in England and Ireland and a large fortune. Lady Wallace turned to the indispensable and brilliant secretary for advice for the rest of her life, and in gratitude for his devotion considered leaving the entire estate to him. He persuaded her that Hertford House and its treasures must go to the British nation, and when she died in 1897, the will showed that she had done so. The residue of the estate went to John Murray Scott, who as a trustee of the Wallace Collection was present when the Prince of Wales opened Hertford House to the public in 1900.

There was much in common between him and Victoria. Both were enviable figures in the eyes of the world, both were privately lonely. Scott had been too submerged in his responsibilities with the Wallaces to make friends of his own, and the Wallaces had led an isolated life among their great possessions. His own family consisted of an old and dominating mother, four rather uninteresting brothers, and two even more uninteresting spinster sisters, all of whom he took care of conscientiously but joylessly, living with the mother and sisters in a large house in Connaught Place where two or three times a year he gave heavy dinners, often embellished by the presence of royalties and other persons who were curious to see what the very new rich Scotts were like. These grand guests did not often ask them back. Yet never has there been a man more made for joy than John Murray Scott. He weighed twenty-five stone and was six feet four inches tall; his majestic progress down St James's Street of a morning all but stopped the traffic. Like Victoria, his appetite for life was inexhaustible and his pleasure in fun and simple jokes childlike. Like her, he loved beautiful things and arranging houses, but she was a novice beside his expertise and he had much to teach her. Both spoke English and French interchangeably; and, most importantly, for all his Scotch blood he understood Latin rows and indulged in them frequently when he was annoyed with her; his generous soul was incapable of nourishing a grudge and the storms passed like summer lightning. What a relief to Victoria, accustomed as she was to the cool Lionel and distant, melancholy Papa to have a man care enough about her to write her two angry letters a day, followed by immediate contrition.

The friendship blossomed speedily. A summer weekend at Knole a month after the luncheon was followed by a visit to a rented shooting lodge in Scotland, Finavon, which lasted from 29 August to 6 October. Seery, Vita's nickname for Sir John, was delighted to have Lord Sackville, as well as Victoria and Vita. Lionel was shooting in the Rockies that autumn. The Scott family were there; and Victoria got on well with old Mrs Scott. Finavon, a fairly large mock-Gothic house built of grey stone was surrounded by gentle woods of larch and birch which led down to the river. Victoria loved the peace of it and used to walk past the ruins of an ancient keep to sit by the river in the evenings, waiting for the fishermen to return and watching the light fail.

The following January Lionel left for the South African war with the Yeomanry horses, returning two months later. Seery came often to Knole, and together Victoria and he would rearrange the pictures in Lady Betty Germain's bedroom and afterwards walk to the Masthead, talking and talking. He teased her, calling her 'a little Spanish gypsy', or 'you little rascal', and Victoria, who had too little sense of humour about herself to appreciate English teasing, loved Seery's form of it. In London they were inseparable, and if they didn't meet every day there was an exchange of letters.

Surely she must have confided in him every detail of her worries about Henry and the inevitable problems that Lord Sackville's death would bring, and she wrote in her diary that no one could be more comforting or understanding than he was. Seery was a great giver, and it must have delighted him to be needed. After one of the Sackville-West visits to his magnificent apartment in Paris at 2 rue Laffitte, Lionel wrote him a thank you note enclosing a small cheque for some expense they had incurred, and Seery responded with a simple but infinitely touching letter of thanks for the happiness that they had brought into his lonely, dull life.

The years fell into a pattern that altered little. Winter and spring were divided between Knole and London, in London Seery bought and paid for a house in Hill Street for the Sackville-Wests, dealing with Lionel. The house was in Victoria's name; it is not clear whether she was aware of the transaction at the time, but if she was, she accepted it as easily as she did the loan of one of Seery's carriages when she required it.

Victoria loved presents – at the end of each diary year her Christmas presents were listed with meticulous care, from plebian penwiper to costly Fabergé jewel, but she was undiscriminating, value meant little to her for she had no sense of proportion about money. Acquisitive she certainly was; she shamelessly stole hotel notepaper, delighted if she could stuff a dozen envelopes into her bag as she left after lunch; but at the same time she might well have given a five pound tip to the waiter had he chanced to tell her that he had a sick wife or baby. The magpie instinct to get something for nothing came straight from Catalina, her gypsy grandmother, and it must have driven her family mad to watch her buy writing paper for Knole at the most fashionable stationer's in London, hardly bothering to inquire the cost of the expensive dies cut to go with it, while she wrote her own letters on half sheets torn from letters that she had received, or on the backs of catalogues or advertisements. Often she was observed cutting up used postage stamps and fitting the pieces together so that no trace of postmark appeared – true Catalina. Vita thought that she had touched the peak when she wrote on toilet paper stolen from the Harrod's ladies cloakroom.

She was always generous and few visitors could leave without a present from Victoria; no newly born baby went without its blue or pink dress, no hospital patient without a rich and generally indigestible offering, no young couple of her acquaintance fell into trouble without her remembering them. Lady Diana Cooper, who had met Victoria as a child at Belvoir Castle, married Duff Cooper, a brilliant but hard-up young man in the Foreign Office; when all her most valued treasures were stolen out of her little car, Victoria read about it in the paper and sent the young Coopers £100, quite a lot for those days.

It was all inconsistent, but she was not systematically grasping. An attempt to make money by establishing a little shop called Spealls in South Audley Street gave her sporadic occupation for a few years, but was a most unbusinesslike venture. She sold lampshades and knick-knacks for presents, but if her friends were slow to pay their bills or attempted to return unwanted goods as they would have in an ordinary shop, she became personally offended, and she turned on her harassed managers and shop assistants for incompetence when in fact the incompetence came from her own lack of experience. Spealls must have been a great bore to her family and even to Seery, who would have had to listen to all her troubles concerning it.

For everyone it must have been a relief to be through with the London season and the quarrels at Spealls and off to stay at Seery's marvellous home in Paris as they did every summer. It was on the corner of the rue Laffitte and the Boulevard des Italiens; the entrance from the noisy boulevard led to the quiet courtyard of the vast house, all of which belonged to Seery. The main apartment was a long series of rooms opening one into the other, the parquet floors gleamed and looking down the glorious vista the visitor heard no sound but that of the eighteenth-century clocks chiming the quarter hours together, exactly on time. There was no electric light, no telephone, no bells except those that could be pulled by a silken cord to summon one of the old servants who seemed too grand to be doing housework or cleaning, but rather priests whose chapel was the Wallace Collection. Seery's heritage of furniture and tapestries was one of the noblest in Europe, his eighteenth-century sculpture the finest in private hands, and besides the marvels of the rue Laffitte there was, until Seery sold it to the City of Paris in 1904, lovely Bagatelle. It was surrounded with leafy gardens, containing fountains and grottoes and hidden statues. Seery and Victoria used to drive out there in the afternoons with little Vita, who loved playing on hot days in the cool caves beside the little lakes with their bridges and tiny islands. Then back to the tranquility of rue Laffitte, where in the evenings the heavy silken curtains were drawn by the quiet servants, the candles lighted in the great ormulu sconces, and noisy Edwardian Paris of the boulevard outside dismissed. At dinner the oldest priest–servant of all, Monsieur Bénard, made it seem almost a holy rite when he set some huge silver dish down before Sir John or brought in a precious wine in his white-gloved hands. These evenings when the three of them were alone were rare – the collection was so famous, Seery's hospitality so generous, that there were nearly always guests. Lionel would arrive, bringing his friend Lady Constance Hatch, who had displaced Lady Camden. She was a society woman married to a man whom Victoria called 'bedint', a private family word meaning middle or lower class and generally implying dullness; Lady Connie was anything but dull.

Quick-witted and amusing, she kept Lionel entertained. Once more, Victoria played up. The diaries of the years 1906–9, when Lady Connie came to Paris every summer, show no hint of strain. They are full of the expeditions to galleries and museums with Seery and Vita, of the fun of rearranging Seery's beloved collection with him, of visits to friends' châteaux in the countryside and of the entertainments at the rue Laffitte.

In mid-August the slatted shutters would be drawn and the house and its treasures put to sleep by reverent hands as the party moved on to Scotland for the annual two-and-a-half-month visit to Seery's rented shooting lodge in the Highlands, Sluie, on the Deeside near Banchory. Lord Sackville and Vita came every year until Lord Sackville's death in 1908. Lionel joined them now and then, enjoying the first-class salmon fishing and the shooting. The Scott family did not join the party as they had at Finavon, the lodge that Seery had taken in 1899. The Misses Alicia and Mary Scott had continued to live with their brother in Connaught Square since the death of their mother. The family ran to fat, and the Scott sisters were heavy physically as well as mentally. Their middle-class minds were filled with suspicion of fashionable goings on and fashionable people; one of them said and both of them probably thought that all aristocratic women automatically took a lover immediately after marriage and that all aristocratic young girls had a baby before they were married. Their empty lives gave them unlimited time to nourish causes for resentment, and their chief cause was Mrs Sackville-West.

If the Scott sisters had come to Sluie during Victoria's time they would have been confounded by what they saw. The luxurious, fashionable woman of the world was happier there than she had been since her early days at Knole, yet it was a most unpretentious establishment. Brand new when Seery first took it in 1903, it was a free standing house with no trees around it, built of pinkish grey granite, with a reddish tile roof and grey trimmed gables. Finavon had been enclosed by its dark evergreens, sunny Sluie was open to the winds. A gay, happy, welcoming house, a good-humoured house, its rooms were and are small and full of light. In the only sitting room there is an unusual feature, thought by the present owners to have been installed by Victoria: a large plate glass window directly over the fireplace. It gives an immense view of the Deeside hills and of range after range of the lower Grampian mountains; in the far distance on good days stand Ben Avon and Morven, snow-covered in early autumn. There must have been dreary days at Sluie, but no one who went there seemed to have remembered them; Victoria's diary gives the impression that the sun was always out, the sky cloudless and the hills glowing pink in the sunset as she went out to call Vita down from the glen. Vita adored Sluie – her mother let her run wild and there was no nonsense about dressing up – she could play with the farm children and come in pink-cheeked, tousled and dirty without any comments being made on her appearance. Her favourite place was the loch behind the house where the hill climbs gently north through the pines and beeches. The loch, with its witches' coven, has a magic feeling as one looks down on it from lichen-covered rocks.

A mile below Sluie runs the river Dee, fast flowing in its hidden valley, its south bank covered with silver birch trees. Then the best season for salmon fishing was the autumn, and the fastness of the river suited a very heavy man like Seery admirably. He was splendidly sporting, perfectly unselfconscious if stone walls crumbled under his weight as he climbed over them, his clumsiness terrifying to his companions if he happened to have a gun in his hand.

Victoria seemed released in the Highland air. The toiling solicitors in Spain were forgotten as was the strain of keeping up the show as she and Lionel drifted apart; she took long walks down the lanes wearing an old tweed cape and a scarf over her head, singing sentimental French songs at the top of her clear, pure voice. Although the rue Laffitte visits and her occasional European travels during those years with Seery and Vita were pleasant interludes, it was at Sluie that she became her old self and each year she found it harder to leave the serene, happy house and the countryside of rust-brown bracken, bright purple heather and golden gorse and broom.

It was a quiet life; for although she read a certain amount, her only distraction beyond her daily walk was the society of Seery, her father, and Vita; visitors were rare nor did she miss them. Were she and Seery lovers? It is impossible to know, but this writer's guess is that the relationship never went beyond a very deep and close *amitié amoureuse*. Both Seery and Victoria were fastidious people, and it would have been unlikely that the sensitive

Seery would have wanted to force his huge and ageing body on Victoria. And in middle life she seemed to lose her desire for sex – perhaps because she was still in love with Lionel.

The last year at magical Sluie was 1907.

During the summer of 1908 Lord Sackville lay dying at Knole and Vita was sent up to Scotland; where, for the first time, the Misses Scott were invited by their brother. Vita described going down to see Seery when the telegram had come announcing her grandfather's death on 3 September:

> I found him sitting in front of his dressing table, clad only in a suit of Jaeger combinations. He was sobbing uncontrollably, and his sobs shook his loose enormous frame like jelly. He was quite oblivious of my appearance.

Seery had loved Lord Sackville.

Seery himself had had his first heart attack that May, from which he recovered, but in November of the next year, 1909, he had a second serious attack while staying at Knole. Three years later, he died suddenly at Hertford House, while Lady Sackville waited for him to come to take her out to lunch. The last few years had been less harmonious than those of the early friendship, the rows were more frequent and their causes always trifling. They bickered over unimportant bills, over imagined slights about failed engagements, and Seery's lovable, generous nature seemed to change. By 1911 his physical condition must have deteriorated more than either of them had realized, and the demanding Victoria would have been the last person to understand that physical illness can sadly alter the personality of the most sweet-tempered person. She was impatient, both of them nagged at each other; but happily, by November 1911, two months before he died, the affectionate relationship was recaptured and the acid was removed from their correspondence as it must have been from their personal encounters. They became very close again towards the end and the old teasing resumed – 'You were a much better Seery this morning and I liked it when you called me repeatedly little rascal.'

Seery was a very rich man, who had made his will in 1900, a year after the commencement of his friendship with Victoria. At the time of his death his estate was £1,180,000 of which he left a cash legacy to her of £150,000 plus the contents of the rue Laffitte, then estimated at £350,000. To his family Seery left the residue of the estate, approximately £410,000, with the exception of other legacies amounting to £223,000. During his lifetime he had made cash gifts to Lionel and Victoria of between £85,000 and £90,000, of which £30,000 had originally been a loan to help to bear the expenses of the illegitimacy case, but which was later converted by Seery into a free gift. In addition Victoria was left a Houdon bust from Connaught Place valued at £30,000–£50,000 and a chandelier valued at £10,000, a necklace that had belonged to Catherine Parr and a pocket book that had belonged to Marie Antoinette.

Throughout the last years of his life Seery constantly told Victoria that he was going to cut her out of his will – in 1911 he wrote: '. . . it would be a terrible thing for you if I were to die suddenly and you were to find all your hopes shattered.' Her reply was affectionate and tolerant, not showing any sense of threat; a generous letter asking him only to spare Vita. Lionel, as early as 1904, had been the one to be practical – when Victoria told him that Seery's vagaries were getting on her nerves, he advised her to put up with them and think of the future.

There is not a mercenary line in her diaries concerning Seery, instead her entries were a mixture of irritation, affection and dignity.

She saw herself as the custodian of Knole and felt that it was natural that Seery, who truly loved beautiful things, should want to give lavishly so that Knole could go on; as for his presents to her, she as a giver herself understood the pleasure that giving can bring. And until the arguments of the years after his illness, their relationship had been of infinite mutual pleasure.

The fortune had been left by Lady Wallace to Seery and he was perfectly free, legally and morally, to leave it to anyone he chose – it was not Scott money. He must have foreseen that his brothers and sisters would cause trouble when he added a codicil to the 1900 will to the effect that any member of his family who disputed the testament would lose his share, which would go to an orphanage. What he did not foresee was that his siblings could find an easy way around that. Filled with the bile that had been accumulating within them for twelve years, heavy with their resentments, self-righteous in their demand for justice against the temptress who had robbed them, the Scotts went to court. The famous case was called Capron v. Scott, in which Lord and Lady Sackville were cited for undue influence. Capron, the firm representing the John

Murray Scott estate, was the plaintiff, the defendants were the Scott family, and the two counsels, assisted by their junior colleagues, were Mr F. E. Smith for the defendants (the Scott family) and Sir Edward Carson for the Sackvilles. The judge was the Rt Honorable Sir Samuel Evans, sitting as President in the High Court of Justice, Probate Division. Public interest was enormous. Ladies arrived early in the morning to be sure of getting seats, carrying cushions for their fashionable behinds and hampers of lunch to be eaten where they sat, lest their place be stolen. It was the event of the season, for in those days famous advocates were like great actors and to watch the two most brilliant barristers of their day, F. E. Smith and Carson, pitted against each other would have made it worth attending the dullest of cases, and here they were embarking on what promised to be a highly dramatic one. The press played up Knole and the Sackvilles for all they were worth, and made Vita a national celebrity under Seery's nickname for her, Kidlet. After the trial was over, the Alhambra put on a popular musical skit depicting it.

On the first day the judge and jury entered the courtroom to find it jammed, for besides the fashionable ladies every junior member of the Bar who could find a corner was there, standing in the back. It was known that F. E. Smith was to lead, and no one wanted to miss an opening speech by the most mesmeric orator of his day. Entering Parliament as a Conservative at the moment when the Liberal sweep of 1906 had left his party in a state of hopeless dejection, his maiden speech had made parliamentary history and injected new life into the Conservatives' gloom. It is rare that one speech by a young and unknown member can have such an effect. His son wrote:

He looked like a young man of fashion, who had wandered into the House on his way back from Ascot. He was thirty-four, but looked much younger, like a youth who has had much experience of life which had turned to Dead Sea fruit in his mouth. Even the members of his own party had for the most part not the slightest idea who he was ... Every sentence held the sting of an adder, but the speaker himself remained absolutely impassive ... The Opposition were now cheering every sentence. Great gusts of laughter passed over the House. The tall, bent figure stood there looking down upon the benches; only

the lips moved, and from them in a passionless, slightly mono-
tonous drawl came forth this astonishing flow of invective . . .

He became a national figure overnight, and in 1908 took silk,
becoming the youngest King's Counsel in the country. Lord
Chancellor in 1919 at the age of forty-six, he took the title of Earl
of Birkenhead. It was not an entirely easy decision, for he was not
a rich man and could have gone on to make a fortune in private
practice. 'Conveying the news to his wife . . . he sent her the
following telegram: "I salute my enobled but impoverished
family." '

It was a happy family. Off stage, F. E. Smith delighted in
pleasure, loved his wife and children and was devoted to his
friends. His closest colleague and intimate friend was Sir Edward
Carson, whom he pronounced, 'the greatest advocate since the
illustrious Erskine'.

Carson was a giant of a man. He dominated physically, standing
out head and shoulders among a crowd of men, and he possessed
in an exceptional degree qualities of character which set him apart
from his fellows. Courage, perseverance and kindness of heart were
among his characteristics, and the adjective 'valiant' was often
applied to him. Primarily a lawyer whom the Irish question had
made into a politician, he was preeminent in both fields. Although
his work was done and his fame made in England, his heart was
in the Ireland from which he came and he had the charm and spoke
the soft brogue of the Irish. His family had emigrated from Scotland in the early 1800s and his youth, like F. E. Smith's, had been
far from luxurious; both married young and beyond their means.
Carson had fifty pounds in the bank when he married the girl with
whom he had fallen in love at first sight, and sixpence was left
when the honeymoon was over.

He rose fast in his chosen career, and participated in a number
of famous trials – Oscar Wilde, the Marconi case and the Archer–
Shee case (the basis for *The Winslow Boy*), when Carson spent
eighteen months of his life, indefatigable in the defence of a young
naval cadet who had been accused of stealing a five-pound note.
The Wilde case was one of the classics of the courts and illustrated
Carson's technique. He appeared plodding and slow in his duel
with Wilde, who flung off epigram after brilliant epigram, but the
quiet cross-examiner was unimpressed by the coruscations of wit

of his fellow-Irishman. Pursuing, probing, until he had broken his witness, he then attacked with a leading question that penetrated to the heart of the matter. His mind was just as fast in the court-room as F. E. Smith's, but he preferred that it should not appear so.

In politics he is mainly remembered as the great Ulster leader, a fierce opponent of Home Rule, but he held very high offices. Attorney-General with Smith as his associate and lieutenant, First Lord of the Admiralty during the war, he turned down the supreme crown, the Lord Chancellorship, twice in order to dedicate his life to the cause of Ulster. In 1921 F. E. Smith and Carson divided bitterly over the question of Home Rule, but were brought together by the tactful Lady Birkenhead who knew how fond the two men were of each other.

Carson was godfather to the Birkenhead's younger daughter, Pamela. He telephoned rather shyly to ask if he could come to tea, as he had a present for the little girl, a gold bracelet. Lady Birken-head asked her husband to drop in casually, and he followed her suggestion. 'Hello, Carson,' said F. E. Smith, and began talking about his daughter, whom he adored. Thus the ugly quarrel was composed between the two old friends.

Smith was quite prepared for Carson's technique; he had watched it often enough. What Sir Edward could not know as he entered the courtroom that June morning was what his client Lady Sackville had just done.

Breaking every rule of legal punctilio and common sense, she had started a correspondence with F. E. Smith:

19 June 1913
Dear Mr Smith,

I hear that Mr Malcolm Scott has approached you on the subject of attacking me and my husband and my daughter in his iniquitous suit, coming next week.

I can't believe that you would let yourself be mixed up in this painful affair when you and I meet among our friends in society and I meet your wife often too.

The whole Defence [sic] put forward by Mr Scott is a tissue of falsehoods against a woman who has behaved well all her life and tried to help saving one of the finest places in England.

I do hope you will think over the undeserved pain you will give so unnecessarily.

I don't know if it is professional or not to write to you and I do only write because I can't believe what I hear of you is true.

I have not told anyone I have written to you.

Yours Sincerely

V. Sackville

I swear on my honour that I have *never* influenced Sir J. over his will, except to leave us much less than he intended and that I have never seen or destroyed any signed Codicil.

On 19 June F. E. Smith replied to Lady Sackville:

I am not in the least annoyed at your writing to me, but I certainly do not think that you would have done so if you had thought more carefully.

Surely you must know that I am an advocate making my living by putting forward cases good or bad in the law courts. I should have been enchanted to take your case had you thought proper to employ me. You did not do so but selected, or your solicitor did, the very able counsel who now represents you. Surely you must see what an impossible position you are trying to put a professional man in. Is he to refuse every case which is offered to him against every agreeable acquaintance he may possess?

I have not read the papers yet. For all I know your description of the merits of your case and the demerits of your opponents may be exactly as you represent. In that case you may await the result with composure.

For myself I shall discharge a disagreeable duty with such consideration as the circumstances render possible.

I am yours faithfully

F. E. Smith

On 20 June 1913 Lady Sackville replied to F. E. Smith:

Yes, you are right. I wrote on the spur of the moment and I have been thinking a great deal about you and your difficult position ever since my letter went. With my sunny nature I have always found a silver lining to any cloud, I thought to the contrary that we were lucky to have a man of the world like you are and a man who knows What's What, to examine us, if you did not return the Brief! I hope now that you will not return it, even after reading the twaddle and the unsubstantiated statements that the Scotts will bring before you. I am really sorry for them, as they have completely lost their heads and perhaps they have refused to realize that Sir J. left *us* only about one third of what was declared for probate by the Executors themselves. He was a bachelor and the money did not come from his family and he was very fond of us.

I don't mind anything as far as I am concerned, in the witness box. I have a clean bill. I only hope very much my poor Lionel will not be tormented, as he is the very soul of honour. He has such an important position in Kent and works so hard. I am awfully sorry for him and for my child. *Do Spare Them*, and attack *me* as much as you like.

I know you must do your best for your clients now, but you will do it, I am sure as a gentleman and I have nothing to fear.

I thank you from my heart for the way you have written.

My letters and yours will be seen by no one and no one will know anything about them.

Yours faighfully
V.S.

Then an undated, unsigned note in a large fierce hand:

Mr F. E. Smith
Before the case I was mistaken and thought you were a gentleman. Since then, I have discovered more and more that you are a *CAD* and as you are so fond of letters, it is good for you to know that I have received dozens of letters, from every rank of society, describing you as a *CAD*.

It is to the credit of F. E. Smith that none of these four letters have been published, until now. The most extraordinary and dangerous was of course the 'cad' letter, written sometime during the trial proceedings.

12
The Seery Trial

The trial opened at 10.30 a.m. on the morning of 24 June 1913.

Mr F. E. Smith, who had had less than four days to study his brief, spoke for nine hours. His theme was the disintegration of Seery's character and will: 'We say, in the first place . . . that his mind in these matters ceased to be his own mind and became in fact Lady Sackville's.'

He built up a moving picture of the happiness of the Scott family until the intrusion of the Sackvilles:

> If you had searched England you could not have found a family of a better type, a simple English home in which the strongest mutual affection and confidence existed between the different members of that family. Sir John Scott . . . was a man of affectionate nature, very easily influenced . . .

There had been the first visit to Knole; Mr F. E. Smith read the account from Seery's diary:

> 25 June 1899. "V. is truly a marvellous woman, clever, sympathetic, unlike most women." 26 June. "Sat under the trees until lunch time with V. She told me all her troubles and worries." You will come to the conclusion, I think, that from first to last the troubles and worries which were poured into the attentive ear of Sir John were very frequently connected with the subject of finance and financial difficulties.

Back to the diary:

> 21 July 1899. "Vicky" – we are getting on as you will observe in the intimacy of the acquaintance – "wrote that she had almost persuaded her father to come to Scotland . . ."

I suggest to you that Lady Sackville had formed in her own

mind the clearest possible intention of exploiting Sir John . . . Let me tell you, at the start, that this lady was so fortunate in her friendship, her sympathy was so fruitful, that in the course of an acquaintance of about ten years duration and apart from the enormous benefits which she has enjoyed under his will, very considerably more than half a million, she was so fortunate as to obtain from him in payments of various kinds a sum of £84,000.

The detailed story of the extortion was then described by F. E. Smith. 'The first step had been £42.10,' the sums mounted . . . 'I do not know what your experiences in these matters has been, but I am bound to say that my experience does not afford me cases in which persons unrelated to me are prepared to make me presents of £1,600 . . .' A splendid line followed: 'At that period of the year the cheques were dropping like the gentle rain from Heaven. They total £29,441 for one year . . . rare and refreshing fruit.'

Careful to impress the jury with the vastness of the sums mentioned, Smith was equally careful to be vague about the amount of the residuary estate left to the Scotts, a sum, he said carelessly, hardly worth mentioning. (It was £410,000.) He painted a picture of a desolate family, abandoned by their formerly devoted brother to the mercies of a woman who had stripped them not only of their money but their independence.

Walter Scott, Sir John's youngest brother, had, according to Mr Smith, suffered harshly at the hands of Lady Sackville:

> . . . It became known to her that it was the intention of Sir John to make his brother Walter his private secretary. You will understand that if you are going to have financial dealings with a man, if you are going to make repeated applications to him for pecuniary help . . . the private secretary will know what is going on. Whatever else happens, I think you will come to the conclusion that Lady Sackville had made up her mind . . . that Mr Walter Scott should not become private secretary to Sir John.
>
> Gentlemen, under those circumstances, Mr Walter Scott is at Finavon, and Lady Sackville invited Mr Walter Scott to come out for a walk. She said to him as they were walking out together, "I want to speak to you, so I take my courage in my two hands . . ." She said, "I know very well that you cannot deceive me, I know that you're in love with me," to which Mr Walter Scott

replied more bluntly than gallantly, "You never made a greater mistake in your life."

Mr F. E. Smith expounded on the importance of what followed. Six weeks later, on 16 November, Mr Walter Scott called on Lady Sackville at her house in London to implore her to leave the family alone. 'You must know,' he said, 'you are simply breaking up our family altogether.' Distressed by Lady Sackville's hostility to his plea, Mr Walter Scott went home, and, feeling that he was bound to warn his brother woke him up at 4 o'clock in the morning for what Smith described as 'a conversation of a somewhat delicate and painful character'. Their mother, Mrs Scott, who happened to be near the door, overheard the conversation and suffered palpitations of the heart, from which she died twenty minutes later. The shock was great to Walter Scott, who suffered a nervous collapse.

According to Smith, Lady Sackville's domination grew stronger year by year. By 1900 she had begun to use Seery's carriages as if they were her own. 'She had gradually insinuated herself into the position of mistress of the house. She gave orders to the servants . . . she utterly ignored the Misses Scott . . .' By June 1903, 'Lady Sackville had apparently made up her own mind that both sisters should not have their meals downstairs. You would have thought this question did not obviously concern her, and involved very great cruelty to one or other of these ladies . . . it sounds almost incredible.' F. E. Smith made it clear that this arrangement was for parties, not for day-to-day living, but by 1904 Lady Sackville was actually planning Seery's parties, making up the guest lists and table plans, and rearranging the furniture in Connaught Place without consulting the sisters. The family referred to Seery's 'Knole manner' after he had been with the Sackvilles. Once, for example, Lady Sackville advised Seery to discharge his faithful cook who had been with him for ten years and to take on instead a chef from Knole, and he did so immediately. Then there had been the occasion when Walter had been asked up from the country for a musical evening, he arrived with his violin but was told that Lady Sackville had decided against music, so he was not allowed to play or indeed to join the dinner party; instead was sent upstairs to Miss Mary Scott. In 1906 Seery had given his sisters a red lacquer cabinet for their boudoir. It was worth £600 and they were attached to it. Lady Sackville admired it and 'it went the way of everything else shortly afterwards. Sir John took it away . . . and gave it to Lady Sackville . . .'

Worst of all was Lady Sackville's disparagement of Alicia and Mary Scott, which was aimed at making them appear dull and frumpy to their brother. Once, only once they got him away and 'a spark of independence' returned to Sir John. In Europe with his sisters 'nothing was more amazing than the complete transformation that he underwent when he was removed from Lady Sackville's influence'.

In contrast to the cosy domesticity of Connaught Place there was the racy life led annually during the Paris visits to rue Laffitte. Here Smith's insinuations must have been humiliating to Lady Sackville, sitting in the courtroom.

MR F. E. SMITH: On the 16th March, 1906, Sir John, Lady Sackville, Lord Sackville and a lady whom I may call Lady X. were staying at the rue Laffitte together . . . the diary records a large number of separate expeditions in which Lord Sackville and Lady X. were together and Sir John and Lady Sackville.
SIR EDWARD CARSON: There is no reason to call her Lady X.
MR F. E. SMITH: I should have mentioned her name but for what I am about to read.

He then read a list of ten separate expeditions. Lady Connie Hatch and Lord Sackville seemed always to be on the golf course or dining at romantic restaurants together. The impression was left that year after year Lord Sackville had been absorbed in his friend, leaving his wife and Sir John to pursue their own private lives.

This could possibly have been the occasion that Lady Sackville wrote her 'cad' letter to F. E. Smith.

The summing up at the end of the speech reiterated the points; Sir John, a weak, vain, easily influenced man, had never known the fashionable world, and it had been possible for Lady Sackville to wean him away from his simple, middle-class family by a systematic campaign of interference and disparagement. F. E. Smith ended with a solemn invocation to the sanctity of the family as an institution:

I ask you to bear in mind that the one party here was of kin to the dead man, bone of his bone, flesh of his flesh, and I shall ask you to examine in comparison . . . the flimsy competition of those who, with no tie of blood and nothing but assiduous candidature to support them, come before a jury and claim to destroy and to defeat the claims of blood.

Mr F. E. Smith sat down.

The fashionable ladies must have felt that it had been well worth while to sit out the nine hours in the courtroom. They had surely hoped for scandal but the attempted seduction of Walter Scott by Lady Sackville followed by Mrs Scott's death after overhearing the 4 a.m. conversation between her sons was too good to be true. And those Paris visits . . .

Sir Edward Carson had hardly opened his mouth during the speech. The first witnesses to be called would be the Scott family, and the impression they made on the judge and jury would be important.

Mr F. E. Smith's opening speech was deeply damaging to Lady Sackville. It was quite true that she had been thoughtless and selfish in relation to Seery's family, insensitive to their feelings and, worst of all, apparently not even conscious of the slights she inflicted on them. 1913, the year of the trial, was a year in which the growing social restlessness of England was increasingly apparent. Class consciousness must affect the most open-minded jury in times of strain, and it would take very little on the part of the Scott family to convince a London juror that the aristocratic beauty who had sent the unfortunate sisters to bed for dinner was not capable of far graver crimes than that. It had been a brilliant performance; one that presented a grave threat to Lady Sackville.

Seery's eldest sister Alicia Florence Scott was the first member of the family to testify, and was examined by F. E. Smith's junior counsel, Mr G. Hemmerde, K.C. Miss Scott was a heavy woman of middle age, dressed in a sternly tailored wool suit, her bosom like a bolster and her lips tightly set. Probably she was shyer than the armoured dragon that she looked, for she spoke in a low voice and had to be encouraged twice to speak up so that the jury could hear her. She grew bolder as the questioning proceeded, along the lines of the intimidation of her brother by Lady Sackville. The grievances came pouring out. Mr Hemmerde brought up Lady Sackville's first visit to Scotland, at Finavon, in 1899.

MR HEMMERDE: At that time, when she arrived, what members of your family were there?

MISS ALICIA SCOTT: My mother, my brother, my sister.

Your brother Sir John?

Yes, Sir John.

Did you notice at that time the relations between Lady Sackville and your brother?

Yes.

Will you tell my Lord and the Jury so that they can hear?

I saw that she was getting a great influence over him in many ways.

SIR EDWARD CARSON: My Lord, surely the lady ought to be asked facts?

THE PRESIDENT: I think so, yes.

SIR EDWARD CARSON: And not opinions of that kind . . .

THE PRESIDENT: They have got to determine, not only whether she gained an influence over him but whether she exercised that influence unduly.

MR HEMMERDE: Will you tell my Lord and the jury any facts that led you to that conclusion?

MISS SCOTT: Well, she tried to make mischief; in one instance she said to my sister one day without any reason; she asked her what she thought of platonic friendship, and she said that she thought it was rather a dangerous thing, as that day we had had a letter about platonic friendship, which ended in disaster. The next day my brother said to her, 'I think it was very tactless on your part to ask Lady Sackville what she thought of platonic friendship' and he was very much annoyed . . . he did not get over that for some few days.

THE PRESIDENT: It is very difficult to see which of the two ladies, in long conversations, said one thing or another.

MR HEMMERDE: I was asking you about a dinner party at Connaught Place on 24 May 1911. Do you remember that dinner party?

MISS SCOTT: Yes.

Do you remember anything Lady Sackville did on that occasion?

Yes – Lady Sackville was dining there, and she took it upon herself to introduce people to one another who already knew each other; and then, after the dinner party, she showed them all over the rooms, the pictures, and everything else, as if she was the hostess . . . and ignored my sister and myself all the time.

When Lady Sackville came to stay at Connaught Place, what was Sir John's demeanour to her?

He was subservient and obsequious and used to leave letters and parcels for her, and seemed exactly like a slave.

On the afternoon of the third day Sir Edward Carson opened his cross-examination of the witness:

SIR EDWARD CARSON: I gather from what you have just told us that you have torn up an immense amount of letters from Lady Sackville to your brother?
MISS ALICIA SCOTT: Only a few.
About how many?
Four or five.
Were they early letters of the years 1899 or 1900?
Yes.
The year in which the will was made?
Yes.
You wrote this letter to Lady Sackville on 26 January: 'It would be affectation on our part to say that we approve of all the provisions of our brother's will, but the money and the property were his own and he had every right to dispose of them as he wished.' Was it before or after that letter that you tore them up?
I cannot quite remember.
Please try. That is only nine days after his death. Do you mean to say that you began tearing up letters before that?
I cannot quite remember.
Please try.

Sir Edward Carson's melodious voice, with its touch of Irish brogue, repeating 'Please try,' would have been soothing to a witness who was slow-witted. His line of questioning was directed to show that had there been anything damaging to Lady Sackville in the letters of 1899–1900 the Scotts would not have torn them up. Sir John made his will on 26 October 1900, so use of undue influence would have had to have been before that.

Under Carson's cross-examination, a new picture of Seery emerged, unconsciously drawn by Alicia herself. A generous Seery,

167

who had supported his brothers and sisters handsomely, giving jewels as well as money to the sisters, and leaving in the residual estate the contents of Connaught Place.

SIR EDWARD CARSON: What is the value of them?
MISS ALICIA SCOTT: I cannot tell you because they are being sold now.
You can tell me what they sold up yesterday; I see that they were being sold at Christie's; how much was got?
I think £84,000, I am not clear . . . the pictures will be sold today.

Seery, as the story continued to develop, had been, at the time that he made his will, a highly competent man of fifty-three, thoroughly in command of his business interests and responsibilities. During later years he had had ample opportunity to change his will had he wished to. Sir Edward reminded Miss Scott of the very important letter that her brother had written in 1900 and deposited with his solicitor to be forwarded to Lady Sackville on his death. This letter, which was already familiar to Miss Scott, was a precise definition of the reasons for Seery's gratitude to Lady Sackville and his wish to express his feelings by banishing her anxiety over her future ways and means. At this time Sir Edward did not read the whole text, but quoted from it, holding it in his hand. His manner changed. It has often been described: the charming Irishman in his shabby robes would become the figure of justice – right arm extended, towering over his witness, boring for the truth. F. E. Smith, who had seen it so often, could only remain impassive and pray that Miss Alicia Scott would prove a sharper witness than she had been up to now. He was to be disappointed.

MR SMITH: Do you suggest to his Lordship and the jury that this, which was written in his own handwriting . . . was not a true expression of his opinion . . . Do you say he was not writing there what was true?
MISS SCOTT: I do not know exactly what to say.
I want to ask you. The man deliberately wrote that down there – he was only fifty-three years old – with his own hand. Do you not believe that that was the true expression of his feeling towards Lady Sackville?

I think Lady Sackville had done her work by then.

I ask you . . . do you not believe that that was the true expression of his feeling . . . or do you think he wrote what was false?

I think that he wrote that under circumstances – I meant to say, he was very much upset by my mother's death then.

I daresay.

I think he was –

Do you say that you do not think he believed that when he wrote it?

I suppose he did.

Have you any reason to doubt that he felt gratitude to Lady Sackville for her sympathy?

No.

Was he not of sufficient capacity? I would like to know what you think of your brother . . .

I think that he was so under Lady Sackville's influence that he –

What was the influence that she had over him?

I think mesmeric.

Do you mean she mesmerised him?

Not exactly mesmerised, but there was a kind of spell over him.

Do you mean that he was fond of her?

No.

Sir Edward Carson continued his cross-examination; gentler now. Mr F. E. Smith was probably not surprised when the gentlest question of all was asked, the innocent, leading question:

Will you tell me up to the 26th of October what is the worst thing you knew Lady Sackville ever to do?

THE PRESIDENT: I do not think she heard what you said.

MISS SCOTT: I did not hear your question.

SIR EDWARD CARSON: Up to the 26th October when the will was made, because that is the date we have to take for undue influence, just tell us the worst thing you knew her to do. The worst complaint you have against her?

She belittled the family to my brother.

She belittled the family?

Yes.

What do you mean by that?

When we were in Scotland at Finavon she used to make mischief so as to get my brother annoyed with us.

Was there anything more? You told us yesterday the incident of
talking about platonic friendships?
I cannot remember, but the whole tone –
Will you tell us the worst thing she did so that we may have
something to start with?
I cannot remember anything at this moment.
Of course a great deal goes on in twelve years.

Sir Edward Carson had finished his cross-examination. Carica-
tures of him in the courtroom show the gesture: the tall, gaunt
figure smoothing his gown and pushing back his worn, torn wig
with an expression of melancholy fatigue.

Miss Scott was a limited and stupid woman. She had come to
recite a pat story, a long list of Lady Sackville's iniquities about
things like dinner parties. Now this man had asked her four times,
in different ways, the same question – had her brother been competent or not to write an important letter expressing his feelings
towards Lady Sackville, and then he had gone on to make her
imply that the platonic friendship conversation was the worst thing
that Lady Sackville had ever done to them, which somehow didn't
sound as important in court as it had when she and her sister had
gone over and over it. He hadn't asked nearly enough about dinner
parties. Perhaps Mr Smith would help her to tell more about what
they had endured.

Mr F. E. Smith was not the man to risk emphasizing the damage
that had just been done. His re-examination of Miss Alicia Scott
lasted about five minutes, and his examination of Miss Mary Scott
was almost cursory. She was a dimmer copy of her older sister,
confirming what Miss Alicia had said.

Mr Walter Scott was an important witness. Twenty-one years
younger than Seery, he suffered particularly from the obesity which
characterized his family. Nevertheless he looked bright and
pleased with himself as he handed his older sisters out of the motor
car to proceed to the courtroom. He wore morning clothes which
appeared to be straining at the seams, but there was a certain
porcine dignity about his appearance. As a witness he was sup-
remely self-confident; a master of the fatuous phrase and the
cliché. He was so talkative that twice his counsel had to pull him
up as he drifted into hearsay evidence.

Walter confirmed F. E. Smith's account of the Finavon visit, adding that Sir John had been fascinated by Lady Sackville 'as an animal is fascinated by a serpent'. However, warned by his sisters that there was danger of a liaison between his brother and Lady Sackville, 'Forewarned is forearmed', Walter himself never formed the slightest affection for the lady. Under stiff cross-examination from Carson he became a little boastful, admitting that during a conversation at Finavon she had said, 'I cannot break my marriage vows with you'.

SIR EDWARD CARSON: How did that come about?
MR WALTER SCOTT: How did that come about?
SIR EDWARD CARSON: Did you not hear what I said?
MR WALTER SCOTT: She said it. Why, I cannot tell you.
SIR EDWARD CARSON: But it must come in some category. She did not race up to you and say "I cannot break my marriage vows"?
MR WALTER SCOTT: We were walking along together, and she said it for some rhyme or reason; I cannot tell you why.

There was a ludicrous quality about the whole episode – poor, fat Walter Scott, the lovely Lady Sackville. Sir Edward fought hard to break Walter's version of his visit to Lady Sackville in London on 16 November, followed by his extraordinary visit to Seery at 4 a.m. the next morning which preceded their mother's death from heart failure, but he stuck to his story: he had gone to beg Lady Sackville to leave the family alone, there had never been protestations of love on his part.

The only definite facts established were that Walter Scott had a nervous breakdown following the episode and Seery had subsequently bought him Nether Swell, a country house presently worth £35,000–£40,000 and that he would also receive, under the terms of the will £12,000 a year.

Following Walter Scott came his brother General Douglas Scott, a firm, self-assured proper British Army officer. As Seery's executor he had found the letter to be delivered to 'Mrs Sackville-West' after Seery's death beginning 'Ma chère petite amie', which he read in full to the court:

Ma chère petite amie,
I have directed my solicitor, Mr Capron, to send you this letter which conveys my last farewell, and the renewed expression of

my sincerest gratitude for all your affectionate kindness to me. It will be found that I have left you in my Will a goodly portion of my objets d'art, furniture etc. and also a sum of money which I hope will make you comfortable for life and cause all anxiety as to your future ways and means to cease. You know the love and affection I have always had for dear little Vita, and I have no doubt that you will leave her such a portion of your fortune as you may deem fit. I thought it best to leave all the money to you as I am sure it will be very well applied – at any rate my wish is that you should have full control over everything and that you should leave the money entirely as you please. I can only say that the idea of making you completely independent out of my superfluity has always been a great pleasure to me, and it is only a fitting reward for such an affectionate interest as you have shown in me. You did everything to make my broken life, and my last words to you are: "I am very grateful." God bless you, dear little friend, and may we meet in the land that knows no sorrow. Ever your affectionate *Vieil Ami*, – J. Murray Scott.

This moving letter had done nothing to change the General's hard opinion of Lady Sackville, and the remaining Scott witnesses looked and seemed like an implacable line of dreadnoughts, following each other without a thought in their minds for poor, dead Seery. There was the stockbroker, Donald, the clergyman Edward, and the gossipy friend Miss Edith Davidson to whom Lady Sackville had confided over tea. 'She practically announced to me that she was going . . . to take him under her charge . . . that the sisters only had dull people.' There was the doctor, Sir Benjamin Franklin, and his wife Harriet. Lady Sackville once snubbed the Franklins in Vienna and had made Seery snub them also. There was the nurse, who remembered Seery's attitude towards Lady Sackville: 'He always seemed to have to do whatever she wanted him to do . . . a peculiar friendship.' There were clerks and secretaries and servants. More interestingly, there was a Major Arbuthnot, who described arriving early at Connaught Place for dinner in July 1911, and walking in on Lady Sackville and Vita in the library, going through a desk drawer. He drew back and then saw the two tiptoeing down the hall. The suggestion was that they had been looking for a codicil to Seery's will.

By this time it was the fifth day of the trial.

Then Sir Edward Carson put Lady Sackville on the stand. She had been sitting by her husband every day, listening intently to the evidence. Vita was near them, and a very good-looking family they were. Lord Sackville was marvellously elegant – he always wore his clothes well and in contrast to the poor fat Scott men he stood out particularly. So did Lady Sackville and tall, graceful Vita. Their clothes were always noted by the press and on this particular day Lady Sackville was in blue, with a blue feather boa and a big hat with an ostrich feather – both blue to match her eyes.

The evidence concerned Walter Scott's allegations re the Finavon visit. Immediately Lady Sackville established herself as a lively, interesting witness; highly stimulating after the long parade of plodding Scotts. Even the judge brightened up and seemed to want her to go on, while F. E. Smith fought desperately to cut off her arresting testimony.

She had described her arrival at Finavon and her father's warning that Walter had fallen in love with her and was following her around. This was in direct contradiction to Walter's own story.

MR F. E. SMITH: We cannot have this. I did not want to stop it as I thought it was going to be a short conversation but we really cannot have all this.
SIR EDWARD CARSON: Why not?
THE WITNESS: This is what happened.

After a testy argument between the two counsels the judge ruled that Lady Sackville could continue with Walter's pursuit of her. She told the story with gusto, the court hanging on her words. The culmination was the evening of 16 November, when Walter Scott had come to see her in her London house on Mount Street, according to himself to prevent her breaking up the family.

SIR EDWARD CARSON: Was there anyone else there?
THE WITNESS: No, nobody. I was rather surprised to see him coming into the room, and I got up and he threw himself on his knees, and he began again to tell me that he loved me.
SIR EDWARD CARSON: Pouring out his love for you?
THE WITNESS: Yes, and he tried to take me around the knees.

Well, of course I have always found him very objectionable and I did mind this very much indeed, and I said: "You know, Mr Walter, if you go on like this I shall have to tell my husband and Sir John," and he said: "If you tell Johnny you will ruin my life because I depend on him entirely, but I love you, I love you and I want you to be my ——." I went to the bell . . . the drawing room was rather large and he followed me across the room on his knees, and I tell you he was dreadful. I went . . . out of the room and left him there in that ridiculous position, and I went straight to my husband's room. I told him: "There is a man in the drawing room making a love scene to me. Will you go and kick him?" And my husband said, "By this time he must be in Mount Street. Now calm yourself . . ."

Lady Sackville went on to describe a later talk with Sir John in which he had told her that Walter had come home and said that Lady Sackville had wished to become his (Walter's) mistress. This was the terrible 4 a.m. conversation which old Mrs Scott overheard, and which caused her death, followed by Walter going off his head.

This was the simple, happy family that F. E. Smith had described in his opening speech.

Sir Edward Carson then opened the case for the Sackvilles:

May it please your Lordship, Gentlemen of the Jury . . . You listened for nine hours to a vitriolic blackwashing of the characters of Lord and Lady Sackville, of trivialities magnified by the eloquence of my friend, and you had an instance of his great powers of mesmerism and fascination . . . I think you will say that they all came to nothing.

Walter's story was 'falsehood from beginning to end'.

'Gentlemen, I will tell you why he got up at four o'clock in the morning . . . because he was suddenly afraid that Lady Sackville would tell Sir John that he had made this objectionable declaration of love.' Typically, Sir John had seen to it that Walter would never have to work again after his breakdown; had bought him a splendid country house and given him £12,000 a year. Pounding away at Sir John's right to give away the money that had come to him from the Wallaces as he pleased, Sir Edward read out what he called 'Sir John's message from the other side' – the 'Ma chère *petite amie*' letter. He dealt with Major Arbuthnot, the witness who had claimed to have caught Lady Sackville and Vita red-handed in the library at Connaught Place; there had been no document to extract and 'we will prove' that neither of them had been near Connaught Place that evening.

Sir Edward reminded the jury of the nature of undue influence:

> If someone puts a pistol to your head and says, "Sign this will," that is undue influence. The man is not then able to exercise his own mind ... The Scotts say that Lady Sackville mesmerised him, fascinated him. That is not undue influence. They were afraid to say that it was affection because they knew that affection is a due influence, a proper influence.

Then Sir Edward brought Lady Sackville back for a long examination in which she once more proved a brilliant witness. Her descriptions of her squabbles with Seery were frank and convincing, the endless threats to change his will had become tiresome. Lady Sackville: 'The best way I could see Sir John was to receive him in the shop. He had a corner where he used to sit and be pleasant or growl to me ... he used to stay two hours every morning.' The day before his death he had asked her to lunch and when she said that she had another engagement, he threatened to change his will.' "Very well, let us go to Mr Capron; we will do it at once ..." He said, "You little rascal, you know very well I would never do such a thing." ' The next day, about to leave for Spealls, he died, in his chair at Hertford House.

This was the sixth day. During it and most of the seventh day Lady Sackville was under cross-examination by Smith and then re-examination by Carson. It was the most interesting part of the trial, not for the evidence that emerged but for the drama of the duel between the two antagonists. Her method was to volunteer information that had not been asked, or sometimes to answer his questions with another question. She was ingenious, witty and maddening. The judge described her in his summing up as 'a lady of high mettle, very high mettle indeed'. Mr F. E. Smith was to remark that she was one of the most troublesome witnesses he had ever encountered.

The question of Miss Davidson, the gossipy Scott witness, came up.

MR F. E. SMITH: I am inviting you to inform me why you asked Miss Davidson to come to your house. I suggest that you wanted to pump her about the Scott family?

LADY SACKVILLE: Why should I?

You have asked me a question. Why do you not say "No"?

This case is a tissue of falsehoods.

The witness box has been filled by liars day after day until you came?

Yes.

This has been the first gleam of truth?

Well, very nearly . . . It is too bad, the way they have gone on.

THE PRESIDENT: Do not get upset. [He was very sympathetic.]

LADY SACKVILLE: My Lord, it has been too dreadful.

MR F. E. SMITH: I must take you now, to see if we can discover a little more falsehood, to the evidence of Walter Scott's visit to Finavon.

This was a mistake on F. E. Smith's part. The Finavon story led to the scene in Mount Street on 16 November.

MR F. E. SMITH: Do you really tell the jury that Mr Walter Scott went down on his knees to you?

I do.

And began to pour out his love to you?

Yes.

And when you went to the door?

He followed me on his knees like that.

At this point Lady Sackville sank to her knees and gave an imitation of fat Walter waddling across the drawing room. The court burst into screams of laughter.

Furious, F. E. Smith hit hard:

MR F. E. SMITH: . . . It is suggested to you that this statement from beginning to end is an invention, without a word of truth in it.

How dare you say that?

I am not wanting in that courage when the necessity arises.

At other times she appealed directly to the judge and jury:

LADY SACKVILLE: My Lord, may I ask you something? My Lord, you may remember, and the gentlemen of the jury.

This is an old trick when a witness is cornered by a brilliant cross-examiner, but how did Lady Sackville know it instinctively? Feminine, charming, she had the judge and the jury eating out of her hand.

Mr F. E. Smith [wearily]: I will sit down.

Sometimes she insisted on treating F. E. Smith as a person she knew socially, as indeed she did. Over a question of an unimportant grievance of one of the Scott sisters:

The Witness: You would have said just the same thing yourself, Mr Smith. We meet at dinners, so I know you would.
Mr F. E. Smith: We will not argue about that, Lady Sackville.

Her answers brought Smith into conflict with Carson; the following sharp exchange is one example. The question concerned the Hertford House jewels to be worn by the Misses Scott at Buckingham Palace. Lady Sackville said that the matter had not been discussed with her.

Mr F. E. Smith: I thought you said it was.
Lady Sackville: I did not.
Sir Edward Carson: You really misinterpret every answer she gives.
Mr F. E. Smith [to Carson]: That is a statement without warrant of any kind. If you think so, you can object before my Lord.
Sir Edward Carson: My Lord, I do object. Over and over again my friend, when she says one thing, pretends to think she has said another.
Mr F. E. Smith: That is a grossly improper statement without warrant.
Sir Edward Carson: I will not take any notice of ill-temper, I have been too long at the Bar to do so . . .
The Judge: It is much more agreeable to go on to the next question.
Sir Edward Carson: I am not the least inclined to be bullied.
The Judge: Now, the next question.

Next to Lady Sackville's habit of answering questions with another question, the tactic that seemed to irritate the opposing counsel most was the cosy way she would take him into her confidence. He was trying to make her admit that she had been disappointed when Sir John threatened to cut her out of his will:

MR F. E. SMITH: You say you did not mind?
LADY SACKVILLE: No, I did not. It is funny but I did not. I got so sick of it, you know, Mr Smith, you do get sick when you are told five or six times a day that you are going to be cut out of a will.

There was only one new point brought out – a letter was produced by Mr F. E. Smith from Lady Sackville to Mrs Cooke, a friend of hers, dated 1911. This lady had been the wife of the agent at Letton, one of Sir John's properties, and Lady Sackville had written to her in 1911 that Sir John was changing his will leaving 'everything he has dangled before my weary eyes for ten years away from us three'. This unexpected letter rattled Lady Sackville badly. She broke down, and the judge, distressed at her distress, told her to dismiss Mrs Cooke from her mind. Lady Sackville said that she would try.

Sir Edward Carson made a strong case for the unimportance of the upsetting letter. It had been written the day after one of Seery's angry threats; so sadly frequent in the year before he died. The letter began, 'Now that you have ruthlessly terminated our friendship' and in writing to her close friend Mrs Cooke it was natural that Lady Sackville should have expressed her irritation.

It took a woman of extraordinary cool nerve and quick mind to stand up to two days of such intensive questioning. There had been much to retain, facts and figures, dates that had to be accurate down to the hour, as well as the effort of thinking out her strategy. No greater compliment was ever paid to Lady Sackville than that interjected by Mr F. E. Smith in his summing up to the jury:

Did you ever see a lady of a more arresting or dominating personality; did you ever see a lady who showed herself at every stage in that cross-examination how completely she was mistress of herself, who displayed a more extraordinary and almost uncanny cleverness dealing with every stage of the case . . . you saw in that box one of the strongest and most striking personalities which any of you has ever met in your lives.

Sir Edward then put his remaining witnesses on the stand. Two younger friends of Seery's, Mr Kenneth Campbell and Mr Sutton

Timmis spoke movingly of what a wonderful man he had been, and also a strong man. The very thought of coercion was absurd. Mr Campbell recalled that not long before his death Seery had said to him, 'Mrs Lionel is the greatest friend I ever had in my life and I shall never forget it'. He also told a charming story: Mr Campbell had borrowed £1,000 from Seery to buy a Stock Exchange partnership and had repaid £100 of it when he got married. As a wedding present, in addition to a Louis XVI desk, Seery had sent him a little clean slate, symbolizing an extra present of the £900 debt.

Mr Timmis added a pleasant touch – Seery had told him that his idea of happiness was to have a fishing in Scotland and a good shooting in England, where he could ask his friends.

Unlike the resentful Scott witnesses, with their tales of snubbings and hurts, the Sackville witnesses brought the real Seery into the courtroom with them, the lovable, fun-loving, generous friend who lived to give pleasure to others. It was as if a fresh breeze was blowing into the stuffy room as these delightful people got up one after another to tell their stories in their clear, upper-class voices. Vita was an excellent witness; she rose to describe the evening of the Major Arbuthnot incident. At the hour that it was alleged to have taken place she was ill in bed at home with her mother sitting beside her, there were plenty of servants to testify that they had dined together in Vita's bedroom. Later Lady Sackville went on to a musicale given by Mrs Walter Rubens. Vita added that even if her mother and she had wanted to break into Seery's desk they could not have done so, as Seery always carried his keys with him.

Lady Constance Hatch was another good witness. Sir John was never intimidated or coerced by Lady Sackville: 'He knew his own mind and spoke it.'

Mr F. E. Smith gave Lady Constance a bad time in cross-examination. He read from Seery's Paris diary:

On March 18th there is this entry: "Lionel took out Lady Connie." March 19th: "Lionel took Lady Connie out in motor." March 20th: "Lionel took Lady Connie out to the Vaudeville." March 21st: 'Lady Connie was taken by Lionel to the Folies Bergères." . . . tennis, lunch, Fontainebleau and finally: "Lionel and Lady Constance left for London at 4 o'clock by the Club train." Does that remind you?
LADY CONSTANCE: Yes.

The intimacy between Lionel and Lady Connie was made excruciatingly clear. Perhaps this was the moment that Lady Sackville wrote the 'cad' letter? The way in which F. E. Smith handled this questioning, only peripherally linked to the case does seem a desperate move, presumably made in order to shock and prejudice the jury against the Sackvilles.

On the eighth day of the trial Sir Samuel Evans, the judge, summed up the case for the jury. It was a long, finely thought out speech, and a fair one, considering that it was clear that the judge's heart lay with Lady Sackville:

> If you think that by reason of the wiles, the domination, the fascination, or the influence of this lady were exercised, not in the ordinary way, but exercised in order to compel him to make a will which he had no desire to make in favour of the Sackvilles, you are entitled to say so. On the other hand, if you think that whatever that influence was, even if you may not commend it ... if it was a legitimate influence, the influence of friendship, the influence arising out of the community of tastes, the influence arising out of the affinity of natures . . . it was perfectly legitimate ... unless it fetters his will to such an extent that he made her will and not his own, it is not an undue influence in the eyes of the law, and you ought to say so by your verdict.

Sir Samuel Evans concluded his summing up with the classic phrase: 'Gentlemen, consider your verdict.'

After twelve minutes of deliberation, the jury returned to court and found that the bequests under the will of Sir John Scott in favour of Lord and Lady Sackville were not obtained by the undue influence of Lord and Lady Sackville and that the said bequests were not obtained by the fraud of Lady Sackville.

It had been a long eight days.

Sir Edward Carson cut an important political meeting in Ulster and collapsed in bed, where he remained for three days prostrate with exhaustion.

There is no record of what Mr F. E. Smith did, but his son wrote that his father could not conceal his admiration for so worthy an antagonist, adding:

> In one of the Sherlock Holmes stories Holmes was foiled by a woman, and with unusual humility asked Watson to remind

him of the fact whenever he appeared in danger of becoming conceited. In like manner F. E. Smith might well have said to his wife: "If ever I show any signs of becoming over-confident in my powers just mention the words Lady Sackville, and I shall be infinitely obliged."

The Judge, Sir Samuel Evans, never forgot Lady Sackville. When in later years he retired with Lady Evans to Brighton they became close friends, and on sunny afternoons he would call on her and they would sometimes walk by the sea, pausing to sit on a friendly bench and run over the juiciest moments of the case together, relishing every memory of F. E. Smith's discomforture. It is pleasant to think of the two old people sitting in the sun, reliving Victoria Sackville's triumph; for triumph it had been, the greatest of her life with the exception of her conquest of Washington.

As for the heroine herself she returned to Knole immediately after the case and from her diary seemed to be suffering badly from reaction:

25 July 1913, Knole
I have written nothing since the case. I've had the most awful times since and during the case. I feel very ill, much more than anyone knows. I've put all the paper reports of the case at the end of this book, giving the account of what happened. I know that F. E. Smith prejudiced many minds by his opening speech. I have heard since that the judge, Sir Samuel Evans thought I was a pretty bad lot until I got into the witness box. As I was not lying, it was easy to defend myself and I did. I had to save Knole and make Vita's future safe, so I fought for all I was worth. I hated to have to give Walter Scott away. The way I showed how he ran after me in the drawing room in November, 1899 made everybody laugh and the papers have taken it up and laughed at him. The music halls even have made a parody on it.

All the Scott witnesses seemed to recite a lesson; all repeating the same words and expressions, one after the other. I could not help crying when Sir Edward read from one of Seery's letters ... the one beginning, "*Ma chère petite amie*," it stabbed me.

Sir Edward told me I was splendid ... my plan was more or less when Mr F. E. Smith asked me some stupid question, to ask him a very embarrassing one.

Lionel went off yesterday to Holland. I shall want a rest and a change very badly; my nerves are shattered.

The press accounts were indeed interesting. The papers had given the sensational case day-by-day coverage, and the editorial comments that followed were in many cases highly thoughtful. The one Lady Sackville seemed to have liked the best was from the *Los Angeles Times*, but she underlined a great many flattering comments.

Lady Sackville deserved her accolades, and it is nice to read that she recovered from her nervous exhaustion sufficiently to take Vita on a shopping spree at the end of the month. As they passed a jeweller's shop in Bond Street a necklace caught her eye. 'How much is that?' 'Two thousand pounds, my lady.' 'Thank you – we'll take it with us. Do you like it, darling? I think it will look very pretty on you.'

Although it is not recorded, Lady Sackville, who hated to be kept waiting, probably wrapped up the necklace herself in a piece of writing paper that she had stolen from the Ritz Hotel at lunchtime, and proceeded down the street, a gleam in her lovely dark blue eyes.

13
Pre-War Adventures

During the last two years of Seery's life, the sad time of increasing illness and irritability, when he was no longer the perfect companion of the preceding years, Lady Sackville had made a new friend, John Pierpont Morgan. Although there are today far bigger banking houses than J. P. Morgan and Co. (now the Morgan Guaranty Bank) prestige is an intangible quality, and no banker since has had the status of this giant world figure. When Lady Sackville came to know him intimately he was seventy-four, but he retained the vitality of the man who had saved the United States federal reserve during the panic of 1895 by raising $62,000,000 in gold overnight and so preserving the redeemability of Treasury notes, a famous episode in the history of Wall Street.

Although he was a convivial man who enjoyed society and the company of women, he frightened people who met him for the first time by his overwhelming personality and his intense eyes which were said to look right through you. His tragic, bulbous nose – the result of *acne rosacea* – was a dreadful disfiguration of which he was very conscious. Mrs Peter A. Jay, one of the few people alive who knew him well has said in 1977:

> It was funny, but after ten minutes one simply didn't notice his nose because he was so compelling. Attractive to women? Fascinating. He had really loved his first wife who died a few months after their marriage; his second wife was a quiet person who stayed at home when he went abroad on his collecting trips and was said not to share his interests. I didn't know her but we all knew his ladyfriend, Winona Wetmore, who was delightful and very popular in New York.

Lady Sackville also forgot his nose, and was mesmerized by the imposing, powerful figure who entered rooms 'like a whirl-

183

wind', and made important financial decisions in ten minutes.

Morgan was adding to his magnificent, eclectic art collection and in early 1911 acquired from Knole Gainsborough's *Miss Linley*, which Lord Sackville sold through the dealer Partridge for £36,000. Lady Sackville had adored this picture, and wrote in her diary in capital letters: 'ALAS! MISS LINLEY IS GONE.'

Meeting Morgan a few months later at a party in London she wrote, 'I avoided Pierpont Morgan most carefully, as we have got tapestries to sell, and I do not want him to think that I am running after him . . .' In fact he was running after her and insisted on a rendezvous at his house in Princes' Gate to discuss the purchase of other heirlooms from Knole. This was the year before Seery died, and despite his generosity the Knole estate needed to sell. Lady Sackville's diary tells the story:

8 July 1911, London

. . . I had rather a shock to be ushered at last into a room, where our ex-Miss Linley and her brother were hanging. The picture had been over-cleaned and had lost its mellow look, so I did not feel as miserable as I might have felt otherwise . . . We sat on a long sofa, yards away from each other! It was most awkward. He asked me what and why we had to sell anything. I said "Lloyd George's super tax and land tax and the death duties." He answered, "Damn Lloyd George . . . I want to help you. What have you got to get rid off?"

"Tapestries."

"I don't want any tapestries, let me come down to Knole and look around."

'No, Mr Morgan . . . it is a case of take it or leave it."

He thought for a few moments and said, "Well, I'll take your tapestries to help you. How much do you want for them?"

It took no time for Lady Sackville and Mr Morgan to settle on the price – £65,000: he was about to show her to the door when,

to my utter astonishment, he folded me in his arms, and said, "I hope you don't mind . . ." Vita was waiting for me in the car and her joy was great when I told her I secured £65,000 for Dada and the Knole estate. The whole interview did not take more than ten minutes . . . I wired at once to L.

20 July 1911, Knole
Pierpont Morgan came here yesterday with four people to see the tapestries he has bought. He was delighted with the Seven Deadly Sins. I've got the house in shape. The heat continues: 89 degrees in the shade.

30 July 1911, Knole
We had a big dinner in the Hall. Mr Pierpont Morgan came. I had a long talk with him in the garden. He told me many of the bothers of being very rich, but the great thing to have was personality, which he has to an infinitive degree. He has a wonderful personality, I have not met anyone as attractive . . . he is full of life and energy; a wonderful man.

Visits to Princes' Gate continued, but Mr Morgan was constantly disturbed by people coming to ask him questions and by papers and telegrams to sign. Lady Sackville, generally impatient at being kept waiting, was intrigued by watching the wheels of power turn.
Morgan left England, returning in May of the next year.

20 May 1912, London
I called on busy Mr Morgan at Princes' Gate. He was arranging a loan with ten men, for China, but he gave me half an hour all the same. He came in like a whirlwind and crushed me, saying he had longed for this moment, that he had told nobody of his return, but wanted to see me at once . . . I went away with mixed feelings of friendship and apprehension of what may follow from this great friendship; as I am so straight. I can think of nothing else. The man has such marvellous personality and attraction for me . . .

22 May 1912, London
Mr Morgan came again and was beaming with joy to be quietly alone with me . . . he repeated several times how much he had cared for me for so long, but had not dared to tell me. He also spoke of the long talk we had in the garden last July. How much he was in love that day that I must have seen it or guessed it. (But I really did not.) He said he would care for me just the same, if I got ill, ugly or an invalid . . .

The following entry came after they had been having a lovers' tiff over *Miss Linley*, which Lady Sackville had asked for permission to buy back, if she ever had the money:

20 May 1912, London

He replied: "I don't think, dear, I don't like to part with it."
I said: "You like *Miss Linley* better than me." ... He held my
hand with so much affection and said that he was very sorry to
be so old, but that I was the only woman he loved and would
never change. He is very careful not to get me talked about and
told me so, and said it would be too dangerous to come to
America this winter. He keeps on saying that there is nothing
better in the world than the affection he has for me. How can he
find time to come as he does, beats me, as I know he is so busy.
I won't talk about *Miss Linley* or money with him; I hate it.
Our friendship must be free from any sordid motive.

Pierpont Morgan died in March 1913, in Rome, following an
archaeological expedition to Egypt. Seery had died just over a year
before, and Lady Sackville must have felt abandoned. But she
never could have hoped to replace Seery with Morgan – it
wouldn't have worked in the long term. The key to Lady Sackville's
happy relationships with men – and this thread ran from Washington with her father to her last admirer – was that they must
need her, be helped by her, drawing warmth from the strong sun
of her strength. She could be petty and mean at times to the people
she loved best, but she was a great giver. What could she have
given Pierpont Morgan? Her body, had he wanted it, but although
she was still a desirable woman it was probably too late for him.
There clearly was no physical relationship between them; had
Morgan wanted to be alone with her he would have emptied
Princes' Gate of the business visitors she always found there on
her visits. And while he was surely genuine when he declared his
love for her it is impossible to imagine that he conceived anything
more serious than a romantic dalliance during his annual visits to
England. Not from him, with his vast responsibilities and pres-
sures, would come two letters a day; there is no record of any
correspondence except one letter from New York and a series of
ardent telegrams announcing his arrival in England and, from the
returning liner, messages of his desolation at leaving her.

Peripheral friendships filled the vacuum. Lady Sackville was
rather flattered to learn that Mrs Rudyard Kipling was becoming
jealous of her. Lord Kitchener occupied some of her time. A
complex man, he was the hero who had driven to Khartoum under

Wolseley to relieve Gordon in the eighties, failing by a few days as all England watched and Queen Victoria thundered at her Prime Minister, Gladstone, in the strongest words a constitutional monarch could employ. Kitchener then avenged Gordon by his annihilation of the Sudanese at Omdurman in 1898 and reoccupied Khartoum; he was Sirdar of the Egyptian army, Chief of Staff to Lord Roberts during the South African war, Commander-in-Chief in India, Secretary of State for War. He was so towering a figure that the posters that went up all over England at the beginning of the First World War, 'YOUR COUNTRY NEEDS YOU!' under the picture of the Mars-like face with its fierce moustache needed no further caption. The youth of England rushed to the recruiting office and the story of 'Kitchener's First Hundred Thousand' is a valourous page of English history.

He was also highly ambitious, given to taking personal slights over-seriously, and throughout his career disliked by his brother officers, with the exception of his intimate personal staff. The troops adored him and would have followed him anywhere.

The women who interested him were great ladies, who besides being charming were extremely useful. Lady Salisbury and Lady Desborough were staunch friends to him, the former especially encouraged his career and their correspondence was enormous. Lady Sackville was a late comer to the field, but during the pre-war years she helped him do up his house.

In 1911 when he first came to Knole she found him 'a rough diamond' but was touched by discovering that the aim and dream of his life was to have a country house in which he could place, in a perfect setting, the collection of objects he had acquired during his long career, and although their relationship was never faintly romantic Kitchener needed help, and he fulfilled her need to give it. She thought little of his taste but did her best to educate him, spending days working with him over designs and scouring the shops for him, dropping in now and then at the War Office to discuss the turning of a newel post on the staircase at Broome, the house that he loved and was destined never to live in, for he was drowned on a mission to Russia before it was ready for occupancy.

But in the summer of 1913, at the age of fifty, Lady Sackville needed something more in her life than being the decorator of a busy and self-centred military hero, and, as she put it bitterly, 'Lionel's unpaid housekeeper'. For one thing, Vita was to be married and she depended greatly on the society of Vita. Practical as always, she had insisted that the engagement should be a long one, not from selfish motives but because she was a little uneasy about whether Vita really loved Harold Nicolson, the young diplomat who was much in love with her. She wrote in her diary that she couldn't understand Vita, who seemed at some moments so reticent and withdrawn, at others genuinely attracted to Harold and eager to become his wife.

In 1913, after a year of reflection, Vita and Harold were determined to be married and Lady Sackville was a great deal more unworldly than her husband. Both recognized that two other suitors were 'better catches' than Harold, for they held great names and great possessions, while the Nicolsons, distinguished and able as they were, had little money, belonging to the caste of English who served the state and ran the Empire, holding eminent positions but likely to retire as poor men. However Lady Sackville liked Harold, and when Vita had convinced her that they were 'in love', she wrote firmly in her diary that she was going to write to Lionel that night telling him that she was delighted and that the wedding would take place in the early autumn, adding, 'I don't look forward much to his reply'.

Thus we have Lady Sackville, at the end of July 1913, sitting at Knole, perhaps a little bored with pasting in the clippings about the Scott case, and perhaps a little uncomfortable about her correspondence with Jacques Seligmann, the Paris dealer to whom she was to sell the rue Laffitte collection. Seery, in his beautiful '*Ma chère petite amie*' letter, had said that he wished to make her financially independent out of his superfluity and to have full control over the money that he left her; but the *objets d'art*? She had declared in court that she was fighting the case for Knole, and Knole would have been greatly enriched by the Paris segment of the Wallace collection. Instead, it was to be scattered about the world. Lady Sackville had done nothing illegal, but Seery had loved Knole and surely would have preferred that his beloved heritage from Sir Richard Wallace remain under one roof. It is unlikely that she suffered from a guilty conscience – she was always ingenious in persuading herself that whatever she did was right; but she was bored and lonely and subconsciously looking for another Seery. The result was a love affair with a curious man indeed.

William Waldorf Astor had been born in New York in 1848, and so was eleven years younger than Lady Sackville's last admirer, Pierpont Morgan. His grandfather, John Jacob Astor, had been a courageous German immigrant who founded the family fortune. The son of a butcher, he left home at the age of seventeen with an extraordinary determination to make his way in the world that enabled him to retire from business as the richest man in New York. This impressive pioneer's descendants possessed his business flair. When William Waldorf Astor's father died in 1890, his son became, according to a biographer of the Astor family, the richest man in America, with an income of six to nine million dollars a year from rents on his properties.

At the age of forty-two he therefore had the world before him, but there must have been a bitter taste in his mouth. Disliking business, he had gone into New York politics and failed. The New York press delighted in his electoral defeats; although part of his universal unpopularity must have been self-inflicted, some of it was inherited – it seems unfair to blame him for the fact that his income came in large parts from the reeking tenements possessed by the estate.

On coming into his fortune he decided to leave America and move with his sweet, rather sad wife to England, where he became a British subject, remarking 'America is good enough for any man who has to make a livelihood, though why traveled people of independent means should remain there more than a week is not readily to be comprehended'. His heirs have denied that he made the often quoted remark, 'America is not a fit place for a gentleman to live,' but it is not denied by anyone that he was snubbed by old-fashioned American patriots – Teddy Roosevelt was one.

In England he bought two splendid country houses, Cliveden and Hever Castle. Later he gave Cliveden to his son Waldorf and his wife Nancy, the famous Virginian beauty who as Lady Astor made her own career in the House of Commons and as a hostess in the 1920s and 30s. Astor also bought the *Pall Mall Gazette*, the *Pall Mall Budget*, and founded the *Pall Mall Magazine* and the Sunday *Observer*. Following munificent gifts to war funds and British charities he was given a peerage, and became Viscount Astor in 1917. His wife had died in 1904; by her he had had two sons and a daughter.

This thin sketch tells nothing of the man, but he was hard to know. An anonymous friend wrote to *The Times* when Astor died:

> In character, as in physique, he was a big man, with a singular capacity for silence and for silent action. He was always scrutinizing, vigilantly on guard . . . Despising all adverse criticism yet too sensitive to cease to resent it, his crust of protective reserve thickened and thickened. In the end he seemed an almost inaccessible personality – an imprisoned soul immured within walls of his own making . . . It was impossible for such as knew him well and could deal with him on frank, independent, human terms to doubt that he had by nature a strong capacity for friendship and affection.

The last sentence is particularly telling. If someone could get past his guard, there was another facet to the unpopular figure who had bought himself a place in English society and led a lonely life at Hever Castle, surrounded by his treasures, for he had learned to love beautiful things and to collect on a large scale. There was a sentimental and very sweet side to this outwardly grim man's nature, as Lady Sackville was to discover when after years of formal acquaintanceship he suddenly fell head over heels in love with her. As the diary is maddeningly discreet on the subject it probably would never have been known had she not kept his love letters. It was unlike her to do so especially as she implored Astor to destroy her letters to him, and he wrote approvingly that he agreed.

His first sentimental letter was dated 15 January 1913, from Sorrento, Italy. In it he told of 'the secluded retreat' at Hever, which he called 'the house of the poetic faun', to which only he had the key. He hoped to show it to her in the summer.

The correspondence was evidently extensive on both sides, but continued on a 'Dear Lady Sackville' – 'Yours, W. W. Astor' level until a certain momentous afternoon, sometime between 17 and 20 July when she visited Hever, that lovely medieval castle which had belonged to Anne Boleyn's family. He must have shown her his 'secluded retreat'. The letters changed entirely in tone:

> Have just come in from a walk . . . I smiled to notice the footprints, large and small, in the wet gravel at the House of the Poetic Faun . . . for anything I may have said and done amiss in that splendid hour's excitement I entreat forgiveness.

He begged like a schoolboy for her photograph, and wrote that he kissed her hands, adding that he hoped she would accept a little present of £10,000 in Bank of England notes, for a new garden. (Besotted as he was, the keen Astor sense of prudence evidently prevented him from writing a cheque.) He then left for a cure at Marienbad from where he wrote daily, and she must have replied daily, from his touching and very German letters. By now it is 'My dear,' and 'Sweetheart, goodbye. Yours, Will.' He wished that she was with him so that they might 'idle in the dim German forest'. He loved the occasional French in her letters. 'That momentous Saturday was the psychological hour for which you and I have unconsciously waited . . .' To think that all these years, he had been afraid of her. Alone in his lonely spa his mind returned to their *après-midi d'un Faune*:

> A woman in the flower of her prime – like yourself – needs a romantic attachment. Without it, the heart grows cold . . . It is the consciousness that someone is thinking of you, desires you, longs for the touch of your beautiful body that keeps the heart young.

The poor man was naturally frantic for the next rendezvous. Venice? No, he did not trust the discretion of Italian hotel keepers. The rather ludicrous solution was ten days at Interlaken, to be chaperoned by the engaged couple, Harold and Vita. Lady Sackville, who apparently signed herself 'B' in her letters, agreed to this and loosely placed in her diary for August 1913, lies a faded Swiss edelweiss.

The autumn brought intimate lunches at the Studio, as Astor called a very secret hide out that he retained in London, attached to the Astor estate office on the Embankment, then he left, following his usual schedule, for his villa in Italy. Perhaps the most sensitive letter from this curious man to Lady Sackville reached her on Vita's wedding day, 1 October 1913, in which he spoke of the sadness he knew that she must be feeling.

She was, in fact, too upset to attend the wedding, and stayed in bed, writing in her diary that she was too ill to go downstairs as it was the first day of her monthly period. A few days later Vita and Harold returned to Knole to say goodbye before leaving for Constantinople and their first diplomatic post abroad together. Cross-examined by her mother on her impressions of 'marriage', i.e. sex, Vita's responses were so happy that Lady Sackville rejoiced and saw them off cheerfully. Settling down at Knole with Lionel for a Vita-less winter was less cheerful. She wrote that they were irritating each other more and more, that he was very hard on her; an evening alone together was a torture. It did not seem to occur to her that small things can drive a man mad, and one of her habits had become intolerable to him. The diary of 26 November describes how she had enjoyed lunching outdoors, well-wrapped in furs, hot-water-bottle girdled. Both Lionel and Vita had been fighting this open-air mania for some time, uselessly. Snow could fall on the lunch or dinner table, and Lady Sackville would remark on the romance of the occasion, while the family and guests either shivered or sat unable to raise knife or fork because of the heavy weight of their Arctic explorer's costume. Even more trying than this was her habit of insisting on having every door at Knole kept open with door stoppers, inducing hideous drafts from room to room. Lionel was very much an outdoors man, but indoors was indoors and it is no wonder that he fled his drafty home as often as possible for the warm and cosy Olive Rubens. In February he and the Rubenses set off for Turkey to visit Harold and Vita, and at about the same time Lady Sackville embarked on a dashing adventure.

The Rolls-Royce with its hard driving chauffeur, Leconteur, tore down the straight roads of France, heading for the Mediterranean. By the chauffeur sat Grey, the discreet lady's maid. It is unlikely that she let out her sight the heavy jewel case that was her responsibility. Lady Sackville would have sat in the back and the windows would have been down, to let in all possible drafts.

Desperately lonely, still beautiful at fifty-one, she had three men waiting for her at different places in the south, and she hurried towards the sunlight, longing for comfort, and for love.

At her first stop she found little; but the story is worth telling. She had met the sculptor Auguste Rodin during one of his triumphal trips to London in 1905 – once, when he came there his carriage was drawn by his admirers, with John Singer Sargent, proud to sit on the box, holding the reins. The following year she had written asking him to do a bust of her, but the plan fell through and he came to Knole for the first time in the spring of 1913. She was charmed by him, he by her, and in the following November she went to Paris to sit for him; the result was the lovely bust now in the Musée Rodin in Paris. She wrote him an enormous number of letters in the lonely months after Vita's marriage and confided her troubles to him; he was sympathetic and immensely flattering, calling her 'my model', and comparing their relationship to that of Michelangelo and Vittoria Colonna, the Roman lady to whom Michelangelo had addressed some of the most beautiful sonnets of the Renaissance. It was arranged that they would meet in the early spring either in Rome or in the South of France, where the bust could be finished.

It has been said that Lady Sackville was a spoilt woman in middle life; but in comparison to Rodin she was nun-like in her modesty. He was now seventy-four, and looked back on a hard climb from poverty and obscurity. He was only recognized when he was forty, and even then the steps to real fame and financial security were slow and painful. It is hardly surprising that the international success he achieved by the end of the century went to his head. Paris society embraced him and he loved it, rich beauties from all over the world flocked to his studio imploring him to do their busts, he enjoyed the flattery as much as he did the dollars and the pounds and the pesos. His friends and students were bitter; calling him 'the God Pan' and 'The Sultan of Meudon' (the suburb of Paris in which he had a house), they laughed at his harem, even as they worried that his genius would suffer. One contemporary wrote that Rodin was 'seeking salvation by sensuality', and this may be true – love and death are the themes of his marvellously sensual works. An exasperated comment showed how his admirers were torn between affection and annoyance at his conduct: 'Rodin is nothing but a sexual organ, but, Good God, what an organ!'

The letters he received from women were revoltingly obsequious. Here is one example among a thousand. 'I will come to see you while you are having coffee, but I won't bother you with my tiresome presence while you are at lunch, I will just take coffee with you if you permit, dear Master. If you want a poodle take me! Until soon –' The writer bore one of the most historic names in France.

Lady Sackville never sank to this sort of thing, and by the time she knew him he was past playing the God Pan, but her curious mixture of vanity and innocence certainly led her to believe that he did love her, and her letters showed that she looked forward to the rendezvous at Cap Martin as a romantic interlude.

Instead she arrived to find a grumpy and worried old man, living in a dark little cottage with Rose Beuret, who had been his companion for fifty years and was the mother of his son. Rose had been an enchanting creature when she was his adored and adoring early model, now she was a bitter old woman who huddled in the kitchen, as jealous of Rodin's grand lady friends as she must have been terrified of them. The visit started badly; although the sculptor seemed delighted to see her and the rich stream of compliments flowed as easily as ever Lady Sackville was disappointed in her bust and even more disappointed to find that Rodin was obsessed by his money troubles. She settled down to help.

13 March 1914, Mentone
I have been doing secretary's work for Rodin every day ... he muddles up all of his letters and as soon as I have put them in order. He does not know how to draw cheques. How he has managed till now! He is in terror of having no money in the future. I lunched with them both today ... She [Rose] said that she was not uncomfortable with me. She told about the days of their poverty, she used to pose for hours and get so cold. When they had left the studio they walked home and went straight to bed without lighting the stove and without food ... she is very humble about herself.

Except for one excursion to lunch with Jean Renoir the other days of the visit appear to have been spent by Lady Sackville working on Rodin's accounts, which she straightened out ably; in between lecturing him on the subject of Rose. Courageously she told him that it was time he married Rose, and he agreed to do so. This accomplished, the Rolls was packed up and Lady Sackville departed for Italy. It was typical of the best side of her to have pitched in to help when she was needed; instead of sulking at the disappointment she must have felt. Certainly she had been in love with Rodin, and her continuing letters to him showed it. He never seemed to answer them, and she appealed pitifully for just one line from him. The archives of the Musée Rodin today contain, with her letters, some pathetic self-addressed envelopes, unused, which she must have sent him in the hopes of encouraging him to write to her.

The heavy car wound its way through the lovely Umbrian hills of early springtime in Sienna. There Lady Sackville found a man who really loved her unselfishly, and she seems to have fallen into his arms, accepting safe harbour gratefully. Baron Bildt, the 'Buggy' of Washington days, who had written to her every year on the 8th of May, the anniversary of his first proposal to her, was waiting for her. She called him R.S. in her diary.

18 March 1914, Sienna

R.S. had come to meet me. He was out buying flowers for me when I arrived . . . he has not changed in the least, except that his moustache is quite white he is the same loving old friend. He reminded me so much of Seery . . . Seery at his best. I was so glad to see him.

For the next two days they sent sightseeing. The weather was deliciously warm and they would come out of the churches and sit talking in the shadows at a café table for hours, sometimes staying up late at night. Perugia was the next hill town at which they stopped.

21 March, Perugia

R.S. and I went again over our lives and talked and talked. How his affection has resisted my hardness of all these years. He is exactly now like he was 32 years ago; it is marvellous and delightful and his affection makes me very happy, and I feel the same towards him. This hotel is very comfortable, we have a nice little sitting room and such happy talks . . . It is a real Renaissance, and as he says so truly: "Italy, spring and love – there is nothing better."

22 March, Rome

R.S. has won me again entirely. He has come at a moment when I felt so terribly lonely, having lost Vita and poor Lionel trying to like me, but being physically absolutely unable to do so. I feel I grate on him and he is tired of me, being so much in love always with somebody else. Now it is 'O' – so evident! I want my share of happiness in this world . . . I have been careful not to be talked about with W.A., but no one can find fault with an affection of 32 years.

The unlucky W.A., William Waldorf Astor, was at that very moment expecting her for a romantic rendezvous at his Villa Sirena near Sorrento, to which he had been looking forward all winter. She went, for four days, but the visit was not a success. Lady Sackville wrote, carefully referring to Astor as 'Tom':

> I feel a little sad for poor Tom; he seems disappointed in me. What else can I do? He has become hard on everybody, even against his own children and so self-centred and unfeeling about everything ... We are parting perfectly good friends, but things have changed, alas.

The Astor affair had been a brief one, but although the correspondence returned to the formality of 'Dear Lady Sackville – yours, W. W. Astor' it continued intermittently and she could not have hurt him, for his later letters were warm in tone. She had a great knack for keeping friends, and when Astor died in 1919 it is not impossible that one of the happiest memories of his dreary life was that summer which began in the 'house of the poetic faun'.

Clearly, Lady Sackville could not wait to get away from Sorrento and she was back in Rome on 7 April, writing:

> Alexandra [Baroness Bildt, wife of R.S.] came to see me and we had a long talk about R.S. How she understands our affection. She told me that he still wore around his neck a little chain with a medal of the Blessed Virgin which I gave him in Washington ... he is to be buried with that medal. She told me that she was incapable of a great and lasting love, like his for me. I told her, I was very fond of him, and she need not fear being humiliated by me in any way. I would always spare her pride and I do try.

Lady Sackville may have tried, but it seems hard to believe that she and Bildt were not the talk of Rome that spring. He was, after all, the Ambassador of Sweden.

By day they wandered at Frascati after a picnic lunch in the woods, they went sightseeing endlessly and sometimes after dining alone at a small restaurant they would visit the Colosseum by moonlight. They appeared at the golf club together, they attended parties together, and there were more excursions to the hill towns; if they happened to run into Roman acquaintances in remote places Lady Sackville would introduce Grey, her maid, as 'Miss Grey, my secretary'. This ingenuous explanation could have deceived nobody, but if Lady Sackville had any worries they must have been allayed by encouraging letters from Vita and Harold,

who had heard of the romance even in Turkey and wrote, egging
it on.

It was a dazzling spring in every capital in Europe; the guns that
were to open the most ghastly war history had ever known still
lay silent and shrouded. Of London Osbert Sitwell has written:

> An air of gaiety, unusual in northern climates, prevailed. Music
> flowed with the lightness and flash of water from under the
> striped awnings and from the balconies; while beyond the open,
> illuminated windows, in the rooms, the young men about to be
> slaughtered still feasted, unconscious of all but the moment.
> For a hundred years the social scene had not been so attractive
> to the eye . . .

Mrs Peter A. Jay, the wife of an American diplomat in Rome,
gave a charming description of two nights in Rome shortly after
Lady Sackville's arrival:

> We went to the Palazzo Colonna, which I still think is the finest
> house I have ever seen. Do you know the gallery with the
> frescoes of the Battle of Lepanto – Tiepolo or Veronese I think
> – it must be two hundred feet long. As we were new to Rome I
> was much struck by the enormous amount of jewelry the ladies
> wore, but it was all rather dirty, and the tiaras didn't shine.
> Princess Teano – her jewelry *was* marvelous, and everyone was
> looking at her. Then Lady Sackville came in on Bildt's arm, and
> she stopped the show. You never saw such jewelry, all gleaming
> and of perfect quality, she wore it beautifully and carried
> herself with such style – everyone forgot about Princess Teano.
>
> The next night we all went to another party – was it at the
> Villa Doria? I remember a long avenue of cypresses with foot-
> men holding torches. Princess Teano was there, wearing only a
> gold wreath in her hair, it could have been Etruscan and was a
> marvellous object. She looked so much better than all the ladies
> in their showy diamonds. But Lady Sackville beat her again;
> she wore nothing in her hair, which was very dark and rich and
> thick. Princess Teano must have been furious.

Every entry in the diary showed the happiness of that Roman
spring. Occasionally there was a brief interruption – a moment of
impatience from the long-suffering Alexandra Bildt, and Easter
Day, when to everyone's irritation Lord Sackville suddenly

appeared from Venice. The unhappy Bildt went to the Villa Doria just because he knew that the Sackvilles were going there for lunch, and that by standing on the corner he would see his beloved drive by.

8 May, Orvieto
It is 32 years since R.S. asked me to be his wife in Washington. Curiously enough, he was playing at proposing to me today at Orvieto between 5 and 6, when we had gone to see the Cathedral, and it was exactly the same hour when he asked me 32 years ago. Palace Hotel rather dreary, but we did not mind. We are quietly happy together.

It must have seemed to Lady Sackville that she could have stayed in Rome forever, for she began to look about for an apartment to buy. But this was unrealistic. Bildt said passionately, 'I will not give you up . . . I cannot . . .' and he clung to his friend, Count Wachtmeister, former Foreign Minister of Sweden, who came to Rome and advised him to stick to Lady Sackville: 'Care not for what people might say.' However, the situation had grown tense in the Bildt household. Alexandra's passivity had changed to jealous rage, and there was the marriage of their daughter Blanca to be considered; she was engaged to Prince Boncompagni, son of a noble house which would not have been pleased by the touch of scandal. It was time for Lady Sackville to go, and she went with Bildt to Siena for a sad farewell on 3 June, then the Rolls-Royce pulled out of the hotel courtyard, northbound. The adventure was over.

14

Difficult Years

Vita and Harold arrived in Paris in mid-June 1914, on their way back to England from Constantinople. They found Lady Sackville waiting for them, and both thought that she was going off her head, as she was obviously in an unbalanced state of mind.

It must have been a bad two weeks, alone in Paris, with the task of dealing with Seery's things from the rue Laffitte, some of which she was sending to England for her own use, but the vast mass of which were destined to be sold to Monsieur Seligmann, one of the most distinguished dealers of his time, and dispersed about the world. There was nothing dishonourable about his purchase; £270,000 was, perhaps, half the real value of the collection, but he had offered it without having been able to see the things, as the apartment was under legal seal, and Lady Sackville had grabbed his offer with the greedy acquisitiveness of her grandmother Catalina, the gypsy from Malaga.

It was an inexcusable thing to do. Seery had been devoted to Sir Richard Wallace and to break up his heritage would have seemed to him criminal. If it was not to go to Knole it should have rejoined the Wallace Collection at Hertford House. Perhaps Lady Sackville felt the reproachful ghost of Seery beside her as she worked with lists and movers in those splendid, shuttered rooms. How could she have borne to sell Seery's favourites – Houdon's *Sophie Arnould* or his *La Frileuse*, those marvellous creations? She had helped him arrange the treasures, and she knew by heart the furniture, the tapestries, the pictures and the sculpture, which was the finest collection of eighteenth-century French sculpture in private hands.

The blind eyes may have seemed to look at her as the men lifted the objects into their excelsior-lined cases, and their regard would not have been a kind one.

Lady Sackville spent her evenings unusually quietly as she waited for the Nicolsons; she wrote that she missed Bildt and felt very much alone. It is highly unlikely that she would have considered breaking up his marriage and retiring with him to Sweden; she was fond of him but she was far too conventional to have taken such a step. Still, it had been a lovely interlude and a flattering experience; it must have been hard to contemplate the cold return to Knole. And she had just had a horrible shock. There is no record of the date it occurred, but on 21 June she wrote to Rodin and on the 22nd to her solicitor of her brother Henry's suicide. She gave no details except to say that he had died leaving many debts, which she wished to pay, as well as his funeral expenses. This must have brought back every sort of memory – the little boy whose poignant letters she had answered from the convent, desperately attempting to be a surrogate mother at the age of twelve, the tall boy whom she had outfitted for boarding school, the young man who wrote affectionate letters to her from South Africa – then, sadly, the paranoid figure across the courtroom in the illegitimacy case.

She returned to England with Harold and Vita to await with them the birth of Vita's first child at Knole. Throughout late July the diary carried the increasingly ominous daily news of impending war – culminating in the terrible night of 4 August 1914, when Vita and she, hardly able to take it in, saw Lionel come downstairs dressed in his khaki uniform. This was no routine departure for Yeomanry manoeuvres, but Lionel was not one for drama. He said to his wife in the familiar tone and words that he had so often used, 'Dear, I must be going now', gave her a quick kiss on the cheek, and jumped into the waiting car.

Benedict Nicolson was born two days later. Lady Sackville had sat up all night waiting for Vita to send for her, but the summons never came, and she felt doubly rejected when the triumphant Harold burst out of Vita's room to announce the news and, on seeing Olive Rubens waiting also, enthusiastically invited her to be godmother.

This nearly spoiled Lady Sackville's pleasure in 'the dear little baby', and she made far too much of the incident, wallowing in self-pity. But everything she did that first month of the war was embarrassing. There was the correspondence with Lord Kitchener, in which she asked him to give Lionel a safe staff job; and when he replied that he could make no exception for an individual officer she wrote back that she understood, but that perhaps the carpenters at Knole might be exempted? She didn't quite ask for the footmen to be let off, but came close to it with the plea that she knew Lord Kitchener would feel as she did that parlourmaids were middle-class, 'I must say that I had never thought that I would see parlourmaids at Knole . . . instead of liveries and even powdered hair.' Lord Kitchener's reply was polite and evasive.

Her next step was to organize a hospital in the Great Hall. This was exactly the sort of administrative work that she should have accomplished admirably, but the effort was unsuccessful after an enthusiastic start. The truth was that Lady Sackville was running into a nervous breakdown, and the diary broke off on 5 September, to start again the following July after a winter during which she had been very ill.

Summing it up, she wrote:

Feeling my mind give way with all of my worries . . . and feeling depressed enough to take my life, I went to see Dr Woods.

Dr Woods must have been an able man. Lady Sackville attri-buted her collapse to Henry's suicide, the declaration of war and her ensuing anxiety for Lionel, Vita's indifference and Harold's rudeness to her at the time of the baby's birth, and above all, Olive. 'I saw Olive's influence growing and growing over Lionel, who is madly in love with her.'

While it can only be conjecture, it is possible that Dr Woods reached back into profounder causes for her breakdown. Perhaps he told her that the human being can only take a certain amount of strain, and he may have reminded her that she had lost her child-hood at the age of eight when Pepita died, that she had no adoles-cence and had been flung straight from the convent into an adult position of great responsibility in Washington, and had found security in her success there, only to be thrown into despair by the humiliation her adored father suffered following the Murchison incident. Marriage to Lionel had brought not only renewed security but also total happiness for nearly ten years, but the shock of finding a love letter from him to Joan Camden in 1899 had opened the Pandora's box of uncertainty which was never again to be closed, and the companionship that Seery brought her, while indispensable, could never replace Lionel, the only man she ever really loved in every sense. Dr Woods might also have asked her about the strain of the sibling relationship, and been told about the agony of the long-drawn-out illegitimacy case and the disloyalty of her sisters, the pain of her ageing father, and the culmination of the notorious trial in which she had to hear her mother's and father's private lives described in the courtroom and know that the story of her own illegitimacy was being blazoned by the press of the world. The Seery trial had been a triumph – but an immense strain. Very few people can have lived more intensively; and those who have done so have often burned out young. Thanks to her own stamina and to Dr Woods's skill Lady Sackville recovered, and less than a year later was writing in her diary of her gratitude to her doctor, of her renewed closeness to Vita, and of her hope that she had attained philosophy and calm. She felt guilty about her maid Grey, who had had a terrible time during the months of depression. Lady Sackville could be impossible with servants, but her own lady's maids seemed to have been devoted to her and they were the ones who saw the most of her and had to put up with the tempers and whims. Grey was in her service for nearly twenty years, to be replaced by a French maid, Louise Genoux, who complained only of the cold in any house inhabited by Lady Sackville; the poor Frenchwoman found that thick layers of brown paper pinned beneath her skirts were some protection against the drafts.

Lady Sackville lost no one close to her in the war; in this she was almost alone among her contemporaries. Lionel fought in hard campaigns, Gallipoli, Palestine and France. They corresponded every day but were separated by far more than geography, and when he came home, once invalided out and twice on leave, she wrote sadly, 'We seem to be worse strangers than ever'. The Rubenses, to the rage of Lady Sackville, spent part of the war installed in the laundry at Knole, which Lionel had arranged for them, and each time he came back to England he spent every moment that he could with Olive. She must have been a hard person to hate; even the jealous Lady Sackville could not help noting her charm and warmth.

> Olive sang charmingly after dinner and danced . . . Olive came to say goodbye and seemed so genuinely grateful to me . . .

Knole was shut up for most of the war, a skeleton staff remained and Stubbs, the head gardener, was ordered by Lady Sackville to neglect the flowers, turn the lawn and the Green Court into hay, force vegetables and 'just keep the greenhouse from freezing'.

She lived in Hill Street, where she wrote long and intelligent daily passages in her diary about the progress of the war. Always shrewd, seldom original, her entries on topical subjects were less interesting than her conversation must have been but they showed a great change from the earlier diaries in which she was rarely observant of public events. She was never 'clever' in the sense of intellectual brilliance, but her chameleon-like nature absorbed the opinions of those around her and the last years of the war brought her many new and clever friends. Loyal to the old ones, she continued to see a good deal of W. W. Astor and through him had become close to J. L. Garvin, the editor of the *Observer*, who brought the news to Hill Street; and, inevitably, he was soon confiding his private troubles to her sympathetic ear. 'He told me the romance of his life, a touching story . . .' There were Lord Leverhulme and Gordon Selfridge, two self-made millionaires whose energy and power appealed to her; they too became close personal friends.

Lady Sackville, freed from her husband's conventional milieu, enjoyed mixing people up and she must have been one of the best hostesses in London.

14 November 1917, London
Have rearranged my yellow and red and rose glass window in spite of the threat of air raids. My windows are all wired outside.

The 'Persian Room' was her great pride. It was not Persian at all; it was Turkish, but as Vita wrote, after her mother had decided it was Persian no one took the risk of contradicting her. This Arabian Nights room must have been very beautiful. It had painted panelling carrying views of imaginary cities, and romantic, mysterious lattice windows which gave onto nothing. Sir Osbert Sitwell described it:

From time to time, I would go there to dine with her alone. I would find her, before dinner, sitting in the Persian Room . . . the arabesques, and small tightly painted roses and cypresses blazoned on the walls recalled Granada, and Andalusia, and thus the strain in her own blood from which sprang the particular strange quality she possessed . . . The decoration of her houses, indeed, mirrored her personality; yet the ancestral cave in the Albaicin was to be detected in it, no less than the ancestral palace ... Indeed, Lady Sackville lived in a world almost imaginary ... but there was nothing petty about her; she was capable of acts of imaginative kindness and of cruelty, she was clever and cunning and silly and brave and timid and avaricious, extravagant and most generous, possessed the best taste and the worst, and was, in all, one of the most vivid personalities I have ever met.

This description missed a side that perhaps Lady Sackville never showed to young Sitwell, whom she received in the dimly lighted room in which she mesmerized those who entered it into thinking that instead of being in foggy London they were actually being protected by the latticed windows from the hot and glaring sunlight of the East. This was the sheer fun of her entertainments. Whether it was the poet Robert Graves, the painter Augustus John, the great French actors Lucien and Sacha Guitry, the writers Somerset Maugham or Arnold Bennett, Lord Berners, the connoisseur, her old friend Jennie Churchill and her new women friends, Lady Cunard and Lady Colefax; the young Duff Coopers or Lytton Strachey; Condé Nast of New York, or Lord Hardinge, Viceroy of India, they all left the house happier for having been in it. Her food was original and very good, combining the best of French cooking with American dishes from long ago to which she remained faithful. 'Waffles are really my favourite dish . . . At last I have got Selfridge's to import peach fed Virginia hams, there is nothing like them.' And thanks to her friendship with Gordon Selfridge she was able to offer a real innovation for dessert after the war – American ice-cream sodas which were sent over from the store with straws through which the guest could suck away to his heart's content.

As Lady Sackville spent a great deal of her time cheering up people whom she thought to be unhappy, and one of her ways of doing it was to feed them well and give them good wine, it was not surprising to have her write in a diary of the early twenties of the farewell *tête-à-tête* lunch she had given a distraught suitor of Vita's before he left England. 'Poor G.S. [Geoffrey Scott] seemed so unhappy, but I think I cheered him up with lobsters stuffed with caviar.' They drank Château-Yquem; that famous white Bordeaux must have been Lady Sackville's favourite, as it appeared frequently in the diaries. Very heavy and very sweet, it was her panacea for all her troubles. The effects of it could be compared to sticking an ice pick into any but an Edwardian liver, but the taste was nectar.

Enid Bagnold, in conversation, has described Lady Sackville as a hostess:

> She made people talk, because they were teased or contradicted. She stirred up men to talk (not women, so much) and if the party was going well she wouldn't say anything herself. But if there was a moment of dullness she knew how to start things up again – one was always on tiptoes, trying to be at one's best.

This was the London Lady Sackville, the brilliant hostess whose chief private pleasure was Vita and her two babies; for Ben's birth was followed by that of the Nicolson's last child, Nigel, in 1917. Knole was another story. Lionel returned to England three times between campaigns, and for good in 1918, but instead of joy in the reunion the unhappy mistress of Knole found only sorrow as Olive Rubens's influence increased.

Walter Rubens and his wife had been friends of Lionel and Victoria's as far back as the Seery days. When Olive became Lionel's mistress is unclear, but this cheerful, kind woman was probably the antithesis of the temperamental Victoria. She had been an opera singer, married to a rather dim figure who suffered from tuberculosis and evidently accepted Lionel's hospitality complacently. Lady Sackville called Olive Rubens 'that snake in the grass' when she wrote her *Book of Reminiscences*, but every record shows her to have been a most open and charming person. The following diary entry shows the pain that Lionel gave his wife at Knole:

19 November 1917
I went back to Knole and found Olive there. L. had altered the library greatly. I had a sad shock when I got to his room, as my two portraits, when I was 2 and 23, which had been hanging there since 1889, had been put out of sight.

She was already thinking about another home, partly because of her insatiable love of decoration and possibly because she may have felt that Knole might become untenable. In May 1918, she bought three contiguous houses on Sussex Square, in Brighton, and started

to plan the arrangement of them with the advice of Sir Edwin
Lutyens, the great architect. Later that summer she sent seven
vans of furniture to Brighton from Knole. 'I don't want to spoil
Knole, and take too many of my things away; I love Knole too
much for that.'

During the autumn and winter of 1918–19 the atmosphere grew
increasingly strained between the Sackvilles:

1 October 1918, Brighton
Letter from L. telling me he proposes the Walter Rubenses
should live in the Green Court . . . What an impossible situation.

5 April 1919, Knole
I arrived about 6.00 and went around the garden calling for
Lionel, as Vita had remained in London. I was amazed to see
under one of the tulip trees, O. and L. in each other's arms and
kissing!! Just like any soldier and his girl in the Park. I got away
as quick as I could and tore to the sycamore seat. They must
have seen me . . .

They had, and both Olive and Lionel apologized humbly to her.
She did not seem to take the episode very seriously at the time,
although she must have been hurt. The end came the next month,
during the weekend of 17 May 1919. The trivial cause was that
Lionel had mentioned that the Rubenses, who had been away,
were coming down to stay for 'a day or two'. Victoria said if they
came she would leave, and went upstairs to pack. Poor Vita spent
an awful weekend running between her parents carrying notes back
and forth. She wrote that she felt sure that if her father had shown
any tenderness her mother would have changed her mind, instead,
in answer to the heartbreaking notes signed 'Vicky' came back
correct, cold answers of which this is an example:

Monday [May 19]
I still think that you are making a great mistake in going away,
but as it is your decision and choice I will say no more about it,
except that if, in course of time, you feel like coming back, the
door will not be entirely closed to you. I cannot take the whole
blame for what has happened but I am sorry for the pain which
you have been caused.

L.

Vita thought that her father, returning from the war as a leader of men, having seen much and suffered much, was a stronger figure than he had been before it and so resented the fact that his wife had become the administrator of Knole, outside and inside. This would be plausible if there was a word of evidence to prove that Lionel had ever been anything but lazy about Knole affairs and delighted to have Victoria do the dirty work from the time of their marriage on. Harold Nicolson had written shrewdly to Vita the preceding Christmas:

Poor B.M.!* Poor Dada! How happy each could be without the other! . . . I have the impression that Dada wants to make Knole more or less impossible for B.M. Perhaps I am wrong, but I feel that he has come to the conclusion that it is only by being rather cruel that he can beat her. I think he is right, of course, because if he is nice to her, she will only take advantage of it.

On the Sunday Lady Sackville went up to Hill Street to collect some things, taking Sir Edwin Lutyens, who happened to be at Knole. with her, Lutyens did not know what had passed, but seeing her distress he attempted to divert her during the drive by talking about future plans for another, small house that she might build. She returned to Knole that same evening. The next day she left for Brighton:

I left at 4.00 with a very heavy heart. The last thing I did was to kiss Ben and Nigel. Grey was so nice in the car as we motored to Brighton and said she was now glad that her Billy had not come to fetch her away, as she could be with me in my great trouble. Vita has been SUCH a comfort and has lavished love on me.

A week later Lady Sackville was back in London, buying Golliwogs for Ben and Nigel and giving a lunch party, to which came the actress Mrs Patrick Campbell and the opera singer Melba.

Melba and Mrs Pat were most amusing. They tore all singers to pieces especially Mary Garden and Olive Rubens. Mr Selfridge sent me some wonderful ice cream sodas for dessert.

This cheerful entry might have suggested that she didn't care about leaving Knole; but she did care, only the pain was less

* B.M. was a family name for Lady Sackville: *Bonne Maman* (grandmother).

intense now that she had crossed her Rubicon. Still she thought and wrote often of Lionel – the above passage ended:

Oh, shade of that tulip tree, where they were kissing and hugging and God knows what, as I did not stop long enough to look, and I ran away in terror of being seen by Lionel, who saw me. Is Walter [Rubens] a rogue or a simpleton?

In June she wrote that she missed Knole much more than she missed Lionel. Vita must have been infinitely relieved that her mother, far from collapsing as she had in 1915, was able to go on as the still vigorous, still fascinating Mama who in turn enchanted and infuriated her. She may not have realized that Lady Sackville was at her worst when she had nothing to do and felt that no one needed her. Now, in 1919, Vita herself was in deep trouble and her mother's mind was, for once, more on her child than it was on herself.

Her daughter's career had been a source of pride to Lady Sackville. The first of the four novels that she was to produce between 1919–24 was *Heritage,* and to Vita's embarrassment Lady Sackville used to rush about London chivvying the booksellers, probably waving in their faces the best reviews. Then the marriage was such a success; the little boys were adorable and the charming Harold was considered by the Foreign Office to be extremely able. Their life was divided between a beautiful London house on Ebury Street and Long Barn, near Knole, where both Nicolsons delighted in the garden they were making.

Lady Sackville could not have known or guessed that Vita had for some time been torn between her natural inclination towards women and her true affection for Harold. During the winter of 1910–11 Lady Sackville had taken a house in the South of France, following Vita's pneumonia, and a childhood playmate of Vita's, Rosamund Grosvenor, had accompanied them. The visit lasted for several months, and Lady Sackville had written happily of how well the girls were getting on. Nothing in her upbringing would have led her to suspect that her child had entered into her first physical love affair; her innocence was complete. Violet Keppel was another childhood friend, and her mother and Lady Sackville had known each other since the nineties. What could have been more natural that Vita and Violet should wander off to Cornwall together during the spring of 1918? They shared a love of wild flowers which Lady Sackville understood were profuse in that beautiful part of England. The visit was extended, but still Lady Sackville, busy with her new house wrote calmly enough from Brighton on 24 October:

> Lovely weather . . . Vita came for tea. Poor H. is rather distressed at her tremendous friendship with V.K. because he says she tries to destroy their love and home life by turning it constantly into ridicule. He says it is so insidious.
>
> Dr George Williamson came to lunch and was interesting about Queen Elizabeth on the researches made as to her curious-shaped body and still more curious insides, which would count for many of her vagaries . . .

This is typical of Lady Sackville's interest in anything new, and she gave more space in that entry to Queen Elizabeth's insides than she did to the Nicolsons. However, two days later the alarm was sounded with a flurry. In a guarded entry Lady Sackville recorded that Harold, utterly miserable, had come to 'open his heart to me'. What she felt was probably best expressed in a cry of pain from a later entry:

> Had another letter from my poor Vita in the same sad strain, like a broken hearted lover. If V.T. [Violet Keppel had by now married Denys Trefusis] was a man, I could understand, but for a woman, such a love beats me and I try so hard to understand.

Understand she could not, but she settled down to fight for her child. Violet came to Brighton the next week and Lady Sackville listened while she recounted how horrid Harold was to Vita, nagging and fault-finding and above all stifling her literary career. If Vita, who was not according to Violet at all in love with Harold, could strike out on her own – why, Hugh Walpole had said that Vita might be one of the leading novelists of the day. Lady Sackville recorded this, adding only one comment at the end. 'I am suspicious.'

A few weeks later she was more than suspicious; she was desperately worried. Vita had come to her for the Armistice, 11 November:

> Day of Days! . . . The nightmare of four years ceased! I heard a merry peal of the neighbouring church. Everybody began

ringing little dinner bells. I rang my big bell, which Harold gave me, out of the window when I saw Ben and Nigel coming home in the distance. Vita and I want to impress on Ben's memory this great event, and he probably will never forget my bell.

But the glorious day was overshadowed by an intimate talk with Vita that night:

Vita's remarks about Harold being physically so cold have made me ill ... it is so hard on her, poor child ... he is always so sleepy and has her in a desperate hurry. So many men are like that and lose.

When Vita and Violet went off together that winter to Monte Carlo Lady Sackville blamed it on the fact that Vita and Harold were both frightened of Violet, 'poor, misguided things', and her adjectives for Violet were 'pernicious' and 'amoral'. Hating the gossip, loathing the whole thing, she remained throughout the affair supportive of and affectionate to Vita, barring one moment that same winter when she lost her temper over what she called the neglect of the two little boys, aged three and one, but partly she meant the boredom of coping with their tiresome governess and discussing plans with her fellow grandmother, Lady Carnock. She telegraphed for Vita to return, and she did, defiantly.

1919 was the year that Lady Sackville left Knole, leaning heavily and gratefully on Vita's love. For poor Vita, it must also have been a terrible year; torn between her parents' drama and her own. In October she left again to join Violet at Monte Carlo. The boys were sent with their nurse to Knole with their grandfather and then to their grandmother at Brighton. Harold was on the British Staff of the newly born League of Nations. By December he was unnerved enough by the uncertainty of his future to send for his formidable mother-in-law.

7 December 1919
I've had an urgent message from Harold asking me to go to Paris to help him with Vita ... when she first comes back to him. I have had an awful time getting passports ...

Lady Sackville was in Paris the next night, to be received by Harold with open arms.

Poor Harold had stayed up to receive me and had prepared supper, cold chicken and potato salad and champagne. Lovely flowers, and he had kept my windows open. He is so touchingly kind. We talked about Vita, who has disappeared again, until four o'clock in the morning. He does not know if she is coming back. He has telegraphed to Monte Carlo four times, no answer. He is so unhappy. I tried to comfort him but I feel pretty miserable and anxious myself.

The next day was worse.

No further news tonight about Vita. He has been six days without any news from her and has no idea where she is. He says she is breaking his career, for which he was so well fitted, and if she does not come back for good and all, he must get divorced and disappear; such as going to China and take up another life.

Poor Harold. Poor Lady Sackville. However, during the days and nights waiting for Vita, who finally returned nearly two weeks later, Lady Sackville was at her best, as always when under severe stress. In the diary there was not a moment of self-pity, not to mention of the psychosomatic headaches and other ills of the flesh to which she was subject when she was not totally engaged, extending herself to the limits of her capacities. She must have tried to give Harold a very good time. Apparently, from the diary entries, she interested herself in his work, and it is not impossible that, displaying the quality that had endeared her to many men, she would have greeted the harassed young diplomat on his return from the office in the evening with an astonishing knowledge of the niceties of the problems before the League of Nations, knowing just the questions to ask, the right compliments to pay to the British Delegation; subtly and soothingly leaving Harold with the impression that without him, Clemenceau and Lloyd George might have had a duel on the Champ de Mars that night. Vita had never heard of the League of Nations when her husband's appointment had been announced. The diary continued:

18 December 1919, Paris
Vita is back with her hair short because she says it comes out by the handful. How I regret it, but I said nothing as she looked lovely all the same, and I was so glad to have her back. She has

been so nice to Harold all day and stayed with him all the time. [Harold had just come down with a badly infected knee.] She told me of her gambling in Monte Carlo and we hardly talked of V.T. She does not look a bit sad, which surprises me, and on the surface shows no change.

Lady Sackville returned to London in January, still uneasy.

Until that beautiful book, *Portrait of a Marriage*, was published in 1973 no one could have had an idea of the white-heat intensity of Vita's passion for Violet. Even Harold was unprepared for the crisis, which came in February. It is impossible to read Vita's account without compassion, and a certain awe, for there can be few love affairs in English literature that have been described so frankly, or more honestly. Less strong than her lover – Harold had truly written to her, 'When you fall into Violet's hands, you become like a jellyfish addicted to cocaine,' – she agreed to leave England forever.

Violet went first, Vita was to join her in France a day later. They took money, and planned to buy a house together, possibly in Sicily. At Dover Violet's husband accosted Vita and followed her to France. On what she thought of as her last night in England Vita had sat up writing letters in the King's Head Hotel, and the first one was to her mother:

I daren't think what you must imagine after my last telegram . . . This afternoon Denys arrived . . . and he will ask her to return to him, and I alas! shall do all I can to make her, but whether I shall succeed I very much doubt . . . if she refuses, God alone knows what is going to happen . . . Oh, Mama, don't think I am not taking it seriously. I know only too well that somebody's heart will be broken by tomorrow night, probably mine – I HOPE mine – and I think of you.

Although her pity for the wretched Denys Trefusis, Violet's husband, made her feel that she must offer to persuade Violet to go back to him, Vita must have been very sure that Violet would refuse. She did so, and the defeated Denys left the defiant pair at Amiens. Then George Keppel, Violet's father, rushed across the Channel to bring back the runaways, but his journey to Amiens was futile. The next rescue operation was conducted by Lady Sackville from Hill Street.

13 February 1920, London

Harold has just arrived from Paris. He told me that he had no idea where Vita was. I persuaded him to see Denys, which he agreed willingly to do. He is in a most pitiful state. After he had left me to go to his conference, I went straight to Grosvenor Street and interviewed Denys ... He is going to fly to Amiens tomorrow at 7, and I asked him to take Harold as he had a two-seater aeroplane, and he most readily said he would. I took him to Cadogan Gardens where he saw Harold and arranged everything with him. Denys was very cool and collected, and fully determined to bring Violet back or have done with her.

14 February 1920

No news from Vita. I have been thinking all day of those two husbands flying to Amiens to try and each get his wife back; quite like a sensational novel.

This entry and the one above it are pure Lady Sackville. Calm and forceful in emergency, she however could never resist the pleasure of drama.

The husbands won, and the Violet–Vita affair gradually subsided. Lady Sackville intervened once more when Vita attempted to publish her novel, *Challenge*, which she had written at the height of her infatuation. This devastating revelation of Violet's character (Eve in the book) is very curious, as it was written while Vita was madly in love with Violet and they went over the manuscript together every night. Lady Sackville got the book suppressed and paid off the publisher. (It was published in America in 1924 and in England in 1973.) The novelist Mrs Belloc Lowndes was the one who brought Vita around; she came to see Lady Sackville after reading the book and said that in her opinion it would be a grave mistake to publish it, adding to Lady Sackville that 'Vita *unconsciously* described the fight which Violet had made to conquer her'.

This was just what Lady Sackville thought, and she further thought the book 'brilliantly boring', but when Mrs Belloc Lowndes said that it contained passages of great beauty she instantly agreed; she was never sure of her literary judgements. *Challenge* is anything but boring once one catches on to the fact that Eve and Julian are Violet and Vita and that Harold is symbolized by a Greek island to which Julian is loyal. But how could Vita have characterized her lover as she did, selfish, lazy, unpleasant to the last degree, except in bed, and still have remained under her spell? As Lady Sackville felt, publication would have shown Vita up as a puppet in the hands of a sorceress, and there had been quite enough scandal.

Nigel Nicolson in his introduction to the most recent edition of *Challenge* wrote, 'This was Vita's declaration of her understanding of love, it should be lit by magnesium, clouded by pain.'

After the crises of the Violet affair the Nicolson marriage became a happy, lasting one, in spite of episodes that might well have broken up other homes. Their secret was to allow each other unlimited freedom, and they were apparently quite frank about their affairs. It is not recorded when Lady Sackville discovered that Harold was also a homosexual, but it must have upset her terribly. She wrote in the *Book of Reminiscences*:

> Vita is absolutely devoted to Harold, but there is nothing whatever sexual between them, which is strange in such a young and good-looking couple. She is not in the least jealous of him, and willingly allows him to relieve himself with anyone. They both openly said so when I was staying at Long Barn, and Reggie Cooper . . . was there too. It shocked me extremely.

15
'Quel Roman est ma Vie!'

When Lady Sackville wrote her *Book of Reminiscences* in 1922, at the age of sixty, she was still a very attractive woman. Everyone who knew her then remembered her beautiful complexion. Never using makeup, she took immense pains to keep her lovely soft skin. Edwardian beauties shielded their faces from the sun with parasols as well as wide-brimmed hats, even an open fire was a possible threat; hence the firescreens were made at face level. Although she was much too fat she knew how to dress and her friends do not today speak of her heavy figure. They instead remember her charm, the seductive, accented low voice and the fun she gave them. Mary Links, the daughter of Sir Edwin Lutyens, has described how as children she and her sisters and brothers looked forward to going to Hill Street:

> She was very kind to us, and I remember a wonderful perfume, which was in her house and on her clothes. It was not very sweet, nor heavy like incense, it was a lovely, rather fresh scent.

This must have been the essence of heliotrope that Lady Sackville used to order from Paris, or the essence of violets which she also favoured.

She went on making new friends. In 1923 she attended the wedding of Prince and Princesse Jean de Faucigny-Lucinge, and found the young French bridegroom enchanting; the bride, Baba d'Erlanger, was the daughter of one of her great friends in London. The Faucigny-Lucinges became one of the most popular couples in European society; invited everywhere, admired and sought after as much in London as they were in Paris, where they lived, they never came to England during the 1920s without looking up Lady Sackville for the sheer pleasure of being with her. They put up with the draughts at Brighton, and the mania for meals outdoors at odd hours, wrapped in rugs. They loved her talk and were touched by her generosity; 'Every time we saw her she had a little present for us.' Like Mary Lutyens and everyone who knew her, 'Johnny' Lucinge above all remembered her foreignness. 'She could never have been mistaken for an Englishwoman, she was never assimilated.' Lucinge thought that she was battling against insecurity to the end; that for the English she was still a foreign adventuress like her mother.

Both reporters spoke of her great taste. The Brighton house on Sussex Square took more than two years to do over, and Vita deplored the immense size and extravagance of it – there were twenty-four bedrooms. Lady Sackville's excuse that it would be a happy holiday home for Ben and Nigel was absurd, for the little boys would probably have preferred a cottage. However, it was a splendid opportunity for their grandmother to employ her truly original taste as a decorator. This description suggests an Arabian Nights quality at Brighton reminiscent of the famous Persian Room in Hill Street:

20 August 1919
What is pretty now is the way I have arranged the long arches in the Privy garden. There is the tulip room with glass doors, then the Ming recess with thick Ming flowers and fruit and green painted chairs. Then a little pantry for Florence and Rose as I have meals out of doors. The other side of the tunnel has two recesses. One done with red chairs, red pots filled with real violet phloxes and a large tin painted red and gold containing China flowers, mostly white and blue, and above this tin is a glass picture, Chinese, with red and blue draperies and harmonizing with my blue and white flowers. That recess is as if it belongs to a Russian ballet. The last recess has green and white chairs and big tin bowls of sweet peas.

It will be noticed that Lady Sackville mixed the blue and white porcelain flowers of the Ming dynasty with 'real violet phloxes' without giving it a thought, and the effect must have been theatrically lovely. But to her daughter Vita, a truly distinguished horticulturalist, her mother's indiscriminate gardening was a torture. Lady Sackville worked very hard over her gardens, both in Brighton and London; in order to find plants for Ebury Street she used to be at Covent Garden Market by eight in the morning, and was always childishly pleased when she pulled off a garden that might please Vita. In 1924 she was delighted with her 'Botticelli' spring garden, and listed yellow primroses, tulips, wall flowers, border of aubretias, carpeting of red daisies, clumps of different coloured primulas. All of this sounds very pretty, but what Vita could not bear was that if there was a gap in the delphinium border Lady Sackville would happily fill in with a line of *tin* delphiniums. 'At least one is rid of *ces détestables* slugs,' she would say.

As unrestrained as she was exuberant, fake flowers suited her just as well as real ones. The last house that she did over was at Streatham, outside London, in 1929. Miss Honey Harris, a talented young woman who had become a close friend recalled how eager Lady Sackville had been to impress Vita. One day it occurred to Lady Sackville that it would be amusing to have the stair treads painted like shelves of books; she was always keen on decorative objects that were not in fact what they seemed to be. Miss Harris worked away on the fake books and was also employed painting door frames to look like tortoiseshell; Lady Sackville was delighted with the results and worried only about what Vita would think of the garden, large, but with no flowers in it; so she sent Honey Harris to buy £30 worth of artificial flowers the morning that Vita was coming to lunch for the first time. Leaning out of the window, she instructed her young friend where the flowers should go. 'She always liked to "buck up" anything,' Miss Harris said, adding, 'Vita must have found it ridiculous. She said nothing, looked very grave and withering, and made no comment before she left.'

In 1920 Lady Sackville left 34 Hill Street for 182 Ebury Street, the house that had been bought for the Nicolsons and in which Nigel had been born in 1917. This was a lovely house, filled with Seery's things, with a fine dining room by Lutyens. The Nicolsons' main base was Long Barn, their country home in Kent. There Vita wrote; her first novels and short stories were followed by an account of her ancestors, *Knole and the Sackvilles*, then came a travel book, *Passenger to Teheran*, and in 1927 she established her reputation as a poet with *The Land*, which won the Hawthornden prize. *The Edwardians* is perhaps the most famous of her later books: the setting is Knole and it is, in the author's opinion, the best novel ever written about the society of the time.

Harold had gone from the Foreign Office during the war to the Paris Peace Conference, then to the League of Nations, the British

Legation at Teheran as counsellor in 1925, the British Embassy at Berlin as its second-ranking official in 1927. He too wrote, brilliantly; *Some People* made a sensation during the twenties, and his later biographies and essays are classics.

Vita loathed the diplomatic life; and except for occasional visits to Harold at his posts abroad remained in England. The boys were brought up between Long Barn and Ebury Street, with visits to Brighton and Knole and occasional holidays at Berlin when Harold was serving there. Lady Sackville's diaries were full of descriptions of her grandsons, typically grandmotherly. There was the day at Brighton when Ben was caught in the nick of time teaching baby Nigel to throw himself out of an upstairs window; there was the terrible episode of Ben swallowing a pin – she was proud of him for being so brave under the X-ray; there was a happier day when Lady Sackville and Ben, aged three, walked solemnly down the drive from Knole to Sevenoaks, each kicking a round stone, to the pleasure of both. There were the usual childish illnesses to worry over, the exchange of letters with Vita about them, and the time that Nigel was operated upon for tonsils and adenoids in the Brighton house. Ever proud of Vita, there was a charming scene in 1921; Lady Sackville reading aloud to six-year-old Ben a glowing review of his mother's latest novel, *The Dragon in Shallow Waters*.

Besides having the family and the decoration of her house to divert her, Lady Sackville in the early twenties was still a very popular member of London society. The two houses that she went to the most were Lady Colefax's and Lady Cunard's, and these two hostesses were not women who would have put up with a bore at their tables. There she continued to meet some of the cleverest men and women in London, and she grew more discriminating than she had been when she had first liberated herself from Lionel's hunting and fishing friends. The novelist Arnold Bennett, she wrote severely, 'paid too many compliments to be sincere'. She herself entertained enormously, both Ebury Street and Brighton were always full of guests. The latter was a second home to the American illustrator George Plank and to Oswald Dickinson, a barrister who held the extraordinary title of Secretary to the Commissioners in Lunacy. Ozzie, as he was called, was a tremendous gossip who amused Lady Sackville enormously. Eve Fleming and Enid Bagnold Jones were the women she saw most often at

Brighton. Mrs Fleming, the widow of Valentine Fleming, was the mother of two boys who were to become famous, Peter and Ian.

But these faithful friends were peripheral figures compared to the man who was central to her life, Sir Edwin Lutyens.

Lady Sackville had met Lutyens for the first time in June 1916, in Lady Cunard's opera box. A few days later she lunched with him and his wife at their house and noted in her diary how amusing he was, how dull was his wife. From then until she could no longer write legibly, sixteen years later, his name occurred in her diaries more often than that of any other except Vita's. It was the longest, most complex love affair of Lady Sackville's life.

He was forty-seven when they met, she fifty-four, and they came together at a time when each needed the other. Lutyens was a highly successful architect, up to then known chiefly for his country houses, but now embarked on his masterpiece, the Viceroy's House in New Delhi, a palace that took twenty years to build. Already a public figure, he was considered one of the wittiest men in London, known for his bubbling, spontaneous fun and for his immense charm. The lion-hunting hostess, Lady Cunard, must have been delighted to have him in her box that night to hear Verdi's *Otello*, just as other hostesses rejoiced in his company all his life. Lady Diana Cooper has said: 'Duff and I would give up anything if Ned Lutyens were free for lunch – he was such fun, oh, you can't think.'

The public figure was much at variance with the essential dedicated man, whose imaginative life, which was his real life, was lived privately. A contemporary wrote of him:

> Years ago Edwin Lutyens was suspected of being the only man in England capable of taking architecture seriously and the suspicion has proved absolutely correct ... He is a rather big man with a phenomenally round, bald head, provocatively innocent eyes, curiously set. He wears a steep butterfly collar and a neat, ordinary tie, and moves with a certain critical, half-humorous deliberation, by no means unimpressive.

Luytens came from an army family; as one of fourteen children he was a poor young man when he fell in love with and married Lady Emily Lytton, a shy, sensitive girl from a very distinguished, aristocratic house. He charmed his way into his mother-in-law's heart by saying to her: 'I would wash your feet with my hair. It is true that I have very little hair, but then you have very little feet.' The Countess of Lytton was delighted by this sally.

His bride had looked forward to a great romance and a wonderful honeymoon, and her disillusion was intense when her husband proved to be a rough and rather cool lover. They produced a family of four girls and a boy, but two years after the birth of the last child Lady Emily broke off sexual relations with Lutyens. Another cause for friction was that although she had tried to learn about architecture in order to share his professional life, he had rejected her efforts to show her love and affection in that way and so perhaps make up for the lack of harmony in their intimate married life. She was probably not a gifted pupil, and it must have bored her husband to have tried to explain his highly original ideas to her. Even today he is admired as having had the same spirit as Frank Lloyd Wright which is called 'organic' by architects, and has to do with designing (unlike Renaissance buildings) from a centre core, moving outwards like a lotus flower; the concept is that of a nautilus shell, the flow of space is in an expanding spiral. Not the sort of thing easily grasped by a young woman brought up by governesses in Victorian England.

Poor Emily Lutyens turned for consolation to the Indian mystics. She became an ardent Theosophist and follower of Annie Besant, and absorbed as she was in her work and her own spiritual experiences the Lutyens home became a cheerless place for a busy husband. Often he would come back from the office to find the house full of Indians eating vegetarian food and his wife too distracted to have thought of ordering a chop for him. Apart from the lack of creature comforts what atmosphere could have been more uncongenial to a hard-working professional who longed for relaxation with people and jokes and fun?

Lady Sackville, her own marriage on the rocks, was just the person Lutyens needed. She gave him 'little meals' of *paté de foie gras* and beefsteak, sauce *Béarnaise*, followed by a delicate *soufflé* and accompanied by Château-Lafitte and a glass or two of Château-Yquem. It must have been very comforting after the dank vegetarian meals at home with the Indian mystics.

And, convinced of his genius, Lady Sackville immediately set to work to further Lutyen's interests. She pursued the meeting at the opera with an effort to 'get Lutyens the Opera House commission', enlisting the support of Lady Cunard. This plot failed, but by the autumn she wrote that she was 'softening Charlie Hardinge's heart towards him'; Lord Hardinge of Penshurst, the 'C.H.' of Washington days, was now Viceroy of India. Lady Sackville had never lost touch with this man who had been so desperately in love with her and she would have known just how to straighten out a misunderstanding over Viceroy's House between Hardinge and the architect.

They had a wonderful time together, McNed and McSack, as they called each other. Arriving at Hill Street he would bring out his pencil and with a speed that much impressed her would dash off drawings – plans for a future house for her, a detail for a staircase, or a garden or a sketch for one of his own projects – she retained all her life the first sketch for the Cenotaph, his war memorial in Whitehall, done during dinner alone with her. And the jokes and the sheer fun of it! She objected to his bad puns, for as is the case with many wits some of his jokes were mere reflexes; for instance he could never see a dish of butter without exclaiming, 'Butter late than never'. Recorded, the Lutyens puns are intolerable, but a man of his enormous charm could get away with a great deal. Lady Sackville, perhaps to amuse him or perhaps to amuse herself began in 1917 to stuff the backs of her diary with funny stories clipped from newspapers; some were off-colour on a childish level, and those she would not have shown to Lutyens who disliked dirty jokes, although he amused himself in idle moments by drawing sketches which Lady Sackville found indecent and offensive.

It was certainly a love affair between them, with deep emotional dependence on both sides, but it is unlikely that they went to bed together. Lady Sackville had found another Seery – the perfect companion, the adoring, brilliant man with whom she could quarrel again and again and make up, certain of his faithfulness. Lutyens may have from time to time made demonstrations of affection – a curious private word occurred in the diary from time to time – 'lully'. She used it first after visiting a place called Lullingstone on one of their many sightseeing trips and possibly something happened there. 'McNed got back from India tonight and came straight here – he was perfect and not a bit lully . . . McNed was not lully today – thank God.'

What she did give him, far more than she had been able to give

Seery, knee-deep in his suspicious, possessive family, was mothering. Fussing over his health, she wrote:

> Please, Nedi, don't let yourself be tempted by too many cocktails! They really are *so* bad for you. I shall never forget the shock I had when I heard of the autopsy of Lord A. whose liver was like a black stone, owing to drinking too much alcohol. I shall give you only a weak whiskey and soda next time ... you are too precious to die: and I think you are shortening your life by drinking a *wee* bit too much ... Now, this is not nagging ...

There was always a comfortable room waiting for Lutyens at Lady Sackville's house, which came as a welcome relief when on return from a long trip abroad he sometimes found that there was no room at his own home, which Lady Emily had filled with disciples of her faith. Lady Emily was very grateful to Lady Sackville for looking after her husband and the following letter is typical of many she wrote. Lutyens had been ill:

> *Chère B.M.*
>
> I was *so* grateful to you for writing to me with news of poor Ned, and shall be more grateful to you for taking such care of him. I expect yr. prompt care saved him from a nasty bout of illness. It was very lucky he came to you, and thank you again. I am glad to know he has such a kind friend near. Should he not get quite well please let me know as I could come up to him at once.
>
> Yours affectionately,
Emmie

Lady Sackville would not have liked Lady Emily's saintly letters. After all, here she was with one of England's leading geniuses head over heels in love with her and what was his wife doing thanking her rival for taking care of him as though he were a charity case? Bed or no bed, there was a violently flirtatious side to the affair and Lady Sackville was incapable of handling any relationship, whether it was with the cook or her lover or her daughter, without the maximum amount of drama.

Edwardian beauties appear to have specialized in the art of torturing the men who loved them. Lady Desborough, a near contemporary of Lady Sackville's and one of the most charming women in England, was an expert at the game of what was called in American slang of the period, 'Treat 'em mean to keep 'em keen'. The Edwardian style was to flirt like mad, then to withdraw with aloof coldness; in Lady Desborough's case the wretched man was left ignorant of his crime, but after a suitable period of penitence he would be permitted to return like a begging dog to be forgiven by the goddess he worshipped, and find ecstasy. Then the cycle would be repeated. The next generation of Englishwomen abandoned this technique, probably because after the First World War there were so many more women than men.

It must be said for Lady Sackville that she left Lutyens in no doubt about his crimes – which always concerned money spent on the alterations to her various houses. Inevitably she had been cheated by the builders and Lutyens was, in her view, personally responsible. A furious letter in the familiar flowing hand would bring McNed down to Brighton in a trice – to be 'sent to his basket' in Lady Sackville's own words. She used the naughty-dog comparison after an episode in 1922 when she wrote, 'Such a good little McNed and so fluffy. Bless him to be so devoted, after all these many years – nearly seven years – and he does not show the slightest sign of abatement.'

The next year she wrote, 'McNed feels very much having been sent to his basket.' She then described with relish the drawings he had given her as a peace offering: 'doleful little pictures of his being in the basket with the lid tight down'.

In 1924, the following year, a typical exchange took place. On 24 August, McNed, hastily summoned to the new house at Roedean, arrived as 'the alterations have been going very badly. He was much upset, said it was dreadful for him to have work done badly and put down to him when he minds a sixteenth part of an inch being wrong in any design.' This rings very true – Lutyens was an architect's architect – a mistake of 1/16th of an inch would have driven him mad.

16 *September*, 'Bungle.' Lady Sackville was furious with McNed. 'He writes by every post.'

29 *September*, letter from the contrite McNed, who was trying to work his way back, calling her 'my darling, a thing he had never done before in a letter'.

30 *September*, McNed came in out of the rain, penitent; she took him back.

22 *October*, 'Emmie asks me to be kind to McNed.'

25 *October*, 'McNed came down to settle the question of the

loggia steps. He is so marvellously quick, he could only stay two hours.'

Two hours was a lot for Sir Edwin Lutyens to give to the question of the loggia steps at Roedean. Lady Sackville particularly enjoyed calling him down when he was at his busiest. On one occasion he abandoned Waterloo Bridge, which could not have been a small commission, to rush to her side, and she complacently noted the fact.

Another weapon was blackmail, which she employed frequently, writing again and again in her diary that she had told him that she must give him up in order to regain her independence. Of course she didn't mean it. Spoilt, vain, famous, Lady Sackville in later life still had a need for security. The illegitimate girl who had made her own way in Washington, fighting her past, still seemed to have to test this hard-fought for security – Lutyens was like a rubber ball that a child flings out on an elastic string, certain that it would return.

But why did he accept being a rubber ball? Why did Lady Desborough's lovers accept their humiliations? They too were highly distinguished men, how could they have put up with the Edwardian rejection–repentance–forgiveness formula? The worries Lady Sackville gave Lutyens would have tried an angel; yet he always came back for more. He earned no money out of the many plans that he made for her which were not executed, no money out of the ones that were.

In 1925 McNed was in India. On 15 January Lady Sackville wrote angrily in her diary that the latest architectural rearrangements in her house at Roedean were a disaster and that she had been obliged to take to her bed, worn out by her problems. She undoubtedly fired off her complaints to poor Lutyens in New Delhi, and Vita evidently tried to propitiate her:

24 February
Vita says that it is a national duty on my part to be nice to McNed.

On 6 March came a letter from Delhi; McNed was speeding home to put everything right.

20 March
McNed is going to pay for all the repairs here . . . I played all

my favorite tunes, and he was sitting on the sofa by me holding my hand and being such a good boy – he does care for me, really.

21 March
He insists upon paying what I owe Cox & [unreadable – the builders].

Occasionally Lady Sackville gave Lutyens presents. There had been a little grey Rolls-Royce in the early years, which he used to go back and forth from the office, and after his above mentioned generosity in the spring of 1925 she wrote that she had paid him back 'with surplus furniture that I do not want – 3 Bon Marché tapestries. He is so childishly happy about it all.'

There *was* a childish side to Lutyens. A 1925 article in *Truth* magazine described him as 'a cross between Peter Pan, who never grew up, and Napoleon'. But there was also a sombre side to his nature of which the public was unaware. A letter to his wife written in 1917 illustrates this part of his character. He had been sitting alone in his London club on an August night, and he was filled with black dejection as he contemplated 'the beastly waste of war, the loss of life and happiness, the church faces that mask animal instincts ... we do, especially I, manage my life badly somehow'. Then his thoughts went to the post-war world, the 'awful quagmire of hideousness and discomfort ahead: a million cottages to be built by a Government that can only work through compromise, leaving its conscience in the hands of accountants ...'

Although he did not say so to his wife, for he was not a vain man, it must have been clear to him on that dreary evening that his sort of building belonged to the past. Who, in a ruined England, would be able to afford a Lutyens country house, who would be left to appreciate the elegant sophistication of a Lutyens moulding, his lovely, sinuous hallmark that must be exact to the last 1/16th of an inch?

For the black side of the artist's nature Lady Sackville provided the perfect escape; there perhaps lay the clue to a relationship that would otherwise have been masochistic on his part. She must have led the romantic Lutyens, and he was a true romantic, into a dream world. At London or Brighton the pencilled projects were deliciously endless, and while she would have been incapable of grasping his serious preoccupations, she was marvellously good at cheering him up. She described an expedition they made to Hampton Court in 1920; he must have been in a blue mood for her diary entry showed that she did not talk about herself for a moment; instead she spent her time telling him that the great Sir Christopher Wren had also been badly treated; this would have been balm to the weary Lutyens. Knowing Lady Sackville, it is possible to conjecture that she had boned up on Wren's career the night before.

Superficial as her knowledge always was, frivolous, self-indulgent, tiresome as she appeared to many people in older age, she never lost the quality that her father had noticed in the ball-room of the Washington Legation in the early 1880s, that she knew what to do without having been taught. The trouble was that as she grew older she applied her instinctive wisdom more and more rarely, and her bad habits deepened with time. Her obsession with money became increasingly eccentric. She varied from great generosity to Catalina-like meanness. Virginia Woolf, writing to Vita, said: 'Your mother writes me long letters on slips of paper with holes through the corners . . .' With Seery's money she had bought Lionel a yacht; she brought central heating to Knole; she installed a very expensive butterfly device in every window at Knole – which made it possible to let in a little fresh air without losing all the heat inside. She bought the Brighton house in 1918 and spent over £50,000 doing it up and adding to it what she called 'bits and pieces', which could be anything from a miniature tea set under a glass dome to a lapis lazuli dining room table. Bored with Brighton, she bought another house, smaller, at nearby Roedean in 1923, and engaged Lutyens to do it over. She moved into this house, White Lodge, before she had sold the Brighton property on which she eventually took a loss of £45,000. In 1924 she owned four houses, Hill Street still unsold, Ebury Street, Brighton and White Lodge, and was to continue looking around for another. Her irresponsibility with money was notorious in the family; it was said that J. P. Morgan had once given her a check for £10,000 drawn to bearer, which she then left in a taxi. Vita wrote that a man on the train to Sevenoaks persuaded her to invest in a gold mine to the tune of £60,000. She never saw him again, but eventually may have got back a few hundred pounds.

In June 1923 when she was moving to Roedean she held a sale

of the major part of the contents of the Brighton house – this must
have been one of the worst-advertised and worst-organized sales in
the history of art dealing, for some of the things were magnificent
furniture and bronzes from the Wallace Collection, yet on the first
day they brought in only £4,500 and on the second day £1,400.
The illustrated catalogue is enough to make the collector today
scream, and although Lady Sackville wrote that she was very
disappointed and in fact bought back some of her own things, the
very fact that she would have had such a sale is reminiscent of the
irrational desire for ready cash that had induced her to sell the
contents of the rue Laffitte to Seligmann after Seery's death.
Another legacy from Seery had been Catherine Parr's necklace;
a jewel of great historic as well as monetary value. She hawked
this about for years, trying to sell it to private and public persons.
At last the jeweller Chaumet accepted it on commission, whereupon
it was stolen from his Bond Street shop, and never retrieved.
Fortunately it was insured.

The sad part of the story was not so much the careless self-
indulgence that reduced her fortune – she still was a rich woman
when she died and left Vita £100,000, but the pain she caused by
using money as an instrument of power when she chose to do so.
McNed was not the only sufferer from her whims. It was Vita who
had to put up with the worst of Lady Sackville's changes of mood
and growing sense of persecution. Yet she loved her mother – how
many daughters would have taken the trouble to write this?

Long Barn
Monday night [4 September 1922]

My darling Mama,
I do miss you so; it seems to have gone in a flash, this little time
that you have been here. I feel quite jealous of McNed, who has
taken you away from me. It was horrid turning back into an
empty house after you had driven away. I wish you could come
back later on? but I suppose that is too much to ask? I have
simply loved your being here, and you are so sweet and appreciative of my little Long Barn and our little parties! I only hope
you did not find all those people too tiring? especially having to
have a real dinner in a real dining room?

The babies were very sorry and angry when they came home
from their tea-party and found that you had gone.

I can't bear to go up to your room to see whether anything has been forgotten.

Your,
Mar*

Lady Sackville loved being Vita's confidante. Her diary in 1924 was typical of the relationship:

23 February
Vita told me that D.C. [Duff Cooper] had declared a *grande passion* for her – what will Diana say? She does not care for him at all but is amused and flattered as he is very clever.

15 March
D.C. continues to pursue her ... I made her give up having Taloola [sic.] Bankhead to luncheon. She says that she is the most accomplished Lesbian in England and I certainly don't approve of V. knowing such an accomplished personality who talks in such a disgusting way.

10 November of the same year brought Lady Sackville a closely written nine-page letter from Vita, which began:

My darling Mama,
I sent you the bluebells – don't be misled by the label, *Scilla nutans*, they are just ordinary bluebells under their grand name! There are about 500, although you wouldn't think it. Plenty more where these came from, if you want them.

Vita then went on to ask her mother's advice about a business proposition that had just been put to her. It sounded very attractive financially but Vita didn't quite trust the woman who suggested the arrangement, and wrote urgently:

I have not even told Harold. Now, the point is ought I to accept or not? I would dearly like to talk it over with you, and as you say you will be in London on Thursday shall I come and fetch you at Osbert's after lunch ... we can go anywhere you have to go, and talk ...

A few days later Vita was writing again to her mother at 1 a.m. about this same business affair, which she had decided to turn down.

* Vita's nickname since babyhood.

These exchanges illustrate the closeness of mother and daughter. 1924 ended happily for Lady Sackville, she celebrated Christmas at Brighton, noting that she had never received so many presents, 114 in all, given by 94 people.

The following years were a slow and tragic decline. Lady Sackville's health had been troubling her since she left Knole, but she always seemed to be able to do anything she really wanted to. Now in 1925 diabetes was diagnosed, colitis complicated the illness and the doctor was worried about her heart. 'It is such an effort to see people,' she wrote, but she continued to see a good many, and was grateful to Vita for her excellent and comforting letters. Occasionally she even went up to Long Barn, and on 1 June mentioned that Vita had had to leave her to go up to London to dine with 'V. Wolff [sic.] to meet Forster, who wrote that charming book'. This was the first mention of Vita's new friend; the next reference came over a year later, 5 November 1926:

> Vita dined at Virginia Woolfe's, [sic.] and told me how brilliant the conversation was. I really understand how and why the child likes the Bloomsbury people, who seem to appreciate her as she deserves.

1926 was another year of illness, the diary became self-pitying, depressed, full of endless money worries and complaints about the servants who were constantly leaving. Even the indispensable lady's maids had become faithless, and were always changing. McNed, George Plank, and Ozzie Dickinson were faithful and solicitous, as was Eve Fleming. Lady Sackville began writing in French again, a sure sign of fatigue or emotional strain, but there were still good moments. In October she wrote that she felt a sort of rebirth, thanks to the devotion of Vita and McNed and George Plank and her grandsons. And she kept up her little acts of kindness – the postman received jelly when he was ill, and the listed presents to friends filled pages at the back of the diary.

The year 1927 brought a steady deterioration, relieved by sudden moments of exhilaration, when she would go to London on a shopping spree. She was very pleased to find maraschino cherries for Vita in one of the stores as she understood that it was quite the rage to put them in cocktails.

1928 was a dreadful year, during which Lady Sackville behaved not only irrationally but cruelly. Lionel's death at Knole on 28

January caused something to snap in her brain, or perhaps the worn motor was ready to give out at about that time. For years she had been on the coldest of terms with Lionel, and although Walter Rubens had died she refused Lionel's request for a divorce again and again. It especially infuriated her to have Ben and Nigel come back from Knole talking cheerfully of Boom-Boom, as they called Olive Rubens because she regaled them with her resounding operatic voice. To the boys she must have seemed a cosy, easy-going grandmother compared to the unpredictable, emotional one they visited at Brighton.

Vita had been at Knole helping Olive nurse the dying man, and it was on Vita that Lady Sackville now turned. The first row was over the funeral; the Nicolsons felt that it would be inappropriate for her to come. Lady Sackville did not go, but she broke with Harold and Vita, using terrible words in her diary:

> Vita has treated me abominably for the last few years . . . I had loved her so. I have finished with that monster of ingratitude.

Virginia Woolf wrote three days after Lord Sackville's death to Clive Bell:

> There's poor dear Vita very miserable about Lord Sackville – in fact it seems a bad business altogether . . . What can we do to prevent Lady Sackville from making a scene at the funeral?

On 12 February Virginia Woolf was writing to Vita's cousin, Edward Sackville-West:

> I have just been down to Long Barn. Vita seems better, and has answered about three hundred letters [about her father] but I'm afraid it is a dismal affair for her, and your aunt's [Lady Sack-ville] behaviour could only be tolerated in an Elizabethan play. That she may take a dagger to her own throat or drink broken glass is rather my hope, I admit.

Lady Sackville's behaviour on 18 April was the last straw for the protective Virginia Woolf. She wrote to Clive Bell:

> Of gossip the chief is that Vita has had a terrific culminating and final scene with Lady Sackville in a solicitor's office, with wit-nesses to take down all insults – The woman seems utterly mad, called her liar, thief and harlot, cut her pearl necklace in half,

and pocketed the twelve best stones, and then announced that she would consider her dead henceforward and stop every penny of her allowance. Vita swears she is going to earn her own living by her pen.

It had indeed been a dreadful scene. Vita wrote to Harold in Berlin that she had gone up to London to see Pemberton, the family solicitor, who had been protecting the family's interests since before the illegitimacy case in the 1890s. She was talking to him when a messenger announced that Lady Sackville was downstairs and wanted to see Vita in Pemberton's presence.

"Give me your pearls!" screamed B.M., "twelve of them belong to me, and I wish to see how many you have changed, you thief." ... Never, *never* have I heard such floods of the vilest abuse, aimed at both Pemberton and me – she was like a madwoman, screaming thief and liar, and shaking her fist at me till I thought that she was going to hit me ... impossible to make out what it was all about.

Vita described that Lady Sackville wanted her to go to a jeweller to have him cut out twelve pearls from the necklace. Vita refused to go but offered to cut out the pearls herself, in her mother's presence, and did so, in the back of the Rolls-Royce. The tirade increased in violence as Vita left the car ...

She screamed that she hated me, and wished that I would die – wished indeed that I must be run over and killed that day – in fact there is no end to the horrors she shrieked at me through the window.

Poor Vita, according to her letter to Harold, went for comfort to Virginia Woolf, who was sympathetic and helpful. Lady Sackville recorded the shocking episode as follows:

18 April 1928
Oh, what a day, another horrible day of my life. I finally repudiated Vita to her face at Pemberton's who were both protecting her in her lying ... It was most melodramatic and Herridge [chauffeur] was shocked at the loud way she spoke to me at the window of my car – I have done with her – Had very bad palpitations and pain.

Vita, in her book *Pepita*, was too dignified to describe the horrors of this period. But she said that her mother's abilities were wasted in later life, and that she should have involved herself in philanthropy or politics. From Lady Sackville's diary descriptions of her health it is hard to know whether this would have been possible, but certainly her unharnessed energies could be dangerous. Lady Sackville was shooting arrows into the air in a desperate need for occupation; some were innocent and ridiculous and others were poisoned, like her treatment of Vita.

The Roof of Friendship Fund in 1928 was an example of the ridiculous. She wrote letters to hundreds of friends asking for money to buy 'a tile of friendship' for the roof of the house that she was planning. The embarrassed friends contributed generously, and it gave her something to do to write back to them thanking them, and to jot down the sums in her diary. A few years later her Million Penny Fund was to pay the National Debt. By then she was blind and often bedridden, but a good morning's mail would arouse her old enthusiasm, for example, a letter from Mr Andrew Mellon, then American Ambassador to Great Britain, enclosing a cheque for a guinea.

The break with Vita lasted nearly two years, during which Lady Sackville referred to her as 'the Vipa' instead of 'the Vita'. The publications of Virginia Woolf's novel *Orlando*, which is a love letter to Vita, caused another outburst. In her own copy of the book Lady Sackville pasted a photograph of Virginia and wrote beside it:

> The awful face of a mad woman whose successful mad desire is to separate people who care for each other. I loathe this woman for having changed my Vita and taken her away from me.

Meanwhile the Nicolsons were having a hard time financially. Under the terms of Vita's marriage settlement her mother legally owed her an allowance. After the break this was cut off and Harold wrote to Lady Sackville in September 1929 that he had been obliged to give up his career and to accept a job from Lord Beaverbrook on the *Evening Standard*. It was very selfish of Lady Sackville to keep the Nicolsons dependent on her financially; they had two sons to educate and she could well have given Vita part of the money that she left her at her death. But it is probable that Harold would have left the service anyhow, for the separations

from Vita that they both minded so much would only have pro-
longed as he rose in his career, and she could not have faced the
social duties into which her mother had entered so joyously fifty
years before. It is impossible to picture Vita as the ambassador's
wife at a large embassy. And Harold himself didn't care for the
pomp that goes with high position, besides which, his friends were
telling him that he was wasting his talents and that he should write
and go into politics.

The reconciliation with Vita for which Lady Sackville must
have longed came in 1930, and no daughter could have been more
devoted during the last sad years of increasing blindness, loneliness
and bitterness. The wind off the English Channel beats hard on the
cliff where White Lodge stands, yet it was there at Roedean, near
Brighton, that Lady Sackville chose to remain, writing long letters
in her disintegrating handwriting, putting down little homilies
and what she called 'Thoughts'. Some were brave ones: 'I am
keener than ever, as I am threatened with total blindness in a few
months.' (1932.) Always casual about time, in her last years she
simply disregarded it, and Vita would arrive, having been summoned for lunch at one o'clock to find her mother still in bed,
possibly asleep. A meal would eventually be served at five o'clock,
and Lady Sackville would rail because the meat was overdone.
Sometimes it was the gardener who did the cooking, the solicitor
who filled the hot-water bottles, and George Plank who ran Lady
Sackville's bath. Yet in good moments she could still dictate an
enthusiastic letter to Vita about doing over yet another house:
'Darling, don't you think it a good idea to buy Turner's house?
We shall talk about it on Thursday.'

Lutyens was loyal and constant; she resented his good advice
and practical common sense as she grew weaker and more neurotic,
but the last letter that exists written by her to him in 1931 was an
affectionate, grateful one. He was at Marseilles, about to sail
again for India.

In longer, darker times poor Vita had to deal with a paranoid old
woman who lashed out at innocent employees and tradespeople;
there were so many law suits that in a moment of McNed-like
humour Lady Sackville called her house 'The Writs Hotel'.

It must have been terrible for Vita, against whom the irrational
complaints were often directed, and it was very hard on the
schoolboys Ben and Nigel, who came faithfully to White Lodge to

see their grandmother, never knowing in what mood they would find her. She paid back their loyalty with the most discreditable action of her life.

Eighteen-year-old Ben went to see his grandmother at White Lodge. He wrote:

> She spent the whole time saying things about M. and D. [Vita and Harold] to put me against them – stories about M. getting hold of women and D. of men – about Violet Keppel, Virginia Woolf etc. All quite without foundation . . . Of course told M. and D. all about it. D. said that she was like Iago . . . M. said that she was a genius gone wrong. I don't think I understand.

The next day:

> After I wrote yesterday's account M. came to my room at midnight and said that what G. [Lady Sackville] had said was true . . .

Forty years later Ben wrote:

> I seek some explanation for her outburst . . . she may just have wished to give vent to her misery and loneliness – this blind old woman with a gardener on a cliff, with nothing to keep her alive but dreams of Washington, Knole and her lost beauty – by poisoning an innocent grandson's mind: so she hoped.

Ben wrote of Virginia Woolf's reaction:

> Virginia and Leonard came to lunch . . . She listened to the whole story of my visit to Brighton with her head bowed. Then she said: "The old woman ought to be shot."

Vita continued her faithful care until the end. Sometimes Lady Sackville's courage surmounted her madness and she could dictate a cheerful description:

> He [a new doctor] and I sang beautifully some duets from Gounod. He has a magnificent voice, and he sang to me, and suddenly I began to accompany him, and he was extremely surprised at the true tone of my singing. It was Verlaine's '*La Lune par-dessus les toits*', but I can't find who set it, it is not Debussy . . .

She slept badly, but wrote that it helped to sing alone at 2 a.m. Other days come to mind reading this sad, brave line; the trip through wild and dangerous Yellowstone Park when the tired German reporter Mohr felt his spirits lift as 'the daughter of the British Ambassador' sang '*Die Wacht am Rhein*' as the party sat around the campfire; the first winter at Knole when Victoria used to go about the house singing '*Plaisir d'amour*' to cheer up her melancholy father, the joyous evening at Buckhurst just after meeting Lionel when she had sung to him, as she did to baby Vita a few years later; teaching her 'Tom, Tom, the Pai-per's son'. And there had been those walks at Sluie in the Highlands, a scarf tied carelessly over her beautiful head, singing from sheer high spirits as she swung down the Scottish lanes.

Perhaps she was singing still as the end approached on the night of 29 January 1936. The next day Harold and Vita, summoned by the doctor, rushed to Brighton to find that she had died quite painlessly three minutes before, without having recovered consciousness from what must have been a stroke or heart attack. She had left a pathetic little typewritten note saying that she was to be cremated, and the ashes flung into the sea.

Harold Nicolson's diary tells the rest of the story. Evidently Vita did not feel up to the ordeal and it was Harold and Lady Sackville's last secretary, Cecil Rhind, who saw that her wishes were fulfilled.

8 February 1936

Go down to Brighton. It is a bitter cold day with a strong east wind. I am met by Cecil Rhind and we lunch at the Metropole. We then go to the oyster-shop of Mr English where B.M.'s ashes have been preserved overnight. The reason for this strange procedure is that the Press had got hold of the story, and it was feared that they would picket the undertakers and take snapshots of us as we carried out the urn. The latter is placed at the back of the car by Mr English. He is anxious to come with us in the boat, but I am very firm on the point. "No, Mr English, we really should prefer to be by ourselves." The boat is there on the shingle – a large open fishing-boat with two sailors and a petrol engine. We climb in, holding the little container in its neat brown-paper parcel. We are launched down the shingle in Homeric fashion and chug along the coast until we get opposite White Lodge. Cecil and I sit there huddled in our coats with a most inadequate rug over our knees, bending our heads from time to time as the spray lashes over us. Sun shining and an angry brown sea. "We're two miles out," says the boatman, at which I undo the string of the parcel. The urn or container is of gun-metal, and one opens it by pressing up the lid with one's thumbs. I am terrified lest the ashes be caught by the wind and I keep the lid on. The two men stand up and take off their hats. So does Cecil. I kneel by the gunwale and spill the ashes over into the sea, saying, "B.M., all who love you are happy that you should now be at peace. We shall remember always your beauty, your courage and your charm." It is merely a handful of dust which slides out of the container into the waves.

Lady Sackville, whose whole life was unorthodox, would have loved her end. Mr English had been a great friend of hers; she was always taking guests to eat oysters at his warm and friendly shop, and what could have been more appropriate than that her ashes should repose on his hospitable premises? She might have said once more, had she known of the arrangements, '*Quel roman est ma vie!*'

Susan Mary Alsop
October 1977
Washington, D.C.

Appendix

The Book of Happy Reminiscences For My Old Age
Started on my 61st Birthday, 23rd Sept. 1922

23rd September 1922:
I am sixty today. I feel as if I was thirty and even younger. But . . .
I am entering *old age* for all that – and I want to have a *golden* old
age ripe with happy reminiscences. and I shall jot them down as I
go along in the down hill Path. I got the idea of this book for my
old age in reading something similar to it in Lady Russell's: in the
Mountains.

I shall often read about the happy things which have happened
to me. I shall quote them quite haphazard. They will often sound
trivial, but they wont be trivial as far as I am concerned. It will be
a sort of precious collection which will lighten the burden of the
inevitable worries which I must necessarily come across. The
one person who will read SOMEDAY, this Golden Book is my Vita.
And she will understand.

I have been so lucky all through life. After all I was born:
enfant naturelle, which is or was a terrible stain and stumbling
block. But Aunt Mary Derby helped me to get over that difficulty
and got Queen Victoria to allow me to go to Washington with
Papa who was H.M.'s Minister there. The Cabale against allowing
'some one who had not been presented' was headed by Mrs
Bloomfield Moore who was won over in a fortnight and showed it
in this way. One of her nieces died and left her a pearl necklace
with the stipulation that, as she did not want any more pearls, she
should give that row of pearls to the most popular girl in Washing-

237

ton. Apparently and unbeknown to me She got up a sort of ballot and the pearls were voted to me. She brought them one morning to the Legation and told me the incredible story of how I had won those pearls, which I sold for 5,000 pounds in 1908, to help Lionel with his death-duties and expenses connected with Knole after Papa's death and the bothers started by Henry. But as nothing unpleasant is to be recorded, I shall not write about my ungrateful brothers and sisters.

My diary contains the doings of my Days – Here I jot down happy events just as I happen to think of them, without any sequence. What flattered my vanity as a young girl was the pro-posal of marriage from President Arthur, after a dinner at the White House; it was the second proposal I had at Washington. I burst out laughing in his face and said: 'Mr President, you have a son older than me and you are as old as my Father.'

I was *la petite chefesse* and went solemnly to big and official dinner-parties like the *chefs de mission's* wives.

I refused to make a lot of money once through Judge Blatchford of the Supreme Court who came to see me and said he and his colleagues knew how the Bell-telephone case was to be settled and if I authorized him to put $100,000 to my name he could double it for me and I need not give him the money; he only told me of this, as I was a good girl and I had done remarkably well in my position at the Legation and he understood I had no money. Instead of being pleased, I was horrified and showed him the door; the old man had not even kissed my hand and was amazed at the effect his doubtful suggestion had on me. I suppose I was a fool, as some one else made that $100,000. But I felt my honour was intact. I felt proud and reported it all to my dear Aunt Mary who always trebled every fiver I could save out of my small allowance. She scolded me a little when I told her I had made (in 1882) 15 pounds at the local races at Ivy Hatch. or some such name. Funny for a 'Derby' to object to racing. But she hated my going to races or betting in the mildest way. It is curious how she made me dislike going Racing, as I have been once to the Derby when King Edward won it with Diamond Jubilee and once for an $\frac{1}{2}$ hour only, to Ascot on Cup day. I've never seen the Grand Prix or the Grand National or the Leger. I dislike racing.

It must have been in 1883 that my Father and I escaped being blown up or poisoned at the Legation by the Fenians after the

Phoenix Park murders. Papa had much to do with the finding of
the murderers in America and every week the Fenian papers were
headed by these lines: 'The British Minister is not bullet-proof.'
I received many post-cards saying we were spared because I was
a Roman Catholic; but when the President found we were going
to be blown up he sent Papa and me on his yacht with General
Sherman and Rachel his daughter, and we remained on board till
all danger was over *What luck!!* – And every day, that great
General took out his map and went through his Georgia Campaign with me and gave me graphic descriptions of the fights and
the wounded. I think it was after Gettysburg that he said he was
on the first floor of a house where the surgeons were operating
with all despatch, and he saw arms and legs getting piled up that
they reached the first floor.

Papa and I loved each other very dearly. I reminded him very
much of Mama who he *adored* and I remember her joy when he
used to come to Arcachon and I was almost jealous of the way he
hugged her and kissed her. I was always with her; she was so
beautiful and I loved looking at her. She had a very happy disposition and was always so cheerful. She loved arranging and re-
arranging her house and I always helped her. She hardly ever saw
anybody. She liked needlework and so did I. I was very fond of
my dolls and a good little mother to them – How I loved afterwards
my live Doll Vita. I adore little babies, tiny littly Mars; I talk to
them in the street, and follow them or watch them out of the
window and long to hold them. I shall never forget the intense
happiness I felt when Lionel brought me Vita on a pillow at five
in the morning after my terrible confinement. One's own little
baby is such a miracle; such an incredible marvel. Nothing else
can be so wonderful! I had the deepest gratitude to Lionel, who I
was madly in love with, for giving me such a gift as that darling
baby. Her little hands were entrancing; and I watched her for
hours, lying or sitting on my lap. Her little sneezes or yawning
were so comic. I hugged her till she screamed, poor Mar –

Lionel and I were so happy with our baby sitting between us in
our big bed; when she could talk a little, she used to look at us in
turn and nod her head, saying: 'Dada – Mama –' This went on
for hours and used to delight us. Vita's babyhood is one of my
happiest recollections. Lionel was perfect to me in those days. He
gave me 10 perfect years of the most complete happiness and

passionate love which I reciprocated heartily. I adored him, and he adored me.

What luck I had to meet him, as I did not want to leave Papa who depended entirely on me – We fell in love with each other the very day we met. We were staying with old Mr Edgar Drummond at ? near Southampton and I heard that my cousin Lionel was one of the guests. I knew Charlie and Bertie, Cecilee and Mary but I had never met Lionel – I remember feeling I was looking my best that night (sometime in June or July 1889). I was wearing a tight fitting bodice and skirt of a pale yellow striped satin dress. Yellow suited me, being rather dark – and I had in my hair a wreath of *épis de blé, a la Cérès* –

Lionel never took his eyes off me during that dinner. I felt much disturbed, as he attracted me immensely. And I was delighted when the next day, he came to fetch me for a walk. It was not long, before he told me how much he cared for me – and he asked me to marry him in Sept. 89, one moonlight evening, in the King's Bed Room, at the Window. The time of our fiancailles, from Sept. 89 till 17 June 1890, was Heaven upon Earth. Oh! the joy of his coming home to Knole for weekends and being together before he returned to London to work at Scoones's – And our wedding-day!!! The immense happiness that filled me when the Clergyman (Mr Curtis or Mr Boyle) said we were man and wife. I felt he was *mine* then absolutely.

We had the most perfect honeymoon and went first – to absolute bliss – to Keston Lodge which Aunt Mary had lent us, near Bromley. What a comfort it was to feel that there was nothing to prevent Lionel coming to my bed-room. Kissing me madly and filling me with such intense pleasure that I would not have cared if the ceiling had fallen down. That is the sort of love that very few people have felt, at least I have been told so very often. I have drunk at the Cup of real Love till I felt absolutely intoxicated. I regret nothing. I have had the most perfect happiness with Lionel that any woman may wish for or expect from a man, being her husband or her Lover. He was both to me, during those ten years. For this, I forgive him what he has done since, under the influence of that snake in the grass: Olive Rubens – Joan Camden in 1899 and Connie Hatch in 1903, never made him behave badly to me. They were *Ladies*. I quite understand that a man's passion may change or he may get tired of his Wife physically. But a man has no right to treat his wife shamefully as L. treated me since 1914 as I never gave him cause – And I have *always* been devoted to his interests.

Another great happiness in my life has been living at Knole between Papa Lionel and Vita for those ten happy years. I got from Mama my love of beautiful things and of great comfort. I had a fine field to work upon at Knole. The first thing I did, after re-arranging the furniture and putting in the Garretts or Barracks the early Victorian horrors, was to begin making Bath-Rooms. The first one one was for Papa, then for me in Cranmer's Bed-Room; then one for Vita near her Nursery; I put it between George III Bed-Room and the Stamp Room. When we married, we first used Cranmer's Rooms and Papa lived in Bouchier's Tower, facing the garden which he loved. I took very little interest in the practical side of gardening while I lived at Knole. It has been a source of infinite pleasure at Eb and at the Cloister and I have succeeded in making two wonderful gardens for those two houses. I work with joy for at least one hour daily in the London Garden. I believe in watering it copiously. The Wistarias love a wet soil.

I enjoyed immensely installing the electric light at Knole and putting in all the modern improvements I could. I made Bath-Rooms with old Jeffrey (and his Son) who was an admirable carpenter – Everybody says that I made Knole the most comfortable large house in England, uniting the beauties of Windsor Castle with the comforts of the Ritz and I never spoilt the old character of Knole. I insisted upon having Electric Light about 1901. And we were the second house which had a motor-car, about 1902 or 1903 – it was a Maudsley. We went all over the place in that curious little car which one entered from the back and the passengers faced each other like in a bus; it had a fixed hood, which we never let down on account of the clouds of dust which immediately enveloped us. The Roads were not treated for Motor traffic in those days. Whenever one of us went to London in the car, or to Maidstone, or any journey of 20 miles, we wired to Knole we had arrived safely!

Besides my stay on the President's yacht in America, I very seldom paid any visits, especially without Papa. We used to go every winter to Ottawa, to stay with Lord Lorne or Lord Lansdowne. And I loved sleighing and tobogganing.

The first time I went, the Duc de Blacas who was staying at

Government House, proposed to me. So did Capt. Drury who became Gen. Drury and was, I believe, at the head of the Canadian army during the War and is the Father of Lady Beaverbrook. He could not believe or realize how innocent I was and kept on telling me this remark, very puzzling to me: 'I see no green in your eyes.' I asked Lord Lorne why his ADC always told me that he saw no green in my eyes which were blue, or why his favourite flower was tulips (two lips). I was almost stupid with that overwhelming state of perfect innocence.

The Duc de Blacas cried bitterly when I refused him and also the morning that I went away. He was ranching in the West, as he was ruined through his father's speculations; he sent me some cheese of his own make when he got back to his ranch. It was a peculiar present, comparing it with the innumerable boxes of chocolate and bunches of flowers which young men sent one, on the slightest pretext. Every time a ball was given, the fashion was to send the young lady of your choice a bouquet. And those bouquets were so numerous that one had to tie them with ribbons all round one's waist. They were so much in the way (and were so expensive for the donors) that I made up my mind to stop that inane fashion of looking like a maypole or a Christmas-tree when one entered a ball-room; the more bouquets one had received, the more popular one appeared. I got together all the well known girls in Washington and proposed to them to do away with that expensive and cumbersome fashion. They agreed. And unwittingly, by having achieved this, I became the most popular girl and the young men were mightily grateful to me.

My father and I paid a long visit in Virginia about 1884 or 5 to what seemed to me an old man: Jesse Tyson. He lived in Baltimore and was a Quaker and a tee-totaller, but his medicine chest contained many bottles of Champagne – and his guests were 'dosed' as soon as they showed the slightest sign of fatigue. He bred trotters at the farm we stayed at. His servants were niggers. I slept in a big room with his niece Miss Tyson. He took us to see the Luray Caves. He proposed to me and was duly refused, which did not prevent him from giving me every year one piece of silver, made by the celebrated Baltimore silversmith: Kirk Till. I had a complete set for my dressing-table.

Very few girls possessed such a thing as a silver dressing-set in those days. It was considered a very great extravagance and great sign of wealth. After I left America, Jesse Tyson finally married a very young and very beautiful girl. Another visit we paid was to Governor Carroll at Carrolton, for All-Hallows Eve. They had a big country house in Virginia and are the smartest and oldest family in the South. We played terrifying games in the evening of the 1st of November, in semi-darkness and invoked the devil who never came. These games remind me of my capacity for lighting an extinguished gas-jet with my nose! I used to do this at Ottawa, on cold and frosty nights, by rubbing my feet in the carpet all along the big corridor and coming in contact, at the end, with the gas-burner. It was Lady Lansdowne who made me try it. I was so successful that I gave people a baddish electric-shock when I touched them. It hurt me too. There was a rug at Knole (black sheepskin) which never failed to charge me with electricity when I rubbed my bare feet on it. It was in our bed-room and the electric game was a delight to Lionel.

I loved the Expedition of August and Sept. 1883, for 'Driving the last Spike of the Northern Pacific Railroad' going to Portland. We went as far as Seattle, where an ox was roasted on the Market place and we went on to Victoria, at Vancouver where Papa was received with great honours and gun firing, by the British fleet; I think it was Admiral Lyons or Tyson who was commanding it on the *Swiftsure*. We saw a great deal of the delightful one-armed General Fairchild going to Vancouver.

This expedition was got up by the President of the Railroad, Mr Willard; he invited Papa and me, and gave us a private car called the De La Warr, as a delicate compliment, as one of Papa's ancestors Lord De La Warr had been governor of Virginia in James 1's time and had had a good deal to do with the Indian Princess Pocahontas. General Sherman took us to see the Church she was christened in at Jamestown on the James River; and I remember stealing a brick from the Church and using it for years as a paper weight for my ever-littered writing-table. Which I never seem able to keep tidy. Why, I cant think! as I am always tidying it up. But I am a hoarder and I hate throwing away anything. And most of those useless, dust-gathering things find a temporary resting-place on my large writing-table.

How I have complicated my life with these senseless accumulations! And also the mania of buying things and putting them away for possible presents when I saw anything that might suit those I cared for. They certainly (the things) came in very useful at times. But how we all complicate our lives with false economies and hoarding! I should have been freer if I had not taken so much thought for 'the morrow'. And yet I like to save a lot of things and papers for Vita and the Boys – I am sure they will be interested when Granwina is not there any more and it will show them how lovingly she thought of them three.

My Vita will never forget the tivas (*les tiroirs*) in my bedroom in Cranmer's Chapel and her petty larcenies of *bonbons* and chocolates which she ate, as she knew they were her own. I put away mercilessly what I thought was bad for her (and forgot to lock the tiva) as I wanted her digestion to be as good as her complexion. I really was very strict about her food (she *hated* Rice puddings) and she must be grateful to me now that she is 30, that her cheeks are like two ripe peaches, with a sun-kissed look and a bloom that is the envy and the admiration of every one – Her complexion is beautiful; so are her eyes, with their double curtain of long eyelashes. She looks at one with such tranquillity. She has such dignity and repose, she is not the least conceited and really does not make the most of her opportunities by leading such a quiet life at Long Barn and hiding herself much too much, while she ought to know everybody of note. She knows a good many writers and has a tremendous lot of silent admirers. I hear it constantly. She is a very difficult person to know. To me, who knows her pretty well, she is 'a beautiful mask'. She has put on a thicker mask since the distressing V. affair. I wont touch on it, as only happy thoughts are to be mentioned in these confidences. I think she will fall in love overwhelmingly with a man some day. I dread that day and therefore I won't dwell on it. Perish the thought. She is or *seems* absolutely devoted to Harold, but there is nothing whatever sexual between them, which is strange in such a young and good-looking couple. She is not in the least jealous of H. and willingly allows him to relieve himself with anyone if such is his want or his fancy. They both openly said so one evening when I was staying at L. Barn and Reggie Cooper was there too. It shocked me extremely. People may do what they like, but it ought to be either sacred or absolutely private. It is nobody's business to know our private lives. The less said about it, the better, unless one has a very great friend with whom one can *exchange* confidences with impunity.

It is good to open one's heart sometimes but how dangerous! Silence is wiser. Vita is practising discretion with me and I never ask her any questions. I always think George P. is always on the brink of falling desperately in love with her, but he checks himself as he realizes the hopelessness of it all. He is always mentioning her name and his eyes are very expressive. Poor boy! I hope he never will get *it* very badly. He might! How marvellously well she writes! and are her descriptions of Love and Passion a revelation of her own feelings? I am so full of the tyranny of both feelings, even in my old age. I have come across so much real Love in my life. And I have had and have so much happiness from my tender affairs that I am very deeply grateful to Nature to have endowed me as She has!

I would not change for anything. And I have all my precious reminiscences to hug *when* or *if* the day comes when I must take a backseat and resign myself to the Inevitable which has not reached me yet. I wait for it without worrying. Things are very satisfactory at the present moment, altho painful at times; such pain as absence is so hard to bear.

But I don't want Vita to suffer again in the way I have seen her suffer, poor child. She seems contented now but the Volcano is there, ready to burst into flame, I am sure. Let us not anticipate anything distressing. And let us enjoy her triumphs in the literary world, where she is getting a sounder reputation every day and is the subject of many flattering and *well-deserved* articles and remarks. Reading her calm descriptions fill me with admiration. She carries into her writings the quiet and tranquility of manner which is so characteristic of her. I only wish she did not choose the kind of subjects she seems so partial to. No one can beat her at her wonderful descriptions of Nature, or analysing a difficult character.

I must go back to the Journey of 1883. We stayed at Portland (Oregon) with a Mr Laidlow the British Consul who had nothing but Chinese servants and had excellent food; this reminds me of a Chinese dinner I had at Portland with a Chinese family. They gave me Birdnest soup and shark's fins. The young wife had a most delightful little yellow baby of a few months, he had a little cap from which hung a pig-tail. I loved him and nursed him and could hardly part with him. They took me afterwards to their Joss House. Papa did not come, as I understood he was not allowed to see the women of the famliy at dinner. They examined my clothes with much curiosity. We had started from Chicago, where I had not been allowed to see much and I certainly did not want to see the slaughtering of pigs. We stayed at the Palmer House, the best hotel of those days. I thought it so bad and so gloomy. I loved the drive along the Lakeshore – The best part of the journey was camping out in the Yellowstone Park. Before getting there, we had stopped at Helena, Montana, to see a War-dance by real Indians. It was really rather dangerous, as the Indians were in an inebriated state and might have made short work of our handful of Britishers, which consisted of Lord and Lady Onslow, Mr and Lady Hilda Broderick (he is now Earl of Midleton), Mr Albert Grey who became Earl Grey, George Holford, Mr Hobhouse (Lord Hobhouse), a Mr Russell (a lawyer) and Mr Robert Benson – who got scalded in the Yellowstone Park sitting on an extinct geyser which woke up suddenly, and burnt his Bobo badly. He could not sit down afterwards for a week. One young Indian, who came towards us after the dance and war whooping was over, said to me: 'You go. Me go,' and wanted to get into my carriage – Buggy and Alan Johnston who were also travelling in our car.

Paper found in the 'Book of Reminiscences':

I don't want to be like a piece of seaweed at ebb and flow and want to settle down. I am full of the gold of enthusiasm for this little place.

I cannot lock up all my feelings in a cupboard and lose the key.

I am fighting against all difficulties and I shall inevitably get the better of bad times, altho' I have not got the sword of un-wearied patience in my hand.

The dull ache of disappointment.

One must put a curb [—?—] appreciation, if one is enthusiastic about anything belonging to someone else.

There is no one in this world as enchanting as you are; one just swims along on a wave of enjoyment.

Paper found in the 'Book of Reminiscences':

Ceux qui m'ont demandé en marriage jusqu'à July 1890

E Le Marquis de Rocca de Torogas
   Marquis de Mollis
A President de l'Amérique USA
   Chester Aster
E Monsieur Chacon (Marquis d'Isari)
F Monsieur Theodore Rouston S. Ex.
E Mr Cecil Spring Rice (Sir Cecil)
E Honb^{le} Charles Hardinge (Sir Ch)
E Maurice de Benson (Sir Maurice)
Germain Egerton (Sir) at St Germain
Reggie West
Eddy Stanley (at D. H^{se})
Middie Rogers
Herrick
Lionel

Notes and Sources

My main sources are the unpublished diaries of Lady Sackville and other unpublished family papers in the possession of Mr Nigel Nicolson at Sissinghurst Castle, to which Lord Sackville contributed additional original material from Knole. These are not listed, as the sources are self-evident in the text of the book, but other sources are listed in the following notes.

1 LIONEL AND PEPITA

page 1 'The weather in Paris . . .' *Moniteur Universel*, Paris.

page 6 'She was better known to the poor than to the rich.' Sackville-West, *Pepita*, p. 136.

page 7 'Pepita was a devoted mother . . .' and the rest of the description of Pepita with her children is taken from Sackville-West, ibid., p. 132, but is not a direct quote.

page 9 '. . . they had festooned the dark branches . . .' Sackville-West, ibid., p. 137.

page 12 ' "Lionel", upon her lips . . .' Sackville-West, ibid., p. 146.

page 15 'My dear sister . . .' Letter in possession of Mr Nigel Nicolson, translated from the French by the author.

page 15 'You are a big girl now . . .' Letter in possession of Mr Nigel Nicolson.

page 16 'Something had to be done about Victoria.' The descriptions of Victoria in the convent and in England come from Sackville-West, ibid., pp. 153ff., but are not directly quoted.

2 POLITICAL WASHINGTON

page 21 'What a pity . . .' Mrs Henry Adams, p. 359.

page 21 'England as against the United States . . .' David Saville Muzzey, cited in Stiller, p. 13.

page 22 'A certain secret jealousy of the British Minister ...' Adams, *Democracy*, p. 23.

page 22 'Oysters on shell ...' Blaine, vol. I, p. 112.

page 23 'And what are your plans, Mrs Blaine?' Mrs Henry Adams, p. 297.

page 23 'Every man in office in this country ...' Knaplund and Clewes, p. 159.

page 24 'So sweet a sister ...' Letter in possession of Mr Nigel Nicolson.

page 26 'Hang it ... let us have some fun.' Adams, cited in Green, p. 87.

page 26 'West, the new Minister ...' Mrs Henry Adams, pp. 317–18.

page 26 'The Sunday papers opened fire ...' ibid., p. 343.

page 27 'She is a funny little church mouse ...' ibid., p. 323.

page 28 'Potomac ...' ibid., p. 269.

page 28 'The new dinner set ...' ibid.

3 WASHINGTON ENTERTAINS

page 34 'I should like ...' Henry James, p. 367.

page 35 '... an air of leisure ...' ibid.

page 38 '... and Miss West!' ibid., p. 408.

page 40 'A charming chief ...' Gwynn, p. 49.

page 42 '... the prominent families of the West End ...' Moore, p. 243.

page 45 'There are three things ...' Hibbert, p. 296.

4 'PLEASE, MISS WEST!'

page 47 'No European spring had shown him ...' Henry Adams, *The Education of Henry Adams*, p. 268.

page 48 'If ever the phrase ...' Sackville-West, *Pepita*, p. 161.

page 49 'My dear Miss West ...' Letter in possession of Mr Nigel Nicolson.

page 51 'Hardinge himself is no courtier ...' Gwynn, p. 400.

page 51 'I hope you may get your exchange ...' ibid., p. 49.

page 52 'They were all such ugly people there ...' ibid., p. 53.

5 NORTH-AMERICAN ADVENTURES

page 60 '... and lesser title holders ...' Mohr, pp. 77ff.

page 60 '... a swarm of politicians ...' ibid., p. 77.

page 61 'To our foreign guests . . .' ibid., pp. 99ff.

page 61 'The Army – Holding the Savages . . .' ibid.

page 61 'The *Pioneer Press* . . .' ibid., pp. 89–90.

page 62 '. . . the criminal element . . .' ibid., p. 125.

page 63 'It was too dark to see . . .' ibid., p. 153.

page 63 'Englishmen, with characteristic good humour . . .' ibid., p. 156.

page 63 '. . . for friends who were not present . . .' ibid., p. 172.

page 64 '. . . in a wooden hotel . . .' ibid., p. 251.

page 64 'You won't believe . . .' ibid., pp. 257, 260.

page 65 'From outside came the light . . .' ibid., pp. 262–3.

page 65 'our awful journey' ibid., p. 264.

6 FINAL YEARS AT THE LEGATION

page 66 'Washington thought the arrival . . .' Legitimacy trial evidence.

page 69 '. . . there were balls of clipped paper . . .' *Evening Star*, 16 January 1888.

page 72 'I am unable to understand . . .' New York *Times Herald*, 25 October 1888, cited in Nevins, p. 429.

page 72 'Sir, I am in receipt . . .' Willson, p. 254.

page 73 'Victoria was one of the most fascinating . . .' Trevor.

page 74 'For the past four months . . .' *Evening Star*, 26 October 1888.

page 75 'Private communication made by an Ambassador . . .' Willson, p. 258.

page 76 'Well, it's all up.' Nevins, p. 439.

page 76 'My Lord, Having read the newspapers . . .' Willson, p. 259.

page 77 'My dear Lord Sackville . . .' Letter in possession of Mr Nigel Nicolson.

page 77 'It is said by those who have know her . . .' *Evening Star*, 3 November 1888.

page 77 'Every day quantities of flowers . . .' ibid., 7 November 1888.

page 77 'After the issue of the President's ultimatum . . .' ibid., 24 November 1888.

pages 77–8 'Lord Sackville and the Misses Sackville-West . . .' ibid., 23 November 1888.

page 78 'A brass hot water kettle . . .' ibid., 20 November 1888.

page 79 'As the train rounded the curve . . .' ibid., 23 November 1888.

7 WINTER IN FRANCE, SPRING IN ENGLAND

page 84 'This unimaginative description . . .' Sackville-West, *Pepita*, p. 180.

8 MISTRESS OF KNOLE

pages 97–9 The history of the family is taken from Sackville-West, *Knole and the Sackvilles*.
page 104 'Lady Airlie . . .' Mosley, p. 10.

9 ENTERTAINING AT KNOLE

page 111 'Hey diddle diddle . . .' D. Cecil, p. 239.
page 114 'Lady Warwick . . .' Warwick.
page 116 '. . . the seventeen letters . . .' King Edward VII's letters to Victoria are in the possession of Lord Sackville at Knole.
page 120 'Another measuring stick . . .' Letter to the author from Sir Claus Moser, KCB, Director of the Central Statistical Office, 1976.
page 124 'Susan McCook' is the maiden name of the author's mother.

10 'THE ROMANCE OF THE SACKVILLE PEERAGE'

This chapter is based on the evidence collected for the case, 1896–1910, by the Sackville solicitors, family letters in the possession of Mr Nigel Nicolson at Sissinghurst Castle and *verbatim* record of the trial.
page 129 'Victoria, never, never let me see . . .' Sackville-West, *Pepita*, p. 127.
page 135 'She was torn . . .' ibid., p. 225.

11 SEERY

page 143 'Lady Diana Manners . . .' Conversation with Lady Diana Cooper, 1976.
page 143 'My mother was adorable . . .' Sackville-West, *Pepita*, p. 201.
page 144 'That particular dish . . .' Sackville-West, *The Edwardians*, p. 33.

page 147 'Rudyard Kipling wrote . . .' Sackville-West, *Pepita*, p. 282.

page 151 Seery's collection in Paris has been superbly described by Monsieur Germain Seligmann in his book, *Merchants of Art*, and by Mr Robert Cecil in the *Burlington Magazine*, June 1950 and April 1956, and in *Apollo*, June 1965.

page 154 'Vita described going down to see Seery . . .' Sackville-West, *Pepita*, p. 222.

page 154 'Seery was a very rich man . . .' From the legal evidence in the Scott trial.

page 156 'He looked like a young man of fashion . . .' Birkenhead, p. 188ff. All descriptions of F. E. Smith in this chapter come from his son's biography.

page 157 'Carson was a giant of a man . . .' Hyde, pp. 1, 222, 336.

page 158 'Dear Mr Smith . . .' Copies of Lady Sackville's correspondence with F. E. Smith are in the possession of Mr Nigel Nicolson.

12 THE SEERY TRIAL

My source is the *verbatim* trial record.

13 PRE-WAR ADVENTURES

page 183 'The man who had saved the United States federal reserve . . .' Canfield, pp. 81–3.

page 183 'Mrs Peter A. Jay . . .' Interview with the author's mother, 1977.

pages 184ff. 'Miss Linley and Her Brother.' The Gainsborough portrait that Lady Sackville and Mr Pierpont Morgan loved so much is now in the Sterling and Francine Clark Art Institute, Williamstown, Massachusetts.

pages 186ff. My information on Lord Kitchener's career comes from Magnus, *Kitchener, Portrait of an Imperialist*.

page 189 'America is good enough . . .' Kavaler, p. 119.

page 189 'America is not a fit place . . .' ibid., p. 114.

page 189 'Teddy Roosevelt . . .' ibid.

page 190 'In character, as in physique . . .' Letter to *The Times* following Astor's death, 20 October 1919.

page 190 'His first sentimental letter . . .' Astor's letters to Lady Sackville are in the possession of Mr Nigel Nicolson.

page 192 'John Singer Sargent . . .' Descharnes and Chabrun, p. 198 (translated from the French).

page 193 'Seeking salvation by sensuality . . .' ibid., p. 158.

page 193 'Rodin is nothing but a sexual organ . . .' ibid., p. 158.

page 193 'I will come to see you . . .' ibid., p. 197.

page 197 'An air of gaiety . . .' Sitwell, p. 254.

14 DIFFICULT YEARS

page 200 'Dear, I must be going now.' Sackville-West, *Pepita*, p. 247.

page 201 'I must say . . .' Sackville-West, ibid., p. 248.

pages 203–4 'From time to time . . .' Sitwell, pp. 245–6.

page 205 'Enid Bagnold.' Interview with Enid Bagnold (Lady Jones), 1975.

page 212 'I daren't think . . .' Nicolson, *Portrait of a Marriage*, p. 169.

15 'QUEL ROMAN EST MA VIE!'

page 215 'Edwardian beauties . . .' Letter to the author from Mrs J. G. Links, 1976.

page 215 'They never came to England . . .' Interview with Prince Jean de Faucigny-Lucinge, 1976.

page 216 'Vita deplored the immense size . . .' Sackville-West, *Pepita*, p. 258.

page 217 'Miss Honey Harris . . .' Interview with Miss Harris, 1976.

page 219 'Lady Sackville had met . . .' Hussey, p. 378.

page 219 'Lady Diana Cooper . . .' Interview with Lady Diana Cooper, 1976.

page 219 'The public figure . . .' Lutyens, Robert, pp. 157ff.

page 219 'He charmed his way . . .' Lutyens, Elizabeth, p. 3.

page 220 'Two years after . . .' Letter to the author from Mrs J. G. Links, 1976.

page 220 'Even today he is admired . . .' Interview with Lord Llewellyn-Davies, RIBA, 1976.

page 221 'Mere reflexes . . .' Lutyens, Mary, p. 140.

page 222 'Lady Desborough . . .' Mosley, p. 55.

page 223 'The next generation . . .' Conversation with Mrs J. G. Links, 1976.

page 225 'Letter to his wife . . .' Hussey, p. 380.

page 226 'Virginia Woolf . . .' Nicolson and Trautmann, p. 353.

page 226 'Brighton house . . .' Sackville-West, *Pepita*, p. 259.

pages 226–7 'She held a sale . . .' Sackville-West, ibid., pp. 259, 264 and catalogue of sale.

page 228 'Duff Cooper' writer, statesman, diplomat, married Lady Diana Manners.

page 229 'That charming book . . .' – *Passage to India*.

page 230 'Virginia Woolf wrote . . .' Nicolson and Trautmann, p. 453.

page 230 'Virginia Woolf was writing . . .' ibid., p. 458.

page 230 'She wrote . . .' ibid., p. 487.

page 231 'Vita wrote to Harold . . .' Letter in possession of Mr Nigel Nicolson.

page 232 'The Roof of Friendship.' Sackville-West, *Pepita*, p. 261.

page 232 'The Million Penny Fund.' ibid., p. 268.

page 232 Harold Nicolson's decision is taken from Nigel Nicolson, ed., *Diaries and Letters of Harold Nicolson*, Introduction, pp. 32ff.

page 233 'Always casual about time . . .' Sackville-West, *Pepita*, p. 270.

page 234 'Eighteen-year-old Ben . . .' Ben's story is taken from Nigel Nicolson, ed., *Diaries and Letters . . .*, pp. 182ff.

page 234 'He and I sang . . .' Sackville-West, *Pepita*, p. 276.

Bibliography

The following have been consulted and the chapter reference notes make clear where particular reliance has been placed on certain sources.

ADAMS, HENRY: *Democracy* (1880). New York: Airmont, 1968.
  The Education of Henry Adams. Edited with an Introduction and Notes by Ernest Samuels. Boston: Houghton Mifflin, 1974.
ADAMS, MRS HENRY: *The Letters of Mrs. Henry Adams 1865–1883.* Edited by Ward Thoron. Boston: Little, Brown, 1936.
BIRKENHEAD, FREDERICK: *Second Earl of Birkenhead.* London: Eyre and Spottiswoode, 1959.
BLAINE, HARRIET BAILEY (STANWOOD): *Letters of Mrs James G. Blaine Vols I and II.* Edited by Harriet S. Blaine Beale. New York: Duffield, 1908.
BOLITHO, HECTOR: *The Reign of Queen Victoria.* New York: Macmillan, 1944.
BRIGGS, EMILY EDSON: *The Olivia Letters.* New York and Washington: Neale, 1906.
BROAD, LEWIS: *Advocates of a Golden Age.* London: John Long, 1958.
BROWNE, CHARLES F. M.: *A Short History of the British Embassy in Washington, D.C.* Washington: Gibson Brothers, 1930.
BURGHCLERE, LADY: *A Great Lady's Friendship: Letters to Mary, Countess of Derby.* London: Macmillan, 1933.
CANFIELD, CASS: *The Incredible Pierpont Morgan.* New York: Harper & Row, 1974.
CARPENTER, FRANK G: *Carp's Washington.* New York: McGraw-Hill, 1960.
CECIL, DAVID: *The Cecils of Hatfield House.* London: Constable, 1973.

CECIL, ROBERT: *Burlington Magazine*, June 1950 and April 1956. *Apollo*, June 1965.

COLVIN, IAN: *Carson the Statesman*. New York: Macmillan, 1935.

CORNWALLIS-WEST, G. F. M.: *Edwardian Hey Days*. New York: Putnam, 1930.

DANGERFIELD, GEORGE: *The Strange Death of Liberal England*. New York: Harrison Smith & Robert Haas, 1935.

Department of State Register. Washington: Government Printing Office, 1882, 1883, 1884, 1886, 1888.

DESCHARNES, R. and CHABRUN, J. F.: *Auguste Rodin*. Paris: Edita Lausanne-Vilo, 1967.

Despatches from the United States Minister to Great Britain (to the Department of State) Feb. 1881–Dec. 1881. United States Archives.

Elite List. Elite Publishing Company, 1889.

FLEXNER, JAMES THOMAS: *George Washington and The New Nation: (1783–1793)*. Boston: Little, Brown, 1969.

FRIEDLANDER, MARK: 'Henry Hobson Richardson, Henry Adams, and John Hay', *Journal of the Society of Architectural Historians*. October 1970.

GARRATY, JOHN A.: *Henry Cabot Lodge: A Biography*. New York: Alfred A. Knopf, 1953.

GIBSON, FLORENCE E.: *The Attitudes of the New York Irish Toward State and National Affairs 1848–1892*. New York: Columbia University Press, 1951.

GREEN, CONSTANCE MCLAUGHLIN: *Washington Capital City 1879–1950*. Princeton: Princeton University Press, 1963.

GWYNN, STEPHEN: *The Letters and Friendships of Sir Cecil Spring Rice Vol I*. London: Constable, 1929.

HALLE, LOUIS J.: *Spring in Washington*. New York: Atheneum, 1963.

HANDLIN, OSCAR: *The History of the United States Vol II*. New York: Holt, Rinehart & Winston, 1968.

BENJAMIN HARRISON Collection. Manuscript Division, Library of Congress.

HIBBERT, CHRISTOPHER: *The Royal Victorians*. Philadelphia and New York: J. B. Lippincott, 1976.

HOWE, GEORGE FREDERICK: *Chester A. Arthur: A Quarter-Century of Machine Politics*. New York: Frederick Ungar, 1957.

HUSSEY, CHRISTOPHER: *The Life of Sir Edward Lutyens*. New York: Scribner's, 1950.

HUTCHINS, STILSON and MOORE, JOSEPH W.: *The National Capital Past and Present*. Washington: The Post Publishing Co., 1885.

HYDE, H. MONTGOMERY: *Carson*. New York: Octagon Books, 1974.

HYNES, SAMUEL: *The Edwardian Turn of Mind*. Princeton: Princeton University Press, 1968.

JAMES, HENRY: *Henry James: Letters Vol II 1875–1883*. Edited by Leon Edel. Cambridge: Harvard University Press, 1975.

JENKINS, BRIAN: *Fenians and Anglo-American Relations During Reconstruction*. Ithaca: Cornell University Press, 1969.

KAVALER, LUCY: *The Astors, An American Legend*. New York: Dodd, Mead, 1966.

KEIM, DE BENNEVILLE: *Handbook of Official and Social Etiquette and Public Ceremonials at Washington*. Washington: 1884.

Keim's Illustrated Handbook of Washington and its Environs. Washington, 1885.

Society in Washington. Harrisburg, Pa. Publishing Company: 1887

KNAPLUND, PAUL and CLEWES, CAROLYN: 'Private Letters from the British Embassy in Washington to the Foreign Secretary Lord Granville 1880–1885', *Annual Report of the American Historical Association* (1941, Vol I). Washington, 1942.

LAVER, J.: *Edwardian Promenade*. London: E. Hulton, 1958.

LESLIE, ANITA: *The Marlborough House Set*. Garden City: Doubleday, 1973.

LOGAN, MARY SIMMERSON: *Thirty Years in Washington*. Hartford: Washington, 1901.

LUTYENS, ELIZABETH: *A Goldfish Bowl*. London: Cassell, 1972.

LUTYENS, MARY: *To Be Young*. London: Rupert Hart-Davis, 1959.

LUTYENS, ROBERT: *Six Great Architects*. Hamish Hamilton, 1959.

MAGNUS, PHILIP: *King Edward VII*. New York: E. P. Dutton, 1964.

Kitchener, Portrait of an Imperialist. London: John Murray, 1958.

Massachusetts Avenue Architecture Vol II. Commission on Fine Arts. Washington: Government Printing Office, 1975.

MAYCOCK, SIR WILLOUGHBY: *With Mr. Chamberlain in the United States and Canada, 1887–88.* London: Chatto & Windus, 1914.

MIDDLEMAS, KEITH: *The Life and Times of Edward VII.* Garden City: Doubleday, 1972.

MILES-CAMERON Collection. Manuscript Division, Library of Congress.

MILLER, BETTY: *Robert Browning: A Portrait.* London: John Murray, 1952.

MOHR, NICOLAUS: *Excursion Through America.* Edited by Ray Allen Billington. Chicago: R. R. Connelley, 1973.

MOORE, JOSEPH WEST: *Picturesque Washington.* Providence: J. A. & R. A. Reid, 1888.

MORISON, SAMUEL ELIOT and COMMAGER, HENRY STEELE: *The Growth of the American Republic.* New York: Oxford University Press, 1962.

MOSLEY, NICHOLAS: *Julian Grenfell.* London: Weidenfeld & Nicolson, 1976.

NEIDHART, W. S.: *Fenianism in North America.* University Park: Pennsylvania State University Press, 1975.

NEVILL, RALPH: *Life and Letters of Lady Dorothy Nevill.* London: Methuen, 1919.

NEVINS, ALLAN: *Grover Cleveland: A Study in Courage.* New York: Dodd, Mead, 1932.

NICOLAY, HELEN: *Our Capital on the Potomac.* New York and London: Century, 1924.

NICOLSON, NIGEL, ed.: *The Diaries and Letters of Harold Nicolson.* New York: Atheneum, 1966.

Portrait of a Marriage. New York: Atheneum, 1973.

NICOLSON, NIGEL and TRAUTMANN, JOANNE, eds.: *Letters of Virginia Woolf* Vol. III, London: Hogarth Press, 1977.

NOWELL-SMITH, SIMON: *Edwardian England, 1901–1914.* New York: Oxford University Press, 1964.

ORR, ALEXANDRA: *Life and Letters of Robert Browning* London: Smith Elder, 1891.

PEARSALL, RONALD: *Edwardian Life and Leisure.* New York: St Martin's Press, 1973.

PLETCHER, DAVID M.: *The Awkward Years: American Foreign*

Relations under Garfield and Arthur. Columbia: University of Missouri Press, 1962.

PONSONBY, ARTHUR: *Henry Ponsonby, His Life from His Letters.* New York: Macmillan, 1944.

QUEEN VICTORIA: *The Letters of Queen Victoria, 1879–1885.* Edited by George Earle Buckle. London: John Murray, 1928.
More Leaves From a Highland Journal (1862–82). London: Smith Elder, 1884.

SACKVILLE, LIONEL: *My Mission to the United States 1881–1889.* Privately printed. In the possession of Lord Sackville.

SACKVILLE-WEST, V.: *Challenge.* Glasgow: Collins, 1924.
The Edwardians. Garden City: Doubleday, Doran & Co., 1930.
Knole and the Sackvilles. Tonbridge, Kent: Ernest Benn, 1922.
Pepita. London: Hogarth Press, 1937.

SCHLESINGER, ARTHUR M.: *Political and Social Growth of the American People 1865–1940.* New York: Macmillan, 1941.

SELIGMANN, GERMAIN: *Merchants of Art: 1880–1960.* New York: Appleton Century, 1961.

SITWELL, OSBERT: *Great Morning.* Boston: Little, Brown, 1947.

STEINER, ZARA S.: *The Foreign Office and Foreign Policy 1898–1914.* Cambridge: Cambridge University Press, 1969.

STILLER, JESSE H.: 'The British Legation in Washington, 1868–1893' (unpublished). 1974.

STURGIS, JOHN: Letter. In the possession of Mr Nigel Nicolson.

TANOCK, JOHN L.: *The Sculpture of Auguste Rodin.* The Philadelphia Museum of Art, 1976.

THAYER, WILLIAM ROSCOE: *The Life and Letters of John Hay.* Boston: Houghton, Mifflin, 1915.

TREVOR, JOHN B.: Memoir. In the possession of Mr John B. Trevor.

TUGWELL, REXFORD G.: *Grover Cleveland.* New York: Macmillan, 1968.

TUCHMAN, BARBARA: *The Proud Tower.* New York: Macmillan, 1966.

VILLARD, HENRY: *Memoirs of Henry Villard Vol II.* New York: Da Capo, 1969.

WALKER, MABEL GREGORY: *The Fenian Movement.* Colorado Springs: Ralph Myles, 1969.

WALKER-SMITH, D. and CLARKE, E.: *The Life of Sir Edward Clarke.* London: Thornton Butterworth, 1939.

WARWICK, FRANCES, COUNTESS OF: *Afterthoughts.* London: Cassell, 1931.

Washington Evening Star, October 1881–November 1888.

WILLSON, BECKLES: *Friendly Relations. A Narrative of Britain's Ministers and Ambassadors to America (1791–1930).* Boston: Little, Brown, 1934.

WOOLF, VIRGINIA: *Orlando.* New York: Harcourt, Brace, 1928.

Index

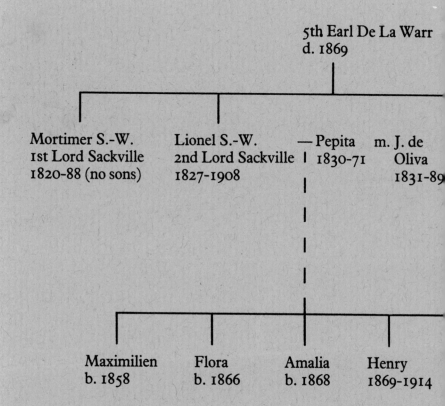

5th Earl De La Warr
d. 1869

Mortimer S.-W.
1st Lord Sackville
1820-88 (no sons)

Lionel S.-W.
2nd Lord Sackville
1827-1908

— Pepita   m. J. de
1830-71   Oliva
             1831-89

Maximilien
b. 1858

Flora
b. 1866

Amalia
b. 1868

Henry
1869-1914